Planning and Organizing for Multicultural Instruction

Second Edition

Gwendolyn Calvert Baker

Addison-Wesley Publishing Company
Menlo Park, California • Reading, Massachusetts • New York
Don Mills, Ontario • Wokingham, England • Amsterdam • Bonn
Paris • Milan • Madrid • Sydney • Singapore • Tokyo
Seoul • Taipei • Mexico City • San Juan

Senior Editor: Lois Fowkes
Project Editor: Jean Nattkemper
Production Manager: Janet Yearian
Production Coordinator: Karen Edmonds
Design Manager: Jeff Kelly
Text Design: Detta Penna
Cover Design: Rachel Gage
Compositor: Publishing Support Services

This book is published by Innovative Learning, an imprint of Addison-Wesley's Alternative Publishing Group.

ISBN 0-201-86112-7
3 4 5 6 7 8 9-ML-97 96 95 94

This book is dedicated to my parents, Viola Lee and Burgess Edward Calvert,
who have provided me with a richness of spirit;
to my children,
JoAnn Elizabeth, Claudia Jayne, and James Grady, Jr.;
and to my grandson Marshall.
All have helped me learn the value of diversity.

Preface

Since the original publication of this book, I have had several professional experiences that have contributed to my interest in a revision. In addition to my experiences, much that has occurred throughout the world and in the United States has sharpened my desire to become even more involved in the promotion of multicultural education.

Immediately upon completing the manuscript for the first edition, I embarked upon a multicultural curriculum revision project at the Bank Street College of Education in New York City. This project gave me an opportunity to apply much of what I had recommended in the original book. The discussion "Institutions of Higher Education" in Chapter 3 reflects that experience.

Following my work at Bank Street College and just as I was settling into my new role as National Executive Director of the YWCA of the U.S.A., I accepted perhaps one of the greatest challenges of my life. I was appointed to the New York City Board of Education, by then president of the Borough of Manhattan, David N. Dinkins. This appointment was important because it gave me additional opportunities to apply what I had promoted both throughout my writings and in my work instituting and supporting multicultural education. Prior to my experiences as a four-year member and later president of the Board of Education, I was keenly aware of the importance of policy. However, serving on that board reinforced, for me, the significance of policy and its utmost importance in creating change. Change does not come about easily and or quickly in any arena, but it faces extraordinary challenges in public education. For that reason, I have highlighted effecting change through policy in Chapter 3.

Public education must respond to changes that have taken place throughout the world in the last few years. Whether we concentrate on recent developments in South Africa, the former Soviet Union, China, Central Europe, Cuba, El Salvador, Haiti, the Middle East, or other parts of the universe, we cannot ignore the importance of diversity. Our responsibilities to respond to change in our own society and in the world have become even more grave. The role of the school, and education in general, in providing what is needed is even more vital. The challenge is ours, and it is one in which multicultural education can definitely offer solutions.

Because of the importance of multicultural education in dealing with widespread change, both in our society and in the world in general, I begin the book with a new chapter (Chapter 1) on the changing mission of schools. It is from the viewpoint presented in this new chapter that the remaining discussions of multicultural education are predicated. Chapter 2 contains material that helps the reader understand the goals and the process of multicultural education, as they are presented throughout the book. Chapter 3 examines what must happen if multicultural education is to become a reality. The importance of policy development as a basis for full implementation is highlighted in this chapter.

Part II will aid educators who are responsible for organizing for instruction. Chapter 4 presents a practical model for preparing teachers to teach. The importance of developing a curriculum embracing multiculturalism is included in Chapter 5. Steps for full implementation are outlined in Chapter 6.

The final section, Part III (Chapters 7–12), is designed to help teachers with instruction. One new chapter has been added, Chapter 9, on math instruction. Although Part III makes use of a subject-matter approach that will help teachers who present their curriculum by subject, those who use an interdisciplinary approach will have no difficulty in adjusting the material to their needs. The teaching strategies included in this part are geared to the primary, intermediate, and advanced levels. They draw heavily on ethnic content. Other aspects of cultural diversity included are integrated throughout. Although this approach may appear to be somewhat subtle, it is my hope that individual teachers will modify the materials to meet the needs of their own teaching styles and learning environments.

Finally, I must acknowledge the many individuals who have contributed to the development of this manuscript. I shall always be grateful to James A. Banks, Professor of Education, University of Washington, Seattle, for the time he has invariably taken to encourage and to support my writing.

For the material in Chapters 7–12, which represents the contributions of subject specialists who provided diversity in the suggested teaching strategies as well as additional expertise in the subject areas, my appreciation goes to Carol Tice, Sharon Artis, Claiborne Richardson, William Ryder, Exyie Ryder, Kathleen Hunter, and Ann Schlitt Kolbell. Special appreciation is due Claudia Zaslavsky for her work on Chapter 9.

I could not have completed this revision without having access to a library, especially a children's library. My thanks to the faculty and staff at Bank Street College for providing this support. I received help in securing photographs from Samuel E. Spaght, Area II Superintendent, Wichita Public Schools; Robert Terte, Division of Public Relations, Board of Education, City of New York; and Renee Creange, Associate Dean for Public Affairs, Bank Street College.

My acknowledgments would not be complete without an expression of appreciation to the National Board and Staff of the YWCA of the U.S.A. A special thanks to the President, Ann Stallard, for her support in providing me the time needed to complete the revision. Joyce Marshall gave much needed assistance. Audrey Lam and Norris Lee were instrumental in teaching me how to use the word processor. I shall always be grateful to them and other valuable staff for helping me develop the skills necessary for functioning in a world that is dependent upon computers.

Finally, I give my thanks to very special friends, Elmer L. Beard, Adrienne Austin, Constance Carter Cooper, Herbert Wilson, Edwin Galley, Reg Claytor, Eddy Bayardelle, and Jimmie James, for their encouragement.

Contents

Part I

Planning for Instruction

1
The Changing Expectations of Public Education

So much more is expected of public education today than was years ago. Because public education has not provided all that has been expected, there has been a growing dissatisfaction with it. This general dissatisfaction has existed longer than many of us can recall. Disappointment with school was expressed in a variety of forums decades before the national report "The Nation at Risk" caused a furor by calling for reform. This document demanded that someone do something about the schools.[1]

There is rarely a conference held, a speech given, an article or a book written on education that does not speak to the need for reform. Our nation and world are plagued with social ills, and it is generally expected that if any one institution in society can help, it can and should be the school. Dropout rates are soaring, teenage pregnancy is on the rise, illiteracy is all around us, violence and racial conflict abound, HIV/AIDS threatens us, and the list grows by the day. The schools must respond.

As the nation has matured and changed, the role for public education has shifted. Yet schools have not changed to keep up with the dramatic changes that have occurred in the United States, let alone the changes that have taken place throughout the world. Nor have they changed to meet the needs of a growing and a different population. Too often, schools do not seem to recognize that students are different today than they were when the common school came into being.

Today it is necessary to create new learning environments, not just new facilities. The curriculum requires more than revisions; it must be new, different, and exciting enough to interest and to educate students who come to public schools from diverse backgrounds. Instructional strategies, too, must be different and challenging. Chester Finn, in his book *We Must Take Charge,* refers to schooling and schools as old and limited institutions. He draws the following conclusion:

> The public school of 1991 is still by and large, an institution designed in the nineteenth century to serve only a part of the population and to do that within a framework of complementary influences. We sometimes forget how good it is—or was—at this mission, while also overlooking how much the mission has changed.[2]

Perhaps it is not so much that the mission has changed. After all, schools are basically still committed to educating all children. However, in order to do this today, those who are daring and bold say that the system needs to change. Louis V. Gerstner, Jr., Chief Executive Officer of RBJ Nabisco, in responding to the failure of schools, said,"Blow up the current public education system. The system doesn't work. No more tinkering at the margins. We need to create fundamentally new learning environments. Traditional approaches simply won't work anymore."[3]

So much change has occurred all around us, impacting schools. The students who attend public schools are ethnically and culturally more diverse than ever before. The structure and responsibility of the family is different. Communities and cities are confronted with more and different kinds of social problems. Technological advances have created opportunities for more communication and interaction. All of these changes, and many more, have placed a grater responsibility on the schools. So much more is expected. We must design approaches that will make education meaningful to all. Traditional approaches are not working and will not work any longer.

In the nation's early years, the schools' primary purpose was to give young people the skills necessary for using and understanding the Bible. As schools developed, the purpose of education, more than ever before, was directed toward the citizenship ideals considered necessary for democracy's survival and the development of an "American" citizen. Although there was a great deal of diversity among public school children during the nineteenth century, success, on the whole, depended on children shedding much of the culture, including the language, of their immigrant parents. A great deal of the resistance to change and to the overhauling of public education today can be traced to this period. Even though schools were expected to do more as the population became increasingly diverse, few changes were instituted to help schools cope with new responsibilities.

Today the school is expected to prepare young people to make successful livings in a society that is becoming ever more diverse. The school is also expected to provide solutions for society's failures. In other words, the school is not only expected to help students adjust to a society undergoing rapid technological change but also deal with and manage the social, economic, and political changes that have occurred throughout the United States and the world.

Our nation's culturally diverse and pluralistic nature makes it imperative for schools to provide educational experiences and training that will not only prepare students to live successfully in a diverse nation but also to base educational content and process on the cultural histories, experiences, languages, and lifestyles of all students. The failure of the public schools to provide this type of instruction lies in the history of American public education. While there has been an expansion in the types of courses and subject matter offered to students, much of public school education is still based on the models of content and instruction used in the past. Little about the structure and/or the curricula of schools has changed to meet the needs of most students, even if we overlook the essential aspects of culture. Today's system is old. If the expectations of public education are to be realized, changes are needed.

Changes Needed

Few will argue with the premise that schools should serve society's needs. The social, economic, and political order depends on the responsible participation of individual citizens.[4] If individuals are to become responsible citizens, it is essential that the school and the process of education help the individual develop his or her capacities. This is a view set forth by the Educational Policies Commission of the National Education Association:

> In any democracy, education is closely bound to the wishes of the people, but the strength of this bond in America has been unique. The American people have traditionally regarded education as a means for improving themselves and their society. Whenever an objective has been judged desirable for the individual or the society, it has tended to be accepted as a valid concern of the school. The American commitment to the free society—to individual dignity, to personal liberty, to equality of opportunity—has set the frame in which the American school grew. The basic American value, respect for the individual, has led to one of the major charges which the American people have placed on their schools; to foster the development of individual capacities which will enable each human being to become the best person he/she is capable of becoming.[5]

Education that can help the individual develop must provide the kind of instruction and experiences that are appropriate for that individual. Schools must change the content of curriculum so that it is compatible with the background and experiences of students. There is no sensible rationale for teaching any subject without first making sure that the content of the material being taught includes some reference to the learner. To attempt to teach American history without an African-American perspective to African-American children will not help the student learn all that he or she needs to learn about American history. Students learn better if they are able to relate to what is being taught. The same rationale should be used for any student or group of students whose ethnic and cultural backgrounds differ from what has been considered traditional or mainstream in American society. Schools must teach the basic skills to all children as the first step in helping them develop their capacities. To achieve this first step, curriculum must change.

The need to change and design instructional strategies to be compatible with the learner's learning style and background is every bit as crucial as the need to change curriculum. The way children learn is often controlled by factors that are part of the way they have learned to learn. Some of these factors originate in ethnic and cultural experiences. Some children learn better when the style of instruction is consistent with their lifestyles. Teachers and schools must be more familiar with the various lifestyles their students bring to the classroom.

Instructional materials are as important to the learning process as curriculum and instruction. Generally there has been an improvement in the kinds of audiovisual materials available for use today. Most publishing companies have begun to reflect aspects of cultural diversity in most of their materials. However, it is still very difficult for one book or a series of books to capture all that may be needed for a particular class or group of students. Teachers sensitive to these needs must be prepared to augment and/or substitute material so that it is appropriate. In some schools, especially those with severe financial constraints, much of the instructional material in use is old and not relevant. Most of the schools in districts where resources are limited are unfortunately heavily attended by children of color. These are the children for whom most of this old material is not relevant. Those who control the purse strings must become aware of the need for different kinds of materials.

Learning environments are also important to the process of learning. Certainly clean and attractive schools and classrooms are important, but the same sensitivity needed to ensure that the curriculum, instructional strategies, and materials are appropriate to the students must also be used in designing the surroundings of the learners. This is the area in which great attention must be given to the attitudes and behavior of teachers and administrators. Equally important, we must make sure that diversity is reflected in the staffing of schools. We must pay attention to every aspect that is a part of the learning environment. The detailed discussion of curriculum in Chapter 5 will clarify some of what has been mentioned here.

The challenge is before us, for we have the power to bring about this kind of change in public education and in our schools. Only by initiating such change can we ensure responsible citizenship for the future. Developing responsible citizens for a democracy means more than preparing students with the education and skills needed for economic security. We need to teach students the value of citizenship, the value of leadership, and the true value of living in a pluralistic democratic society.

Multicultural instruction can help schools to change. If the implementation of multicultural instruction includes adequate planning and comprehensive organizing, the results could be a new and enlightened group of citizens, wise and courageous enough to foster the types of change and reform needed in a changing society and world.

The Promise of Multicultural Education

Let us begin by acknowledging that our society is diverse. We live not only in a world but in a country inhabited by individuals belonging to many different ethnic and cultural groups. It then becomes reasonable to expect schools to prove the kind of education that will help groups from diverse cultures not only to coexist but to live together in some degree of harmony. Education can, at the same time, help students develop the essential skills and knowledge required for successful living in a democratic society. Multicultural education can provide what is needed. However, it is important for those interested in multicultural education to come to a basic understanding of what multicultural education is and what it promises to accomplish.

Multicultural education must be thought of as a process and not simply as a program. In other words, all education should be multicultural. Education, in general, should be viewed as the process through which students are provided with instruction and experiences acknowledging the cultural backgrounds of all individuals and through which they are prepared to develop a more just and equal society.

Multicultural education is not only a process but a comprehensive one. All that is the responsibility of education, and therefore of schools, should be imbued with concepts and behavior that acknowledge cultural diversity.

Principles of Multicultural Education

Chapters 2 through 6 of this revised edition have been revised around eight basic principles. These principles, listed below, should serve to guide the discussion and help move us from theory into practice:

1. Multicultural education is a process.
2. The development of a multicultural approach to education should be comprehensive and complete.
3. Multicultural education should be developed in an environment that is conducive and supportive.
4. All of the participants in the school community should be involved in the development of multicultural education.

5. The training and education of staff, teachers, parents, and community leaders is essential.
6. Multicultural education should begin with the background of the students for whom the process is intended.
7. The development of multicultural education should take place over an extended period of time.
8. The instructional component of multicultural education must be integrated throughout the curriculum.

Notes

1. Catherine Marshall, Douglas Mitchell, and Frederick Wirt, "A Cultural Framework for Studying State Policy," *Culture and Education Policy in the American States* (Bristol, PA: Palmer, 1989), p. 3.
2. Finn, Chester, *We Must Take Charge: Our Schools and Our Future,* (New York: The Free Press, 1991), p. 20.
3. Ibid., p. 52.
4. National Education Association, "The Central Purpose of American Education," in *Education and Society,* ed. W. Warren Kallenback and Harold M. Hodges, Jr. (Columbus, OH: Charles E. Merrill Books, 1963), p. 457.
5. Ibid., p. 457.

2
Defining Multicultural Education

Principle I: Multicultural education is a process.

Multicultural education is a process through which individuals are exposed to the diversity that exists in the United States and the world. Diversity includes ethnic and racial minority populations, religious groups, language differences, gender differences, economic conditions, regional limitations, physical and mental disabilities, age groups, and other distinctions. Through multicultural education, individuals are given the opportunity and option to support and maintain one or more cultures, e.g., value systems, lifestyles, and/or languages. However, multicultural education also stresses the role of the individual, as a citizen of a particular nation, in contributing to and maintaining the culture common to all who live in that nation.[1] According to Louise Berman, "the task of the school then is to foster diversity but within a framework containing some common understandings."[2]

In a discussion on the nature of multicultural education, James Banks writes:

> Multicultural education is at least three things: an idea or concept, an educational reform movement, and a process. Multicultural education incorporates the idea that all students—regardless of their gender and social class, and their ethnic, racial, or cultural characteristics—should have an equal opportunity to learn in school.[3]

It is not enough for schools to share the responsibility for helping individuals learn how to function in a constantly changing and diverse society and world; schools must provide the leadership. Schools need to provide the kind of education that helps individuals become knowledgeable about diversity. They need to create environments conducive to the free expression of a variety of lifestyles, values, and beliefs.

Dewey stated that "education is a process of transmission, partly incidental to the ordinary companionship or intercourse of adults and youth, partly deliberately instituted to effect social continuity."[4] Because the educational process involves the transmission of knowledge and this knowledge bears upon how human beings live and deal with each other, schools are responsible for transmitting the culture of all students in a free and democratic society.[5]

The public school, because of its nature, is expected to address the educational needs of all learners. Past attempts have failed to provide the type of learning that took into consideration students' diverse backgrounds. Schools were designed to meet the needs of one group of students; these students represented the mainstream, and the schools failed to make adjustments for those whose lifestyles differed. As a result, all students have been denied the opportunity to learn about the heterogeneous nature of society in the United States and in the world. Some children have received ethnocentric views of their places in a democratic society. At the same time, still other students, largely those who differ most from the mainstream, do not feel they are a part of society.

The child referred to as the nonminority child, generally meaning the white child, is perhaps the most disadvantaged child in soci-

Multicultural education is a process through which individuals are exposed to the diversity that exists in the United States and the world.

ety today. While the school was designed to meet the needs of these students, and the curriculum geared to them, they have been given a narrow perspective of themselves. This perspective has contributed to feelings of isolation regarding their place in society and in the world. The more the world changes and the more schools stay the same, the more isolated the nonminority child may become. Schools simply cannot continue to lead nonminority children to believe that their values, lifestyles, and language are the only ones that really matter. Often nonminority children are taught tolerance rather than being helped to understand the ideas and thought that may differ from what is familiar and common to them. Those who deviate from these patterned responses are considered ill-mannered, lacking in cultural refinement, and even inferior.

Children come to school with negative attitudes previously established about people who are different from them.[6,7,8] Our total educational system must assume the responsibility and share the guilt for propagating a monocultural view of society that is totally inconsistent with past and present realities of life in the United States.[9] Educators must begin to realize that multicultural education can benefit all children. If multicultural education is seen as a process —a process for helping *all* children, including the nonminority child, understand their place in society and in the universe—then and only then will the goals and aims of education be achieved. Schools must stop limiting the opportunities of the nonminority child to develop, through classroom instruction, attitudes and behavior conducive to living in a culturally diverse environment.

The educational plight of the child who is not white and who continues to be referred to as the minority child, even in areas of this nation where he or she is in the majority, is one of devastation. The African-American, Latino, Native American, Asian, and Pacific Islander child, along with other children whose needs are not being met by the existing system of public education, are also disadvantaged. The disadvantage they confront has seriously affected their academic achievement. Because the curriculum of schools is designed for the nonminority child, academic achievement, in most instances, is not as much a problem for them. However, it is important to keep in mind that all nonminority children are not achievers but that the percentage of achievers for this population is larger than that of other children. The inability of schools to design curriculum and instruction appropriate for minority students is closely tied to the perceptions educators have about them. To a great extent, the behavior and attitudes exhibited by schools toward minority children have produced educational environments that have not facilitated pupil growth but have retarded it. There appears to be a high correlation between achievement in school and students' self-concept of academic ability as determined by the expectations and evaluations of significant others. Those significant others—teachers and other school personnel—make up the environment of the school. If the school projects low regard and low expectations for the minority child, low academic achievement may be partially explained and expected. Some students who have high self-concepts do not achieve, but research clearly indicates that the evaluations of others does affect the student's perception of his or her academic ability and thus sets limits on school achievement.[10] Education that is not structured on the ethnic and cultural experiences of children—in other words, education that is not multicultural—carries with it a subtle but devastating message to children. All children must be able to relate in positive ways to society. Multicultural education can contribute to the understanding all children have of their relationship to society and to the world in which they live.

Unfortunately, as with any new approach to education, too many practitioners, perhaps eager to become involved, do so without taking the time to understand the philosophy or rationale that girds the approach. Therefore, attempts to implement multicultural education often involve a variety of projects and programs that have little to do with the process itself. Multicultural education, as a process, evolves from the history and experiences of this nation. It is a process that is consistent with how we view the relationship between school and society. In discussing the relationship between multicultural education and the American democratic tradition, James Banks concludes:

> Multicultural education in the United States emerged out of the conflicts and struggles of the sixties and seventies. Thus it is a legitimate child of American participatory democracy. It is consistent with the American democratic tradition that views the school as an important socializing institution that helps the nation's youth to acquire the democratic values, knowledge and skills essential for the survival of participatory democracy.
>
> The rich potential of multicultural education, despite its problems and brief troubled history, is that it promises to reform the school within the context of the basic assumptions about schooling held by most teachers and to help schools better to realize American democratic values. Thus multicultural education does not envision new goals for schools but rather asks schools to expand their concepts of political and cultural democracy to include large groups of students who have been historically denied opportunities to realize fully American democratic values and ideals.[11]

Multicultural education is not a project or a program but a process. Its value to and for all children must be acknowledged if it is to have any success at all.

Conceptualizing Multicultural Education

It is important for educators to be aware of the comprehensive nature of multicultural education. The inclusive aspect of this process is one of the reasons why multicultural education can be of value.

The process of multicultural education is illustrated by the concentric diagram in Fig. 2.1. As the model is examined, the inclusiveness of multicultural education will become more obvious. This three-circle model is one way of conceptualizing the process. This is a comprehensive model and distinguishes between three different approaches to education in order to show the relationship between multiethnic, multicultural, and international/global education. Too

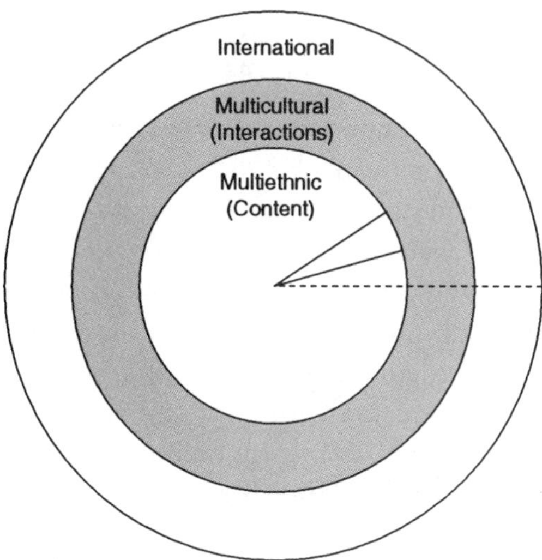

Fig. 2.1 Model for Multicultural Education

frequently these three terms are used interchangeably. However, the definition and conceptual approach presented in this book emphasizes the differences between each type as well as the relationship among all three.

Multiethnic Education

In the early sixties, African Americans, Latinos, Native Americans, and Asian and Pacific Islanders were demanding that greater efforts be made toward equality. The Civil Rights Act of 1964 was a triumph, giving support to the movement that public education reflect greater sensitivity to the needs and values of these and other ethnic groups.

Professional organizations, encouraged by a relatively small group of educators who supported more emphasis on ethnicity in schools, provided a great deal of the leadership in involving the public schools. Much of the early writings about multiethnic education came from publications published by the National Council for the Social Studies. In the forward to the *43rd Yearbook: Teaching Ethnic Studies: Con-*

cepts and Strategies, Harris L. Dante, president of the Council, describes that period in the following manner:

> The demands of minority groups for an equal opportunity to sit at the American table of abundance and for an equal chance at the starting block became a major part of the great social upheavals of the 1960s. There were many who believed that the conscience of America was speaking and that we were in turmoil because we took our ideals seriously and, in spite of everything, have guilt feelings over our shortcomings. Some have said that the self-criticism in which we have engaged and the tolerance granted the protestors indicate that as a society the United States is receptive to change and that many share in part, at least, the belief that things could be better.[12]

The early seventies saw efforts to include ethnic content in the curriculum of schools. Not all schools responded, but some took the lead. Throughout the educational literature of the late sixties, reference is made to the inclusion of ethnic content in the curriculum as "ethnic studies," "ethnic-minority education," "ethnic education," and, finally, "multiethnic education." By the early seventies, multiethnic education had come to mean the study of the involvement of various ethnic groups in the United States and of ethnicity in general. Ethnicity is defined and used in this discussion in the broadest sense. Marden and Meyer define ethnicity as "a term which emphasizes the cultural ethos (values, expectations, symbols) of a group and formerly, quite properly, was limited in reference to groups whose cultural characteristics are their prime distinguishing factor."[13]

However, Banks feels that ethnicity is determined by those who "share a sense of group identification, a common set of values, political and economic interests, behavior patterns and other cultural elements which differ from those of other groups within a society."[14] Regardless of how ethnicity was perceived, multiethnic education often took the form of separate courses of study that focused on specific groups but fell within the parameter of specific disciplines.

Schools commonly offered courses in black history, Chicano literature, and Asian studies. The separate-course approach is not as evident in schools today. Much of the instruction and activity currently focusing on ethnicity takes place under the guise of multicultural education. This often distorts the real value of multicultural education which is comprehensive in nature. What is beginning to take place that does focus on ethnic content and should and can be a viable part of multicultural education is ethnic-centric instruction. A discussion on the value of ethnic-centric instruction and its relationship to the development of multicultural curricula is included in Part II of this book.

Although multiethnic education encompasses ethnic studies and ethnic content, it provides the basis of multicultural education. Depending on how multiethnic education is implemented, it can require a restructuring of the educational environment so that it more closely meets the educational and social needs of all students; in this way, multiethnic and multicultural education have a common thrust. Learning about the history and the involvement of ethnic groups in the development of the United States is the basis for multiethnic education but this same kind of knowledge and information is also important to multicultural instruction. The core of the diagram in Fig. 2.1 represents the type of information and/or understandings offered through a study of ethnic groups.

Multicultural Education

The implementation of multiethnic education paved the way for multicultural education. It laid the foundation for a greater emphasis on the acknowledgment of differences. Attention soon began to focus on the concept of ethnic diversity, and the concept of cultural pluralism became more widely accepted by the mid-seventies. Cultural pluralism was based on the acknowledgement of cultural diversity.

During the early seventies, there was a movement to encourage schools to broaden the study of ethnic groups to include other cultural groups, resulting in a more comprehensive recognition of cultural diversity. In 1972 the American Association for Colleges of Teacher Education (AACTE) adopted a statement that gave support to this more global approach to diversity. In an AACTE official statement, "No One Model American," the introductory paragraph clearly endorses multicultural education.

> Multicultural education is education which values cultural pluralism. Multicultural education rejects the view that schools should seek to melt away cultural differences or the view that schools should merely tolerate cultural pluralism. Instead, multicultural education affirms that schools should be oriented toward the cultural enrichment of all children and youth through programs rooted to the preservation and extension of cultural diversity as a fact of life in American Society, and it affirms that this cultural diversity is a valuable resource that should be preserved and extended. It affirms that major educational institutions should strive to preserve and enhance cultural pluralism.[15]

The center circle of the diagram in Fig. 2.1 represents multicultural education and is designed to show the difference and the relationship between multiethnic and multicultural education. While multiethnic education has as its focus the content of the study of ethnic groups, multicultural education emphasizes the larger cultural groups that make up society and seeks to examine and respond to the impact of ethnicity upon the larger cultural group. Multicultural education looks at the many facets of diversity and helps to explain the concurrent involvement of individuals in more than one cultural group. Individuals may very well be a part of more than one cultural group. Culture, as defined by Ina Corrine Brown, an anthropologist, is

> ...all the accepted and patterned ways of behavior of a given people. It is a body of common understandings. It is the sum total and the organization or arrangement of all the group's ways of thinking, feeling, and acting. It also includes

the physical manifestations of the group as exhibited in the objects they make—the clothing, shelter, tools, weapons, implements, utensils, and so on.[16]

If this definition is applied to larger groups within a society, then it is feasible to assume that almost everyone can claim identity with at least two cultural groups. This point becomes clearer when the society is divided, for example, into two larger cultural groups according to gender. Further distinction is made when the definition of culture is applied to nationality. People who either by birth or through the process of nationalization assume the status of a member of a particular country share a nationality. National membership generally implies that individuals have similar interests and aims and participate in customs and duties dictated by national consensus. In this context, broadly applying Brown's definition, we can say, for example, that a female citizen of the United States is participating in at least two cultural groups. Whether or not an individual chooses to identify with a particular group depends on many things. However, the degree to which a person chooses to identify often depends on how comfortable it is to do so and how beneficial the association is to the individual. Some individuals choose the groups in which they will participate, while others, because of certain physical and linguistic traits, may be so assigned automatically.

It is also possible, using the criteria Brown has established for culture, to think of religious groups as cultural groups. Religious groups evolve from bodies of common understandings that tend to organize these groups and, in general, control the thoughts, feelings, and behavior of members of the group. Brown points out that religious beliefs and practices are aspects of culture. She also states that religion "is best understood in terms of its function; that is, what it means to and does for its adherents, and the part it plays in the total life of the community."[17] A religious group, in a broader sense, can be said to have a culture unique to the group.

If these same criteria are applied broadly to other groups that have common lifestyles based upon shared experiences and understandings, then there are many groups that can be thought of as having a culture of their own. One such group could be determined by geographic considerations—for example the people who live in Appalachia. The 18 million persons who live in the area ranging from southern New York to eastern Mississippi share a common lifestyle as a result of their economic deprivation.

Language, too, is an important aspect of culture, and people who speak the same language often share a common culture. An example of this may be observed in some of the Spanish-speaking populations in this country. As the diversity in the United States expands, so does diversity in language. While, in the past, a response to language and cultural diversity has been bilingual education, it is imperative for all students to have a command of more than one language. One of the tools for successful living in a culturally diverse nation and world is bilingualism.

In applying Brown further, we can expand the list of cultures to include many other groups. People who are poor share a culture of poverty. Individuals who are physically challenged comprise groups of persons who, because of certain physical characteristics, have developed mutual understanding. Young people today have so much in common that there is a youth culture. In keeping with this discussion, it is appropriate to include the culture of the aged. Older people have many things in common and therefore are a distinct group of individuals who form a culture all their own. This list could be expanded to include other groups of people who meet the same criteria. Furthermore, participation in cultures overlaps; the involvement of an individual in one cultural group may influence how that person participates in yet another group. In fact, ethnicity and gender often determine how one responds to and is involved in other cultural groups.

The groups included in the expanded illustration of the concept of multicultural education in Fig. 2.2 serve to suggest the many possibilities for grouping according to lifestyles and values. Multiethnic education can be an entity in itself, but multicultural education cannot exist without the inclusion of ethnic content. To further illustrate the

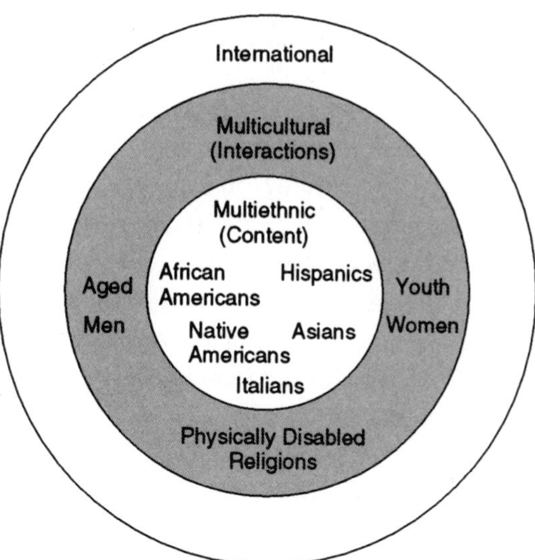

Fig. 2.2 Model for Multicultural Education (Ethnic and Cultural Groups)

Source: G. C. Baker in J. Hartley, ed. *Comment, A Research/Action Report on Women,* vol. 12, no. 1 (Washington, D. C., 1979), p. 2.

relationship between multiethnic and multicultural education, let us consider an African-American woman who clearly identifies with the African-American experience. The ethnic identification of an African American woman will more than likely influence the manner in which she responds to various dimensions of the larger cultural group. This is generally true because most African American women have lived an experience in the United States that is unique to African Americans, and the needs of these women are thus different from those of women from other ethnic backgrounds. These differences may be evident in the way in which African American women express themselves in some of the activities common to all women. All women who comprise the culture of women have many of the same characteristics. However, depending on their identification with and participation in other cultures, their responses and reactions will differ. Socioeconomic dimensions can also affect the manner in which individuals participate. It is thus somewhat easier to understand why women of different ethnic groups respond differently to the feminist movement.

International/Global Education

Because international and global education are used interchangeably to describe the same kind of education, international education will be the term used in this discussion. International education is represented by the outer circle of Fig. 2.2. In most schools, some type of international study takes place. Most teachers are eager to teach a unit and/or lessons about other countries because it is not only fun and exciting but most teachers experience foreign travel during the summer months. Teaching about a personal experience brings with it a degree of comfort that adds to the pleasure of teaching about another country.

There is also something exotic about exposing students to the unfamiliar characteristics of another country. Teaching about the different lifestyles, manner of dress, eating habits, religious practices, and forms of government all combine to make for an interesting study of another nation. Perhaps another reason for the frequent inclusion of international study in curricula is that it requires less personal identification on the part of the teacher; sometimes objectivity is more easily achieved than when teaching about one's own country. International education is taught much more frequently in schools than either multiethnic or multicultural education.

International education is a viable approach to helping students understand diversity from a global perspective. It differs from multiethnic and/or multicultural education in that it does not focus on a study of ethnicity and/or cultural diversity per se. Further, it is not especially concerned with the modification of educational environments so that they respond to the ethnic and cultural needs of all students. However, the study of other countries can provide an excellent mechanism for assisting students in understanding these differences. This can best be accomplished when relationships between groups in different countries are identified. For example, if a relationship between the political behavior of Nigerians and African-Americans can be identified and studied, then the international dimension contributes to a comprehensive analysis of the behavior and the relationship between these two groups. The bridges thus established can serve to promote connecting links between international, multiethnic, and multicultural education. Multiethnic education can be an entity unto itself. Multicultural education requires the input of multiethnic education, and its foundation builds on the knowledge that is gained from the exploration of ethnic cultures. Multicultural education is enhanced by examining the relationships between diverse ethnic groups and the impact ethnicity has on the behavior of the members of larger cultural groups. International education, like multiethnic education, is an area of study of its own but has the potential for contributing to and expanding the various dimensions of multicultural education. Multicultural education can expose individuals to diversity in the United States and in the world. This exposure can create an understanding and a degree of freedom that will allow individuals to maintain one or more cultures and at the same time help them become contributing members of their own countries and the world at large.

Goals of Multicultural Education

According to Dewey, the general features of education can be viewed as the process by which social groups maintain their existence.[18] If social groups maintain their existence through the contributions of their members, education can be seen as one of the processes through which individuals become aware of themselves, of their groups, and of their place in the world at large. Therefore, the goals of multicultural education presented in this chapter focus on the individual.

Goal I: One goal of multicultural education is to help students become more aware of themselves as individuals and of their culture and/or cultures.

Acquiring an understanding of oneself and of the cultures that influence one's behavior and thoughts is a requisite for understanding the cultures and behaviors of others. Understanding and awareness of the diversity of cultures prevalent in our society and the world can help one live successfully in a country and a world filled with diversity.

Goal II: A second goal of multicultural education is to help individuals develop an understanding and appreciation for the cultures of others.

According to Brown, an understanding of others helps us to increase knowledge of ourselves and to be more objective. Peoples of the world are so bound together that survival depends on how well we can live together. In other words, survival depends on knowledge and understanding of one another and respect for peoples whose ways are different from our own.[19]

Goal III: A third goal of multicultural education is to encourage individuals to support and to participate in as many different cultural groups as they choose.

Multicultural education encourages the freedom of individuals to maintain the lifestyles, values, and beliefs of any ethnic and/or cultural group. At the same time, however, multicultural education places responsibility upon each person for maintaining a culture shared by most who live in a given nation. A shared culture can be thought of as a national culture, one embraced by the majority of the citizens of a specific country. Multicultural education supports the idea that the individual has some responsibility for participating in a national culture; the degree of participation is not always left to the discretion of the person but can be determined partially by the rules, regulations, and traditions of the culture. Multicultural education provides an opportunity for helping individuals feel comfortable about the options available to them in the maintenance of more than one culture.

Goal IV: A fourth goal is to help individuals reach their full potential so that they are in control of their lives and thereby become empowered.

An individual who has achieved academically and has developed the skills needed for productive living can be said to have reached the level or stage where he or she is empowered. Christine Sleeter believes that empowerment can be achieved through multicultural education and that empowerment is a fundamental goal of this process. Sleeter also maintains that, through the acquisition of knowledge and skills, individuals who are empowered will also be able to help bring about constructive social change.[20] Multicultural instruction can provide the basis for what one may need in order to acquire that sense of strength and power over self. Power and strength provided through the acquisition of skills and knowledge contribute to feelings of independence and control of one's life and future.

The goals of multicultural education support and encourage individuals to become more aware of their cultures, to have an understanding and appreciation of other cultures, to participate in one or more cultures while assuming responsibility for maintaining a shared national culture.

Where, When, and How to Begin

The process of multicultural education is one that ideally should begin at the very early stages of socialization. The family still remains the individual's first and most influential social system and provides children with their most significant social training situations. The family differs from other social systems primarily because relationships are intimate; there is a well-defined hierarchy of status based on age, and the individual is provided with a primary-group membership throughout all of life.[21] However, because diversity in any form has not been highly regarded in most parts of society, including the family, children have not, to any degree, been taught to accept and to appreciate differences. Therefore, for the time being, the process of multicultural education will need to begin in school.

The process of multicultural education should begin with the very earliest experiences a child has with school. The entire educational environment should reflect the pluralistic nature of society and not be confined to the immediate school community and/or classroom. A total approach will involve far more than the academic curriculum, although the general trend is to make changes in the content taught in classrooms. A total approach means a revamping of educational objectives and goals. It means making sure that hiring policies ensure diverse staffing patterns, that curricula revisions are comprehensive and include ethnic and cultural content, that instructional materials are bias-free, and that inservice training programs provide teachers and staff with information and assistance on how to make education multicultural. A total approach will certainly include and involve the entire school community and will capitalize on the richness of resources that can be provided through students, parents, and other members of the school community.

Successful implementation will depend on support throughout the school community and on the state level. At each level of involvement, there will need to be demonstrated commitment. State boards of education and local school boards have the responsibility for initiating and developing legislation that can affect policy and vice versa. Policy and legislation that support the implementation of multicultural education are needed.

In developing multicultural education, we must create a process of education that will benefit all children. Applying the Principles of Multicultural Education, as discussed in Chapter 1, to the development efforts can help to insure success.

Notes

1. Gwendolyn C. Baker, "Multicultural Imperatives for Curriculum Development," *Teacher Education 2 (1):73.*
2. Louise Berman and Jessie Roderick, eds., *Feeling, Valuing and the Art of Growing: Insights into the Affective* (Washington, D.C.: Association for Supervision and Curriculum Development, 1977), p. 255.

3. James Banks, "Multicultural Education: Characteristics and Goals," in *Multicultural Education: Issues and Perspectives,* ed. James A. Banks and Cherry A. McGee Banks (Boston: Allyn and Bacon, 1989), p. 2.
4. John Dewey, *Democracy and Education* (New York: Macmillan, 1916), p. 115.
5. Gwendolyn C. Baker, "The Role of the School in Transmitting the Culture of All Learners in a Free and Democratic Society," *Educational Leadership 36* (November 1978): 134–38.
6. Kenneth Clark, *Prejudice and Your Child* (Boston: Beacon Press, 1955).
7. Mary Ellen Goodman, *Race Awareness in Young Children* (London: Collier-Macmillan, 1952).
8. Bruno Lasker, *Racial Attitudes in Children* (New York: New American Library, 1970).
9. William W. Joyce and James A. Banks, *Teaching the Language Arts to Culturally Different Children* (Reading, MA: Addison-Wesley, 1971), p. 262.
10. Wilbur B. Brooker, Edsel Erickson, and Lee Joiner, "Self-Concept of Ability and School Achievement," in *Teaching Social Studies to Culturally Different Children,* ed. James A. Banks and William A. Joyce (Reading, MA: Addison-Wesley, 1971), pp. 105–111.
11. James A. Banks, "Multicultural Education and Its Critics: Britain and the United States," in *Multicultural Education: The Interminable Debate,* Johan Modgil, Gajendrak Verma, Kanka Mallick and Celia Modgil, eds. (Philadelphia: The Falmer Press, 1986), p. 229.
12. Harris L. Dante, "Forward to Teaching Ethnic Studies: Concepts and Strategies," *43rd Yearbook*, ed. James A. Banks, Washington, D.C., 1973), p. vii.
13. Charles F. Marden and Gladys Meyer, *Minorities in American Society* (New York: Van Nostrand, 1973), p. 44.
14. James A. Banks, *Teaching Strategies for Ethnic Studies,* 2nd ed. (Boston: Allyn and Bacon, 1979), p. 10.

15. William A. Hunter, ed. *Multicultural Education Through Competency-Based Teacher Education* "Antecedents to Development of and Emphasis on Multicultural Education." (Washington, D.C.: American Association for Colleges of Teacher Education, 1974), p. 21.
16. Ina Corrine Brown, *Understanding Other Cultures* (Englewood Cliffs, N.J.: Prentice-Hall, 1963), p. 3.
17. Ibid., p. 133.
18. Dewey, p. 375.
19. Brown, p. 3–4.
20. Christine Sleeter, *Empowerment Through Multicultural Education* (Albany: State University of New York Press, 1991), p. 91.
21. Robert J. Havinghurst and Bernice L Neugarten, "The Family and the School," in *Society and Education* (Boston: Allyn and Bacon, 1975), p. 135.

3
What Is Needed?

Principle II: The development of a multicultural approach to education should be comprehensive and complete.

Principle III: Multicultural education should be developed in an environment that is conducive and supportive.

Principle IV: All of the participants in the school community should be involved in the development of multicultural education.

The development and implementation of multicultural education will require total involvement and commitment of all of the participants in an educational setting. What is needed to accomplish this level of involvement will be discussed in this chapter. As is indicated in Principle II, the development of a multicultural approach to education should be comprehensive and complete. Every facet of the educational environment must be considered and involved. Committed leadership can offer much in the way of garnering the necessary support. Principles III and IV address the need for the environment to be supportive and inclusive.

Leadership and Advocacy

The success of any effort depends on effective and committed leadership. Leadership, in this context, is not limited to the superintendent of the local school district nor is it confined to the efforts of a building principal. The kind of leadership that is needed to ensure the successful implementation of education that is multicultural will require that all who have the responsibility for making decisions provide leadership. Leaders who are committed often will be able to provide the advocacy needed. However, the advocacy needed to promote multicultural education will also require the commitment of those who represent the full spectrum of the community.

Advocates must be clear and definite about the importance of multicultural education in providing a quality education for all children. The possibility that this approach can offer an opportunity for both minority and nonminority children to gain a realistic view of their place in the nation and the world must be stressed. Unfortunately too many nonminority children have been made to feel that nearly everything revolves around them and their culture. Far too many minority children have learned that they influence little and not much emanates from them. Through the process of multicultural education, all children have an opportunity to learn about their histories and about the involvement of different peoples in the development of this nation. As a result, nonminority children may be able to shake loose ethnocentric attitudes that too often control their thinking. Minority children will and can begin to have a sense of belonging that may have a positive impact on their futures. According to Ornstein, research done in the sixties found a correlation between the teaching of black pride and culture and increased student achievement.[1]

The value of a multicultural approach to all children, minority and nonminority alike, must be clearly articulated. It is also important for advocates to point out the value of multicultural education in helping individuals understand differences so as to develop a greater appreciation for diversity. Increased understanding may lead individuals to become more comfortable with diversity, seek it out, acknowledge it, and accept it as part of the reality of life.

Policy and Legislation

Effective advocacy can result in the development of policy and legislation at all levels. Policy, especially informal policy, often precedes the legislative process. Policy practices and procedures can provide what is needed for the implementation of multicultural education at all levels. Once advocacy has achieved this level of support, the evidence needed to stimulate legislation may be available. For example, if a school district becomes able to support the development of multicultural education through the establishment of procedures and guidelines, much will have been accomplished. This level of support indicates some interest and commitment and will serve to provide a valuable step in the process of achieving greater support. However, most school districts will need much more than guidelines to aid them in this process. The development of clear and distinct policy on several levels may be necessary. Certainly, policy made and adopted by the governing body of the school district will go a long way toward supporting the development of the process. The formal adoption of policy and the legalization of intent, will provide support and enforcement mechanisms that can be helpful in the application of a comprehensive approach. Legislation is a means through which total implementation can be achieved.

Betty Atwell Wright discusses the need for community-school policies, curricula, and facilities to be designed intelligently and creatively so as to meet the needs of educating for diversity. She stresses the importance of alert groups of community policymakers, boards of education, and professionally trained staffs who are attitudinally prepared to treat every child with respect and fairness. She continues by citing the need for monetarily and morally supportive innovations that will permit school personnel to work at the level of their highest competence. Education that teaches children about cultural diversity cannot exist in a vacuum. It does not develop from books and laws alone but will thrive and successfully educate students for life in a democratic society if embraced by the entire educational environment.[2] Total involvement will require action and support at all levels. The following section includes suggestions for taking a comprehensive approach to the attainment of multicultural education.

Governing Bodies

The only way the educational environment can demonstrate total support for multicultural education is to have every segment of the environment actively involved. This means that no group is allowed to sit idly but rather should take whatever action is needed to show support. The best place to begin is with those who are legally responsible for the school, the district, and/or the institution. The boards of trustees, directors, and school boards should take an open position in support of multicultural education. As was stated in the preceding section, while a general statement demonstrating support is needed and valuable in itself, such a statement should be strong in intent and should state a comprehensive commitment by those in charge. A comprehensive statement can provide the chief administrator and others in central administration with the support they will need to direct the implementation. A strong statement will indicate the full intent of the board.

However, strong and inclusive policy statement is not always easily obtained. Most governing bodies will need to spend a great deal of time and expend considerable effort in developing such a statement. Concepts, definition, and intent will need to be clearly stated if the policy statement is to be meaningful. A brief description of the process used by the Board of Education of the City of New York, as well as the resulting policy, is included in the discussion on local school boards.

Policy and legislation established by boards of trustees or boards of regents in institutions of higher education needs to include the entire college or university. To involve only the school or college of education in the process of preparing educators for multicultural education is to use a segmented approach. To effect a total approach, the entire institution will need to be involved. If that occurs, all of the experiences offered to the student will be multicultural. This includes a multicultural approach to staffing, curriculum, and all policies that govern the institution. In order to achieve a total approach at the level of the school district, the same process must be followed. The first step in achieving a comprehensive approach in any type of educational environment is to obtain the commitment of the responsible governing body. However, there are some instances in which a particular college or unit of an institution of higher education may provide the leadership for the institutionalizing of the approach. Also, in smaller settings in which the focus is on educational theory, the opportunity to provide what is needed to transform the entire institution may be more readily available. A discussion of how this was achieved in just such a setting, the Bank Street College of Education, will be included in the section on schools and colleges of education.

Central Administration

In describing strategies for eliminating racism in American education, William E. Sedlacek and Glenwood C. Brooks, Jr., mention the necessity to obtain support for the elimination of racism from the central administration. This strategy is of extreme importance to multicultural education and is discussed by Sedlacek and Brooks in the following manner:

> It is important to have the open support of the top people for effective antiracism efforts. "Open support" means written or public statements, as specific as possible, on the actions to be taken by a school. Aside from committing the top people, this will persuade some of the more cautious in the organization to get involved.[3]

The commitment of the governing body and the central administration to multicultural education is most important. This involvement is crucial because it sets the tone in the institution and/or in the district for implementation. It is through the chief administrator and central staff that deans of colleges and principals of schools receive direction and the kinds of support needed to carry out the approach in their colleges and schools. Once the top administrators have displayed open support through their behavior, the process of achieving a total approach is well under way. It is at this level that various coordinators, counselors, psychologists, and other school personnel receive specific instructions about how they are to operate.

An excellent example of a total approach to multicultural education is illustrated in the writings of John Dillard and his colleagues on special education. The utilization of a multicultural approach to mainstreaming and its effect on counselors, psychologists, and administrators is described as follows:

> Advocates of multicultural education emphasize the necessity for increased awareness and sensitivity among counselors, teachers, psychologists, and administrators that our physically disabled students come from diverse ethnic and cultural backgrounds. Special education is only one of many dimensions under the umbrella of multicultural education, while mainstreaming is one process that operationalizes or places both (multicultural education and mainstreaming) into a degree of practice in meeting handicapped students' personal, cultural, and specialized academic needs.[4]

Although this discussion pertains to the needs of students who are physically disabled, much of it is applicable to any part of the school program. The counselor who works with physically disabled students and who is prepared to take a multicultural approach will be equally well prepared to work with other students. Dillard comments on the effectiveness of counselors who employ a multicultural approach:

> Culturally competent counselors share their special skills with others to produce constructive changes among other school personnel and the institution in which they function. Such counselors interpret handicapped students' needs to the

> institution. A multicultural approach to counseling requires an expansion of counselors' roles to help integrate developmental tasks of handicapped and normal students into the total educational structure, including ethnic and cultural factors, as well as academic and curricular areas.[5]

Integrating ethnic and cultural factors into academic and other curricular areas is the essence of the implementation of multicultural education. Equally as important to the effective operation of an educational environment is the psychologist. A culturally oriented psychologist is one who works well with students, parents, teachers, and administrators. The sensitive psychologist is aware of the variations in parents' cultural experiences and is able to communicate the value of this diversity to other school personnel. A psychologist who is multiculturally oriented emphasizes the need for seriously considering cultural and environmental factors in testing, reporting on, and making recommendations for ethnic minority physically disabled students. The same sensitivity and skills needed to work with physically disabled students are those needed for working with all children.[6]

As a leader, the administrator is responsible for orchestrating the process of implementation and therefore needs to be culturally sensitive to such differences, as well as to the needs of various staff members. A comprehensive approach will require that the administrator makes sure the secretaries, custodians, and bus drivers are all sensitive to the needs of children in a culturally diverse setting.

Local School Districts

Community, Parents, and Students

A concrete way of beginning to involve the entire school district in the process is for parents, students, and community residents to be exposed to cultural diversity. This can be achieved in a variety of ways. Schools have a wonderful opportunity to display diversity through assemblies, theatrical productions, concerts, art displays, radio and television shows, and a host of other events. Parents, friends, and neighbors are always eager to witness events in which their children participate. Sensitive administrators and teachers will be able, through school-sponsored functions and other community events, to identify those individuals who can to help foster interest in the development of a more formal approach to establishing a multicultural school environment.

Sensitive leadership will determine when committees and task forces will need to be organized in order to achieve input and support. The involvement of already established groups such as parent-teacher organizations and associations will be vital to the process. There is no one method or process that guarantees success. However, if efforts are focused on involving representatives from all segments of the school community, the efforts should prove successful. Gollnick and Chinn emphasize the importance of such involvement:

> Although all schools are multicultural, the cultural diversity that exists is not always positively reflected. A school that affirms multiculturalism will integrate the community in its total program. Not only will the educators know and understand the community, but the parents and the community will know and participate in the school activities. The first step in multiculturalizing the school is the development of positive and supportive relations between school and the community.[7]

However, once the community is organized, it is essential that the outcome, either through recommendations and/or discussion, be shared with the school board. The school board should guide the process for developing policy.

The School Board

All initial steps taken to sensitize the school community and to stimulate interest in cultural diversity should involve the school board. Depending on the size of the school district and the style of governance, however, the introductory steps may be planned by the administrators and staff in charge. Regardless of the means through which the need for multicultural education is brought to the attention of the community, the school board is the critical link in ensuring success. Much of the leadership and advocacy, and certainly the policy, needed to guide the development of the approach must come from this governing body.

In order to develop and adopt the kind of policy that will be needed to ensure successful implementation of multicultural education, each member of the board and the members of central administration will need to work together in order to establish a common definition. This is a process that, if done in a thorough way, should lead to a definition of multicultural education that all will be able to embrace. Once a clear definition has been established, the next step is to develop policy that will guide implementation. Again, this will take time and should allow for input from the entire community. In school districts where a committee has been appointed to oversee the development of multicultural education, this committee must work closely with the board and staff and help in developing the definition and in crafting the policy. Each school district should select a process that will be compatible with the operating style of the district and the local community. However, no matter what process is followed, it should involve participation from all segments of the community. Public hearings and discussions should be part of the process.

Guidelines for Policy Development

In developing the policy, the following steps may provide guidance:

1. The mission statement of the school board should serve as a basis for the policy.
2. The definition of multicultural education adopted by the school board should be included.
3. Reports and recommendations made to the school board should include reference to the contributions made by other groups, because these will strengthen the document.

4. The scope of the policy should be clearly stated; in other words, the ethnic and cultural groups targeted by the policy should be included.
5. The goal(s) of the policy should be defined and included.
6. Implementation steps that give the superintendent the authority to develop a plan of action are essential.
7. A method for monitoring the progress helps to ensure effective implementation.

In 1989, the Board of Education, City of New York, adopted policy for multicultural education and for the promotion of positive intergroup relations. In this district, the largest in the nation, the process included almost every step previously discussed. The leadership for the development of the policy came from some members of the School Board, interested staff and advocacy groups in the city at large. The involvement of constituents was extensive and helpful to the adoption and acceptance of the policy. The policy may be viewed as a model of what can be achieved.

Statement of Policy on
Multicultural Education and Promotion of
Positive Intergroup Relations
(November 15, 1989)

WHEREAS, all students are entitled to a quality education which enables them to achieve to their fullest potential; and

WHEREAS, people from all parts of the world live and work in New York City, necessitating a multicultural education which fosters intergroup knowledge and understanding and equips students to function effectively in a global society; and

WHEREAS, multicultural education values cultural pluralism and rejects the view that schools should seek to melt away cultural differences or merely tolerate cultural diversity; rather, multicultural education accepts cultural diversity as a valuable resource that should be preserved and extended; and

WHEREAS, on February 15, 1989, the Board of Education accepted the report and recommendations of the Human Relations Task Force insofar as it identified the need for a comprehensive multicultural education program to foster positive intergroup relations and to eliminate bias of all forms; and

WHEREAS, this resolution extends the policy for Intergroup Relations established by the Board of Education on November 20, 1985 directing the Chancellor to "take appropriate steps to bring about the elimination of practices which foster attitudes and/or actions leading to discrimination against students, parents, or school personnel on the basis of race, color, religion, national origin, gender, age, sexual orientation, and/or handicapping condition"; now be it therefore

RESOLVED, that the New York City Board, by adoption of this resolution, hereby ratifies a policy of multicultural education and commits itself and its resources to providing an education to achieve the following goals:

- To develop an appreciation and understanding of the heritage of students' and staffs' own ethnic, racial, cultural, and linguistic groups.
- To promote and foster intergroup understanding, awareness and appreciation by students and staff of the diverse ethnic, racial, cultural, and linguistic groups represented in the New York City public schools and the general population.
- To enhance New York City youngsters' self-worth and self-respect.
- To encourage a variety of teaching strategies to address differences in learning styles.

- To identify the impact of racism and other barriers to acceptance of differences.
- To develop opportunities for all students to become bilingual and proficient in at least two languages.
- To develop a multicultural perspective (interpreting history and culture from a variety of perspectives).
- To analyze human rights violations in our global society and the progress made in obtaining human rights.
- To develop an appreciation of the cultural and historical contributions of a variety of racial and ethnic groups to the growth of the United States and world civilizations.
- To develop the human relations skills needed in interpersonal and intergroup relations as well as conflict resolution, with a special emphasis on conflict arising from bias and discrimination based on race, color, religion, national origin, gender, age, sexual orientation, and/or handicapping condition; and be it further

RESOLVED, that the Chancellor shall develop procedures and guidelines for textbook selection; shall review all text-books and instructional materials to ensure that they are free of stereotypical views of any group whether expressed or implied, by statement, visual image or by omission; and shall, when necessary, develop supplementary materials when commercially available material fails to meet guidelines for comprehensive and accurate instruction; and be it further

RESOLVED, that the Chancellor shall submit to the Board a comprehensive multicultural education plan which shall include guidelines and procedures for program, staff, and curriculum development.

This policy was adopted by the Board of Education with an additional explanation. The following statement was included in the document.

Explanation

This resolution formalizes the recognition by the Chancellor and the New York City Board of Education of the need for a multicultural education initiative.

The commitment to multicultural education will permeate every aspect of educational policy, including counseling programs, assessment and testing, curriculum and instruction, representative staffing at all levels, and teaching materials. Cultural diversity is to be viewed as an enrichment to learning and not as a deficit.

There will be opportunities for community-based organizations, cultural institutions, and institutions of higher learning to cooperate in developing and maintaining multicultural education in the schools.

The input and cooperation of parents and students are of critical importance in the design and implementation of multicultural education programs. Therefore, a high priority will be placed on their involvement in all aspects of this initiative.

Staff development which emphasizes the philosophy, attitudes, skills, knowledge, practices, and procedures essential to a sound program of multicultural education is to be provided on a continuous, consistent basis for all staff involved in the education process. There must be multicultural staff recruitment and development to aid in the implementation of this policy.

The explanation makes the intent of the policy very clear. It also outlines, generally, what is to happen next. In other words it has included the thrust of the implementation. The suggested steps delineated in the Guidelines for Policy Development have all been included in the development of this statement.

Once the policy has been developed and is adopted by the School Board, it should be publicized and disseminated throughout the community. The implementation process is the next important step and one that should be carefully planned and monitored. The plan for implementation should clearly indicate what action will be taken. In an effort to ensure successful progress, the action steps should include time lines and indicate areas and individuals responsible for the action.

Superintendents

The policy adopted by the board will provide the direction and support needed for implementation. Superintendents have the responsibility for the following:

1. The superintendent will need to openly support the policy of the board and make a statement as to the manner in which he or she will proceed for implementation.
2. A plan of action should be submitted to the board for approval. Once approved, the plan should be presented to the central staff, clearly defining what is expected of all staff. The plan of action should not be a mandate from the chief executive but should reflect the input of all involved in the central office. The plan should include the following:
   a. A statement as to personnel practices and policy so as to create a pattern of staffing that is culturally diverse. This statement should include the need and or requirement for all new teachers to have some exposure and training in multicultural education before they are officially employed. Procedures and requirements for multicultural in-service training should be clearly spelled out.
   b. The effects the policy will have for the academic curriculum should be included in the plan. Some attention should be given to the overall process for restructuring the curriculum and indicating the requirement for all staff to be involved in this effort.
   c. It will also be important to make some reference to the commitment to provide necessary resources.
   d. A general statement as to the expectations of the role and the responsibility of all staff should be included. This

statement should include support staff as well as the professional staff. No group of staff should be excluded, including the maintenance workers and bus drivers.

e. The plan should include student expectations and outcomes.

f. Finally, a time line for completion of the plan will be essential. Most plans will be able to achieve goals in a three-to-five year time span.

3. All of the above must be carefully shared with the community and with the school district staff via newspapers, bulletins, staff meetings, and other effective means of communication.

Central Staff

Each central staff member should be required to develop a subplan indicating his or her role and responsibilities in restructuring the assigned area so that it incorporates a multicultural approach. These plans should be developed with input from as many staff members and teachers as possible. Time lines and budgets can be valuable and should be included. For example, the following list suggests what specific staff members might include in a subplan.

1. *The assistant superintendent for finance* should develop a plan that will incorporate the financial costs of implementation. The budget needed to carry out the plan of action should not necessarily exceed the existing budget. Multicultural education can be implemented without extra funds, but the budget will need to reflect the reallocation of funds to adequately support the implementation.
2. *The assistant superintendent for administration* should make sure that the overall plan is one that includes all staff and one will insure coordination.
3. *The assistant superintendent for curriculum* should include plans for proceeding with the restructuring of the curriculum by level and subject matter. A comprehensive

plan should also speak to the evaluation of existing instructional materials and plans for developing a system for selecting new materials to ensure their appropriateness for multicultural education.

4. *The director of personnel* should formulate a plan that includes the process to be followed in the recruitment and selection of new teachers to ensure that minorities and women are included in significant numbers. Detailed plans for developing a multicultural in-service training program will be needed, complete with identification of staff needs, selection of trainers and/or consultants, procedures, and requirements.

All other central staff should follow the same format and submit their subplans to the superintendent for approval.

Principals

Building principals must also make a commitment to support the policy of the board and the superintendent's plan of action for the district. This commitment should be in writing and communicated to the staff, students, and the school community. The principal will also need to develop a subplan of action for the school. This should be developed in collaboration with the entire staff. The subplan should address the following areas:

1. A process must be established to ensure future hiring of individuals who will contribute to the diversity of the staff.
2. Plans for building inservice training will need to be definite and include a statement as to how this will be accomplished so as to include all staff.
3. Plans for how teachers are to proceed with the restructuring of their instructional content should be included.
4. Some attention should also be given to the importance of involving all support staff in an assessment of what their

roles and responsibilities are to be in the process. This would include the secretarial staff, custodians, bus drivers, lunchroom supervisors, and others.

5. Too often little attention is given to the building itself, and plans for creating an environment conducive to multicultural education should be helpful. This should include bulletin boards, signs, written announcements, lunch and snack menus, and other means of communication.
6. The plans for the building should include a time line and a plan for assessing progress.

Teachers

How the teachers proceed to restructure the instructional content will depend on the plan of action for the district and the subplan for the school. Teachers should be involved in the following:

1. Identify areas they can immediately affect, such as developing bulletin boards that display diversity via pictures and/or language, room book collections, selection of materials to be read to the children, and many other areas that will not necessitate detailed planning. (The material included in Part II may be helpful.)
2. Each teacher should make a list of the kinds of help he or she needs in order to begin to develop instructional content and methodology that are multicultural.

Support Staff

Support staff should be required to identify their contributions to the process. For example, the chef might pledge to plan menus that will reflect the kinds of food children eat at home. A secretary might decide to use a bilingual approach to the office bulletin board. Everyone in the building can contribute something to the restructuring-process and should be encouraged to do so.

Parents

Individual parents and parent organizations should be invited to participate. There are many activities that parents are involved in that can be approached multiculturally. Parents should be invited to participate in the inservice training programs and they should be encouraged to plan programs that will help them to become sensitive and aware of the benefits of a multicultural approach to the entire school community. Parents are a marvelous resource and should be included in providing instruction about specific ethnic and cultural groups to students.

Students

Students will become involved in the classroom through the instruction presented by the teacher. However, students can also serve as resources and should be encouraged to share information about their ethnic and cultural backgrounds in meaningful and appropriate ways.

Multicultural education can permeate an entire school district; a total approach to the process can create the kind of learning environment that produces students who will achieve academically and who will be prepared to live effectively in a diverse society. What is needed is commitment and a plan of action that will involve everyone and every aspect of the local school district.

State Departments of Education

State Governing Bodies

Ideally, the catalyst for implementation on the state level should be the state governing body that has the responsibility for education. The ultimate goal of this body should be to ensure that all education in the state is multicultural. Achieving this goal will, of course, require legislation. However, it would be a mistake to delay efforts to achieve this goal until legislation is adopted. There is much this body can do to ensure progress without legislation. The state board of education can proceed in similar fashion to that suggested for the local school boards and accomplish the following:

1. The body, whether it is the state board of education, trustees, or regents will need to establish policy and legislation that will identify the need, make a commitment, and require a multicultural approach to be integrated throughout every facet of the department.
2. Further, this body will need to plan how best to develop the mechanism that will help achieve the goal of making education multicultural throughout the state. (The mechanism developed will depend on how the state is structured and how best to accomplish the desired outcomes).
3. A comprehensive plan should be developed that must include all that is intended in steps 1 and 2. Because of the comprehensive nature of a state plan of action, careful attention will need to be given to ensuring the input and involvement of as many different constituents as possible.
4. During all stages of the development of policy, legislation, and a plan, the leadership, state superintendent, and the head of the elected or appointed governing body must publicly support the efforts.
5. It will be important for the implementation plan to give special consideration to the following:
   Personnel—Plans for an assessment of the existing staffing pattern in the department should be made. Plans for overcoming deficiencies with regard to cultural diversity should be included.
   Policies, guidelines, certification requirements—The plan should carefully outline the approach to be used in evaluating all departmental policies, sets of guidelines, and requirements for all certification. The approach should include plans for the revisions that may be necessary to make them multicultural.

Guidelines for multicultural education—The plan for implementation should include provisions for the development of a set of guidelines that can be used by all schools in the state.

Technical assistance—Attention should be given to the kinds of assistance the state can provide to schools to assist in the restructuring process. This would include such areas as textbook evaluations.

Financial resources—School districts can be encouraged to adopt the approach through the allocation of state funds, and plans for accomplishing this should be included in the plan.

The plan for implementation prepared by the superintendent for the board's approval must represent the input of the entire department, and participation can be achieved if the plan is approached in a manner that is similar to that suggested for local districts. Planning on the state level may necessitate a longer period of time to develop but should contain time elements and a plan for monitoring progress in the department and throughout the state as well. Currently, where there is some activity that may be considered multicultural on the state level, it is generally confined to those offices within the department that focus on ethnic and minority concerns. A total approach to the implementation of multicultural education in a state department of education must involve the entire department, including every person at every level.

Institutions of Higher Education

Board of Regents/Trustees

If an institution of higher education is to become involved in multicultural education, the process for achieving a total approach is again very similar to that outlined for local school districts and state departments. The mandate for action should come directly from the governing body. The stimulus for adopting a multicultural approach could be directly related to the impact of external forces that may encourage the move. For example, in states where the state department of education becomes immersed in the approach, the outreach will more than likely include the state institutions of higher education. Plans could include the involvement of both public and private institutions. The state is in an excellent position to make a positive difference in this area because of its responsibility for certification, regulations, and funding. Whatever the reason for an institution's move towards the adoption of the process, the governing bodies will need to do the following:

1. A commitment to the adoption of a multicultural approach should come in the form of the adoption of policy and/or legislation incorporating a definition and the intended impact of the policy on the entire school, college, or university.
2. The chief executive officer of the institution and the Chair of the governing body will need to publicly support all of the efforts in this regard.
3. The chief executive officer of the institution should be requested to develop a plan for adoption that will provide specific directions for all segments of the institution. The planning process should involve the following:

   Subplans should be required from each vice-presidential area, and these plans should be as detailed as those suggested for the top-level administrators in the public schools.

   The chancellors, provosts, and deans should be required to submit plans that will reflect how their campus and/or school will respond.

   The involvement of the staff and faculty should be solicited in accord with the mode of operation that is particular to higher education.

The size and type of the institution will help to determine the time it takes to develop a plan. The length of time needed for various stages of implementation and the way the institution will proceed to integrate multicultural education throughout should be included. Attention must be given to as many of the various elements as suggested for local school districts and state departments and also to those areas that may be unique to higher education. Institutions of higher education have built into their system of operation many valuable resources that can help to disseminate information about multiculturalism, i.e., radio stations, campus newspapers, alumni journals, and a myriad of other forms of communication. A carefully developed plan with full participation of all can ensure the success of integrating multicultural education throughout the entire institution.

Schools and Colleges of Education

The current trend in institutions of higher education has been for schools and colleges of education to become involved in developing a multicultural teacher-training program. This approach is limited and should not be substituted for proceeding to involve the total institution. There are several reasons some schools and colleges of education are becoming involved in the restructuring of their programs so they are multicultural. Some institutions are aware of the need; others have been prodded to do so by external forces, such as a requirement of local school districts to place only student teachers who have received multicultural teacher training. Still other teacher-training institutions have been encouraged to do so by the accrediting requirement set forth in the accreditation standards of the National Council for the Accreditation of Teacher Education (NCATE). NCATE is devoted to the evaluation and accreditation of teacher education programs throughout the country. The National Council has been authorized by the Council on Post-Secondary Accreditation (COPA) to adopt standards and procedures for accreditation and to determine the accreditation status of institutional programs for preparing teachers and other professional school personnel.[8]

An institution is approved for NCATE accreditation once it has been assessed by the standards used in the evaluation. Until 1979 the NCATE standards did not include requirements for multicultural education. Therefore, unless a particular school or college of education felt the need to include this approach in its program for training teachers, there were no provisions for multicultural education. The revised NCATE standards were ratified January 1, 1985. These standards reflected a totally integrated approach. In 1988 these standards were reaffirmed. It is interesting to note that the standards were revised to include multicultural education by several groups and individuals external to the association. Today standards are thoroughly integrated with multicultural definitions, concepts, and requirements.

The requirements of these standards can be included in the teacher-training model presented in Chapter 4. In order to accomplish that which is intended in these standards, the institution will need to take specific steps. These steps should include the following:

1. The dean of the school or college, in collaboration with the governing body of the institution (i.e., the executive committee), should develop a statement of commitment to the goals and objectives of multicultural education that includes a definition or provides the opportunity for the faculty to develop a definition that will be adopted by this body at a later time.
2. A committee should be appointed for the purpose of assisting the dean and the executive committee in developing a plan of implementation. This committee should be composed of individuals who are respected in the school and in the school community. The members should represent as much diversity as possible and have some knowledge of multicultural education. The plan of implementation should address as many aspects of the school or college as will be needed to insure the involvement of the total institution. The following are a few issues that should be attended to:
   a. The process needed to involve all faculty and staff in development of the plan.
   b. Restructuring the curriculum and planning for the impact this will have on faculty, staff, and students in the school and in the larger university environment.

c. Identifying policy and practices that will need to be modified to ensure consistency.
d. The time it will take to effect the changes in the curriculum and in the requirements for certification.
e. Inservice experiences for faculty and staff.
f. Student teaching, practicum placements, and supervision.
g. Financial support and commitment.
h. Staffing patterns.
i. Student admissions and recruitment.
j. Accountability and assessment.

If there is strong commitment from the leadership in the school and support for the work of the committee responsible for developing a plan, total integration can be achieved. As previously noted, some teacher-training institutions made the move toward restructuring their programs so they could provide their students with multicultural training before the NCATE standards were revised. Several institutions around the country started moving in this direction. The following description of what occurred at one institution may provide a helpful example of the process.

A Case Study: The University of Michigan

The School of Education, University of Michigan, was one of the first institutions to develop a multicultural teaching training program. The school was encouraged to move in this direction by a mandate from the local school district. Student unrest in the late sixties and early seventies in the Ann Arbor, Michigan, public schools brought forth a report. Titled "The Humaneness Report," it included provisions for the preparation of teachers in the area of multiethnic education and specifically addressed preservice training. This provision had a definite effect on the contract between the teachers and the school board. The 1972–73 master agreement between Ann Arbor Teachers Association and the Board of Education contained a provision calling for the assignment of only student teachers who had been trained to teach a multiethnic curriculum. This provision served as the catalyst for the School of Education at the University of Michigan to provide such training for their student teachers. The school went through several trial approaches before organizing a program that eventually involved the entire school. Although these events took place two decades ago, they involve a process that is still timely, appropriate, and applicable to most colleges and schools of education.

Before the faculty was able to adopt a set of multicultural objectives, two very important steps were taken. First a committee was appointed for the purpose of planning and directing the restructuring process. Second, faculty forums were held to enlist the help of all faculty in the development of a set of objectives. The process was well organized and inclusive.

The following objectives applied to any member of the School of Education—students, faculty, or other staff—who was responsible for academic programs of the school or who was a participant in such programs. The objectives were developed by the multicultural committee and adopted at the November 15, 1973, faculty meeting of the School of Education.

Knowledge

1. To expand the participants' knowledge of their own and other cultures.
2. To deepen and to increase the participants' awareness of their own cultural identity.
3. To help participants develop a better understanding of various ways to expand their contact with other cultural groups and to become better acquainted with their own cultural roles.

Philosophy

1. To develop the participants' capacities for humane, sensitive, and critical inquiry into the nature of cultural issues, particularly as these may relate to education.
2. To study the aesthetic, epistomological, and ethnic interrelationships of cultural life in the United States and

elsewhere through their psychological, social, economic, and political dimensions.
3. To increase the participants' capacity for examining their own cultural attitudes and values in the light of history and the current situation.
4. To augment participants' abilities for envisaging future developments and engaging in planning for cultural interchange within an emerging world society.

Methodology

To help participants develop the ability to develop and plan multicultural learning experiences by

1. Investigating, developing, and testing suitable teaching strategies for multicultural curriculum.
2. Increasing skills in locating, developing, and using instructional resources for multicultural education.
3. Learning to assess the effectiveness of a multicultural curriculum.

The Program was implemented in the following manner:

- A course list was established that represented all of the courses offered throughout the university that were relevant to multicultural education.
- A requirement was instituted directing students to elect three courses from the approved list to satisfy the multicultural requirement for teacher certification.
- Mechanisms were established to equate student experiences and/or courses taken at other institutions for satisfying the three course requirement.
- All courses in the school were required to include a multicultural approach.
- Special courses were introduced.
- Enrichment activities were scheduled to give students and faculty opportunities for more extensive considerations into certain aspects of multicultural education.

- Research was undertaken to compare the effectiveness of the approaches to teacher training.
- The university established with the school system a means for accountability.[9]

The multicultural teacher-training program at the University of Michigan took about three years to get under way. This program represents one approach used to establish training for teachers in multicultural education.

Federal Support Systems

The Department of Education can play an important role in establishing mechanisms in support of multicultural education on the federal level. Presently little has been done to encourage the concept but some of the past legislation has been somewhat supportive. The following represent pieces of legislation that have resulted in the formulation of programs on the federal level that can be considered supportive of multicultural education:

- *Title IX of the Elementary and Secondary Education Act of 1965* (ESEA). The Ethnic Heritage Program that emerged from ESEA and its funding history supported projects that focused on ethnicity.
- *Title IV of the Civil Rights Act of 1964.* This act provides technical and financial assistance, when requested, for desegregation of school systems.
- *Title VII of the Emergency School Aid Act of 1972.* This act was designed to meet the needs of students and faculty who have faced discrimination and group isolation.
- *Title VII of the Elementary and Secondary Education Act* (ESEA). The emphasis in this legislation is on language; it is known as the bilingual education act. This act provides assistance to programs that address language differences.
- *Title IX of the 1972 Education Amendments.* This act prohibits discrimination on the basis of sex and provides for federally assisted educational programs or activities.

Donna Gollnick and Raymond Giles, in their study "Ethnic Cultural Diversity as Reflected in Federal and State Educational State Educational Legislation and Policies," conclude the following:

> All of the above education laws were politically motivated. They were designed either to promote U.S. foreign policy objectives or to facilitate school desegregation and integration and racial harmony on the domestic scene. Thus the concern of Congress for education to promote intercultural understanding, either internationally or domestic, was perceived as a means towards achieving broader international interests or domestic goals.[10]

Whatever has been achieved through legislation at the federal level, it has not been sufficient to establish a comprehensive approach to multicultural education in schools throughout the nation. This does not mean that the federal government cannot take specific steps to create such an environment. On the contrary, there is much that can be done on the national level to encourage education that is more responsive to diversity. In summarizing the major focus of the Conference on Education and Teacher Education for Cultural Pluralism held in Chicago in 1971, Madelon D. Stent and her colleagues make several recommendations that are of particular importance to the involvement of the federal government in helping to promote education that acknowledges cultural pluralism. The following list of specific steps the federal government might take incorporated many of the ideas that also appear in the recommendations by Stent:[11]

1. The federal government, and more specifically the Department of Education, should begin to involve staff at the decision-making level who are either minority or who clearly represent the concerns of minorities to ensure the establishment of policy reflecting their needs and interests.
2. Guidelines for funding opportunities at the federal level should include requirements that would encourage multicultural education and require evidence of implementation and/or involvement.

3. All review panels making decisions with regard to funding should be required to have sufficient numbers of minorities and women involved.
4. The federal government should organize to provide technical assistance to the field in all areas of multicultural education. This would include assistance to school districts, state departments, and to institutions of higher education as well.
5. A multicultural education clearinghouse should be established for the purpose of disseminating multicultural materials.
6. Provisions that would ensure the publication of commercially prepared multicultural instructional materials should be developed.
7. Research that would contribute to the improvement of multicultural education should be encouraged.
8. Mechanisms that stimulate the upgrading of faculty in institutions of higher education need to be promoted.

Even though these recommendations were made two decades ago, they represent needs that are still with us today. No one is advocating federal control of education in order to achieve multicultural education. Nevertheless, the federal government should take a more active role in supporting education that can be relevant and meaningful to all citizens. The mechanisms for achieving the level of support needed are currently built into the system, and what is needed is the total integration of a multicultural approach at the federal level.

National Organizations and Associations

Clearly, the NCATE standards have had noticeable impact. If NCATE continues to monitor the progress of the multicultural aspects of the standards, much more progress should be forthcoming. What is needed also is a formal commitment to multicultural education by all national organizations and associations. Currently there is evidence that some organizations are moving in that direction. The Association for Supervision and Curriculum Development was one of the first associations to incorporate a multicultural approach throughout its program. The National Council for the Social Studies is another pioneer in the field and one of the first to issue a set of guidelines for multiethnic education. The American Association for Colleges of Teacher Education has been most active and has produced a variety of valuable publications. The National Education Association also has provided leadership in helping teachers prepare for a multicultural curriculum. This list is not all-inclusive but serves to demonstrate that some professional organizations are providing support on the national level. What is needed is more evidence that other professional organizations and associations have become and are also becoming involved in helping to create a supportive environment for multicultural education.

To ensure that all facets of the educational system in this country will be integrated with approaches that are multicultural, advocacy at every level is needed. To achieve a system of education that will respond to cultural diversity and provide quality education for all citizens will require a comprehensive approach. Advocacy and steps to achieve total integration of local school districts, state departments of education, institutions of higher education, the federal government, and national professional organizations and associations with multicultural concepts and approaches are needed to achieve quality education for all.

Notes

1. Allen C. Ornstein, *Race and Politics in School/Community Organizations* (Pacific Palisades, CA: Goodyear, 1974), p. 238.
2. Betty Atwell Wright, *Educating for Diversity* (New York: John Day, 1965), p. 80.
3. William E. Sedlacek and Glenwood C. Brooks, Jr., *Racism in American Education: A Model for Change* (Chicago: Nelson-Hall, 1976), p. 105.
4. John M. Dillard, Lloyd R. Kinnison, and Barbara Peel, "Multicultural Approach to Mainstreaming: A Challenge to Counselors,

Teachers, Psychologists, and Administrators," *Peabody Journal of Education* 57, no. 4 (July 1980):276.

5. Ibid., p. 286.
6. Ibid., pp. 286–287.
7. Donna Gollnick and Philip C. Chinn, *Multicultural Education in a Pluralistic Society* (Columbus, Ohio: Merrill, 1990), p. 299.
8. National Council for the Accreditation of Teacher Education (NCATE), *Standards for the Accreditation of Teacher Education* (Washington, D.C.: NCATE, May 1977).
9. University of Michigan School of Education, *Innovator* (Fall 1974):5.
10. Donna M. Gollnick and Raymond H. Giles, "Ethnic/Cultural Diversity as Reflected in State and Federal Educational Legislation and Policies," in *Pluralism and the American Teacher: Issues and Case Studies*, ed. Frank H. Klassen and Donna M. Gollnick (Washington, D.C.: American Association of Colleges for Teacher Education, Ethnic Heritage Center for Teacher Education, 1977), p. 117.
11. Madelon D. Stent, William R. Hazard, and Harry N. Rivlin, *Cultural Pluralism in Education: A Mandate for Change* (New York: Appleton-Century-Crofts, 1973), pp. 8–9.

Part II

Organizing for Instruction

4
Preparing Teachers to Teach

▲▲▲▲▲▲▲▲▲▲▲▲▲▲▲▲▲▲▲▲▲▲▲▲▲▲▲▲▲▲▲▲▲▲▲▲▲▲▲

Principle V: The training and education of staff, teachers, parents, and community leaders is essential.

The training and education of teachers is an important component in the implementation of multicultural education. This chapter discusses the roles and responsibilities of the teacher and of the teacher-training institution. The discussion includes a set of instructional priorities and a series of faculty and student considerations that should be explored within the context of the training of teachers. Finally, a model for the training of teachers is presented followed by a set of imperatives for multicultural teacher education programs.

It was concluded in Chapter 2 that the process of multicultural education should begin in the schools. It was suggested that this process begin with the very earliest experiences a child has with the school and that multicultural education become an integral part of every aspect of the educational environment. The educational environment includes a variety of people, each with a different set of responsibilities and each with a specific role to play. A superintendent's role is to orchestrate the total system so that it is in accord with local and state policy. A principal's task is one of ensuring that a particular school within the larger system functions according to the policies set forth by central administration and the board of education. A teacher has the responsibility for implementing policy and for playing a vital role in directing and guiding students' learning experiences in the classroom. Although parents and community leaders also have responsibilities, the discussion in this chapter will concentrate on the role and responsibility of the teacher.

The Role and Responsibility of the Teacher

What and how a student learns depends largely on what the teacher decides the student should learn; how the student learns is generally under the control of the teacher. According to Lawrence Stenhouse, "The role of the teacher is to control and to direct the learning of his [her] class, and this he [she] most commonly achieves through asserting his [her] legitimacy, deploying his [her] charisma or organizing for interest."[1]

A teacher's legitimacy is established quickly and somewhat easily because society has prescribed the role and the responsibility of the teacher. Research has suggested that, next to parents, teachers are the most significant people in the lives of children and therefore they play a significant role in the formation of children's attitudes.[2]

Educators, especially teachers, are responsible for helping schools achieve the goals and objectives of a democratic society. Charlotte Epstein describes education as a process in a democratic society that can excite students with the possibility of a full life. Schools have a responsibility for helping people to broaden their expectations and to live fuller lives. In fulfilling this responsibility, they must help students understand the pressures in society that lead to isolation and prejudice. They must also help students resist these pressures.[3] Because of his or her unique role, the teacher determines how and when students begin to explore the societal pressures that encourage racist and sexist attitudes. The attitude of the teacher is crucial in helping students develop attitudes that will prepare them for a harmonious existence in a culturally diverse society.

The teacher is placed in a key position. The task of fostering positive attitudes is a great challenge. Kenneth Morland concludes that in spite of this challenge, there is little being done to counter the prejudiced attitudes that develop among young people in the United States. The young are rarely exposed to accurate information about racial, ethnic, and cultural differences. The failure to present children with this kind of information limits their understanding of others, and such silence can lead to the perpetuation of myths that are prevalent in the larger society. The task of counteracting racial biases is a difficult one but is essential for the maintenance and continued development of a democratic society.[4]

The writings of Jean Grambs and John Carr stress the importance of educators formulating policies that support democratic ideology. Schools are expected to institute policies that are consistent with a democratic heritage. If schools fail to do this, the community has the right and a responsibility to demand change. But as long as educators and teachers plan for and perform their duties with the interests of all children in mind, they have the right to determine policy and the means to obtain educational goals. This professional status of teachers and educators gives them the ultimate responsibility for the education of children.[5] Because of the professional status teachers have, they are directly involved in the process of helping to fulfill the mission of education in a democratic society. The role and responsibility placed upon the teacher is great.

Studies by Kenneth Clark,[6] Mary Ellen Goodman,[7] and Bruno Lasker,[8] have found that children come to school with negative attitudes previously established about people different from them. The teacher has the added responsibility for changing these attitudes and at the same time building learning experiences into the educational process that will encourage positive attitudes about racial, ethnic, and cultural differences.

The teacher and the school have the responsibility for preparing students to live effectively in a democratic society. In fulfilling this responsibility, they must teach students how to live and how to relate to people of all cultures. Students need to understand diversity and learn how to appreciate the value of lifestyles, cultures, religions, and languages that may be different from their own. Because the teacher is the primary agent in the classroom, the teacher must be prepared to teach content that is multicultural in nature and to exhibit behavior that is consistent with the principles involved. If teachers are to gear instruction and guide the learning experiences of children toward developing attitudes conducive to positive intercultural living, they too need preparation.

Teachers are products of their environments and of their education. Therefore the majority of teachers are not prepared in either the cognitive or affective domain to function effectively in the area of multicultural education. It then becomes the responsibility of teacher-training institutions to plan for this kind of training. Teachers need information and support in developing an awareness of cultural diversity.

The Education and Training of Teachers

"If the school is to assume the role of transmitting the cultures of all learners in our society, then the curricula of the school must reflect the cultural diversity of its students."[9] The teacher plays a significant part in helping the school to achieve its task. However, teachers cannot be expected to shoulder the obligation of responding to diversity without some support. Teachers need help, and this assistance should come in the form of inservice and preservice training. The importance of inservice training has increased during the past decade due to declining student enrollments and other factors. The responsibility for preparing teachers falls on those institutions that train teachers. Unfortunately, schools and colleges of education have neither aggressively nor consistently reorganized teacher education programs so that they respond to the needs of the teacher, who must be prepared to function and teach in a society that is diverse. William R. Hazard, Madelon D. Stent, and Harry N. Rivlin, in their work on the need for change in teacher education, have concluded that:

> The implications of cultural pluralism for education and teacher education are monumental. For schools and universities to accept cultural pluralism as both fact and concept would revolutionize what passes now for schooling and teacher training. The basic assumptions underlying school governance, curriculum, academic and nonacademic standards, and educational reward systems would be dramatically reformed....The school mission, now focused on conformity to monolithic, social and intellectual expectation, necessarily would broaden and, paradoxically, would narrow on a new focus. At the present time schools (and teacher-producing institutions, for that matter) struggle to build defensible rationales for failure. Elaborate justifications emerge to explain why substantial numbers of children do not learn and substantial numbers of teachers cannot teach.[10]

Teacher-training institutions have the responsibility for training and educating teachers so they will be able to guide the learning experiences of children in such a way as to prepare them for the complex social realities.

Institutions that educate and train teachers need to restructure their programs so that both the education and training of teachers is multicultural. This means that the content of what is imparted to the student in preservice training must be consistent with the reality of cultural diversity. Courses can no longer be void of information and discussions about ethnic/racial minorities and other cultural groups. This information must be objective, with emphasis given to the particular needs of these groups and the educational process that can best meet these needs. Careful attention must be given to ensuring that what is taught is not in conflict with the principles, goals, and focus of multicultural education. A restructuring of the educational process is one way of helping society meet the needs of a diverse population; it is not society that needs the restructuring. The experiences that are planned for students who are trained to become teachers will also need to take into account the necessity for those experiences to be multicultural in nature. In some instances, depending on geographic location and the ethnic/racial composition of a given community, the kinds of experiences that provide direct contact with diverse populations are readily available. In other situations, careful planning will be needed to ensure that there are various kinds of experiences that may be adequately substituted. How this is accomplished will depend on the resources of the institution, and more importantly, on how committed the school and/or college is to the education and training of individuals who must be prepared to function effectively in a diverse society. B. Othanel Smith and his colleagues stress the value of competent teachers in ensuring that students receive effective and appropriate education:

> If education of the teacher is viewed in the context of the great variation among the people of the United States, the enormous dimensions of the teacher's task are obvious. The educational system in the United States is devoted to the idea of a common school. The school is the only institution through which all children of all cultures can share the heritage and life of this nation. The teacher who can work only with children from one socioeconomic or cultural group is inadequately prepared to teach in the common school. If children are to receive effective and appropriate education, the interests and cultural backgrounds of these children must be understood. The skills and techniques effective with children of diverse backgrounds must be built into the competency of every teacher.[11]

Instructional Priorities for Training Teachers

Programs that are geared toward the education of teachers will need to set instructional priorities. These priorities should be those tenets that form the basis of teacher preparation. Often the priorities for teacher preparation overlap with the priorities for curriculum development.

Priority I: Ethnic and cultural content must be integrated throughout the curriculum.

This goal is crucial for at least two reasons. First, negative attitudes about differences of all kinds, but especially those involving ethnic and cultural differences, are often reinforced in subtle ways. Often, this is accomplished without teachers and/or students aware of what has taken place. However, when curriculum content and instructional materials are monocultural, this subtly conveys to students that other groups are not significant enough to be included. The subtle process of exclusion encourages racist and sexist attitudes. Integrating information about other groups throughout the curriculum can serve to accomplish the reverse. Second, separating ethnic and cultural content from other parts of the curriculum can have the effect of perpetuating stereotypes and myths based on discriminatory practices. In some instances, a focus on ethnic and cultural content can be viewed as positive when it is done for the purpose of pointing out the uniqueness of various groups. However, the central focus of multicultural instruction should continue to be helping to promote understanding and valuing of diversity for the maintenance of our pluralistic society. Teaching multicultural content in an integrated fashion can serve to help children better understand, value, and live in our culturally diverse society.

Priority II: The ethnic and cultural content taught must reflect experiences within the context of the United States.

In Chapter 2, the discussion on conceptualizing multicultural education made the distinction between multicultural education and education that is global, or international. While the latter type of instruction is necessary and encouraged, it is not to be confused with multicultural education. Instruction that is confined to teaching about another nation is classified as international education and only becomes multicultural in nature when and if a bridge is established between the other nation and events in this country. For example, a unit

The attitude of the teacher is crucial in helping students develop viewpoints that will prepare them for a harmonious existence in a culturally diverse country and world.

of instruction about a West African country can be considered multicultural when relationships between the West African nation and the United States are clearly identified. These relationships, historical in nature, often explain the behavior of certain ethnic groups and serve to establish the bridge necessary for combining aspects of international with multiethnic education so that it becomes multicultural. This approach gives students a global perspective on understanding ethnic groups and the way ethnic cultures have developed in the United States.

However, the history and development of cultures that are not specifically related to ethnicity but transcend it must also be examined within the context of this country. How various religious groups function and exist in a society as diverse as the United States is worthy of understanding and appreciation. The culture(s) of women is very different in this country for very definite reasons; this deserves to be analyzed within the cultural context of the United States. Racism, sexism, and other forms of biased behavior take a form in the United States quite unlike discriminatory behavior elsewhere. Therefore, efforts to help individuals value diversity must involve teaching about the ethnic and cultural experiences of the United States.

Priority III: The content taught must build on the individual differences that exist among and between people.

This priority is basic to good pedagogy. Multicultural education must build appreciation of the individual differences that exist among and between people. "Individual differences refers to those mental abilities, physical characteristics, personality traits, cultural backgrounds, interests, motivations, behavioral and response mechanisms that make each person unique."[12] Teachers should know something about the cultures to which their students belong. This kind of information forms a knowledge base that is crucial in determining what and how to teach students. Don Hamachek, in citing the characteristics of good teachers, states:

> The choice of instructional methods makes a big difference for certain kinds of pupils and a search for the "best" way to teach can succeed only when learners' intellectual and personality differences are taken into account. Available evidence does not support the belief that successful teaching is possible only through the use of some specific methodology. A reasonable inference from existing data is that methods which provide for adaptation to individual differences, encourage student initiative, and stimulate individual and group participation are superior to methods which do not. In order for things of this sort to happen, perhaps what we need first of all are flexible, "total" teachers who are as capable of planning around people as they are around ideas.[13]

Multicultural education is not the same for all children, classrooms, and schools. If a school is predominantly African American, instruction should be structured to reflect the cultural base of the African-American experience. The same holds true for the classroom that is predominantly Hispanic, Asian, Native American, and/or white. This does not mean that the instructional content should be confined to informing students only about their own ethnic group but rather that the instruction be geared from that perspective. A recent and refreshing contribution comes from the work and writings of Molefi Kete Asante. Asante supports focusing the information presented to children in such a way as to have them feel a part of the information. He refers to this process as "centering." The "centric" curriculum focuses instruction on the ethnic and cultural experiences of the child, empowering him or her and thus fostering achievement.[14]

The importance and value of differences should be stressed before similarities. Too often, differences are deliberately overlooked for the sake of pointing out similarities. This approach tends to minimize differences and, in so doing, places a negative connotation on diversity. Young children need to recognize that the characteristics that make them different from others are the attributes that serve to distinguish them from one another. Education that is truly multicultural must make individual and group differences the basis for planning instructional content and classroom processes. William E. Sedlacek and Glenwood C. Brooks, Jr., in their discussion of cultural and racial differences, point out the importance of recognizing differences:

> (1) Cultural and racial differences exist, and they should be openly discussed and understood by all. (2) Differences should be approved and presented positively in and out of the classroom. (3) Expressions of racial and cultural identity are necessary and healthy for cultural and racial minorities, and also for the rest of society.... (8) The characteristics associated with cultural-racial groups are dynamic rather than static. (9) Understanding cultural and racial differences and designing appropriate educational experiences, and reinforcing that context, are crucial to any educational system.[15]

Setting instructional priorities early in the planning for preparing teachers to teach will benefit the planning process and ultimately make for a more effective teacher-training program. The priorities established will vary according to need, but all planning should consider the value of teaching multicultural content in an integrated approach. Such an approach requires teaching about the ethnic and cultural experiences in the United States, and making individual and group differences the basis for planning instructional content and teaching techniques.

Faculty, Curriculum, and Instructional Considerations

There are several areas in teacher training that need to be considered before a restructuring of training programs occurs. These concerns can be grouped into three major headings: faculty preparation, relevancy of curriculum, and student population.

Faculty Preparation

Unfortunately the majority of the faculty in schools and colleges that educate and train teachers are not prepared to respond positively to cultural differences, particularly with regard to their area of specialization. This is not to place the blame on a particular group of individuals but rather to point out that most of the instruction provided for in schools of education comes from professors who were educated and trained during a period when ethnic and cultural differences were not accepted as positive differences but rather as deficits to be ignored or handled as disadvantages. Although the climate in the nation and world have encouraged more consideration of the need for multicultural education, this approach still does not have the hearty endorsement of most faculty. However, those who are responsible for the education and training of teachers can no longer continue to ignore the importance and value of preparing teachers to impart information that is multicultural.[16]

Relevancy of Curriculum

In planning for the reorganization of the education and training of teachers, much attention will need to be given to curriculum content. The content of the curriculum needs to be examined for multicultural relevancy in order to determine ways through which the existing curricula can be revised and integrated with content that is multicultural. The content of courses, required reading, supplementary bibliographies, audiovisual aids, and other learning experiences will need to reflect a culturally heterogeneous population. Careful attention must be given to the kinds of materials that are used. Equally important is how the material about racial/ethnic minorities and other cultural groups is presented. Therefore a consideration of a given curriculum must take into account the relevancy of course content, methodology, and instructional materials to the objectives of multicultural education.[17]

Student Population

Often there is some concern over "uniformity" in the preparation of teachers. Presenting the same kind of education and training to preservice teachers would be inconsistent with multiculturalism. In planning for the restructuring of teacher education programs, it should be remembered that the individuals involved in teacher training come from a faculty that is culturally diverse, which means they too bring a great deal of diversity to the classroom. Whatever is imparted to these students through the content of courses must be done in full recognition of their diverse cultural backgrounds and varied sets of experiences. The training programs for students who plan to teach must prepare them to function both from a set of specifics and a set of generalities. The specifics will deal with information about various ethnic/racial characteristics as well as religion and gender. These generalities should focus on developing a comprehensive set of concepts and guidelines that will ensure behavior that is consistent with multicultural education. Students who are in the preservice stage of teacher education will need different sets of learning experiences commensurate with their backgrounds; they will also need to have a firm grasp of the generalities that relate to an understanding of ethnic and cultural diversity.[18]

How a particular teacher-training program responds to these three considerations will vary. Some institutions will permit faculty to struggle with the responsibility for preparing to incorporate multicultural concepts, content, and materials in their courses. Others will develop plans for providing support via faculty retreats, workshops, and/or other forms of inservice experiences. Whatever approach is used, if it is planned with these considerations in mind as around the instructional priorities discussed in the preceding paragraphs, the results should be useful.

A Model for Teacher Preparation

The first section of this chapter highlighted the role and responsibility of the teacher and the importance of teacher preparation for the promotion of multicultural education. The necessity for establishing instructional priorities and the need for attending to some other considerations were also discussed. If teachers are to be prepared so they will be able to help children learn how to function successfully in a culturally diverse society, some serious consideration needs to be given to the manner through which teachers are prepared.

According to James Banks, the teacher who can function effectively in ethnically pluralistic environments is one who has democratic attitudes and values, a clarified pluralistic ideology, a process conceptualization of ethnic studies, the ability to view society from diverse ethnic perspectives and points of view, knowledge of the emerging stages of ethnicity, and the ability to function in such a manner in the classroom so as to demonstrate all of the above.[19] Banks feels that the programs of the schools and colleges of education should be designed so as to assist teachers in preservice and inservice training programs to acquire what is needed. Geneva Gay has suggested that the curriculum of multicultural teacher education programs should be designed around three major components. These components are categorized as knowledge, attitudes, and skills.[20]

The characteristics of a teacher who can function effectively in a pluralistic environment as delineated by Banks can be grouped so as to fit the categorization suggested by Gay. The model for preparing teachers introduced in Fig. 4.1 is one that includes the characteristics suggested by Banks and also supports Gay's suggestion that curricula for preparing teachers should be designed to include knowledge, attitudes, and skills. The model, as presented in Fig. 4.1, organizes the preparation of teachers around three distinct stages. The three stages are acquisition, development, and involvement. Theses stages are generally consistent with the manner in which most schools and colleges of education structure their curricula. For example, the acquisition stage can be satisfied through most courses offered in social foundations. The type of study necessary for helping students develop a philosophy for multiculturalism can be best offered through psychological foundations and can thus serve to satisfy the requirements of the second stage, development. The implementation of a multicultural curriculum is the essence of the third stage and is easily facilitated through methods courses offered in teacher-training insti-

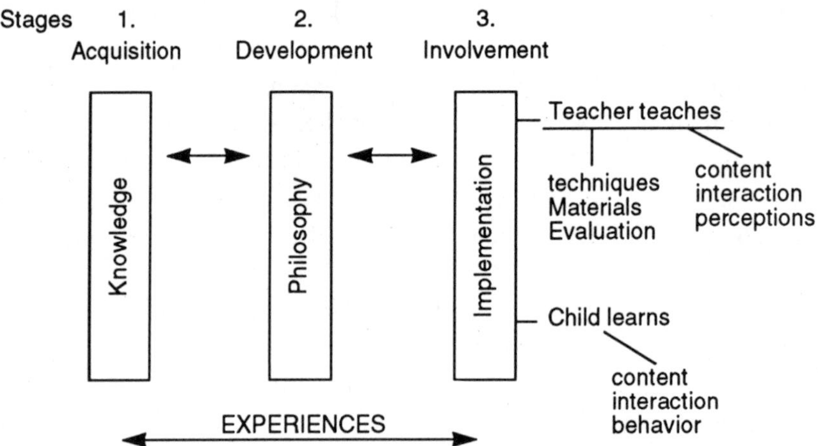

Fig. 4.1 A Model for Training Teachers to Teach Multicultural Education

Source: G.C. Baker, "*Instructional Priorities in a Culturally Pluralistic School,* "*Educational Leadership,* vol. 32, no. 3 (December 1974), p. 117.

tutions. The application of this model to existing curricula makes it easy to use. The curriculum-restructuring process becomes one of reorganizing course content and integrating course offerings with culturally relevant information and experiences. For example, the history of education courses that are offered through social foundations can begin by integrating the facts about how education did or did not meet the needs of minorities and about the effect this situation has had on minorities and on education in the United States. If this type of exploration is accomplished from an objective historical basis, it will begin to take on a multicultural approach. It will also serve to make the students not only knowledgeable about the effects of the past on the present but certainly more sensitive to the need to address ethnic and cultural diversity in schools today.

The same approach can be taken in the integration of multicultural content into sociology of education courses. The impact of education on the development of society and on social groups, and vice versa, certainly makes this area of study an appropriate place to include a multicultural focus. Consequently, when lectures and discussions address those issues that are pertinent to the exploration of the educational needs of all groups, bibliographies, audiovisual aids, and other kinds of instructional aids and learning experiences will also reflect this approach. Once students have established a knowledge base and a rationale supportive of multicultural education, planning for implementation can build on this knowledge and sensitivity. The methods courses and practical experiences often required during the final stages of teacher training can be designed so as to assist students in developing instructional components, lesson plans, materials, techniques, and strategies consistent with the priorities set for effective multicultural education. The material in Chapters 5 and 6 will focus on specific suggestions for implementation of a multicultural curriculum through teacher-prepared units of instruction.

This model can be used effectively in restructuring teacher education programs but is also an efficient method for designing inservice programs. Too often, inservice training programs are planned without direction and structure. This model can be the basis for what is needed when planning a short- or long-term program to aid teachers in service. For example, if teachers in a school and/or a district are limited to three days for inservice education, those three days can be structured around the three stages presented in this model. A day can be devoted to providing information to teachers that will help expand their knowledge base about a specific ethnic group and/or culture. This can be done via a series of lectures, films, or a variety of other forms of instruction. The second day could be filled with group discussions, role plays, and a host of other activities that could serve to reinforce the experience gained during the first day. The third day could then very easily center around teaching strategies, techniques, and the development and selection of instructional materials. This same approach to planning can be used to design a three-hour, a six-week, or two-year education program.

Another interesting aspect of this model is that it is easily applicable to individual situations. An individual can follow this plan to prepare him or herself for teaching a multicultural curriculum. A teacher may decide independently to organize the study program for an advanced degree based on this three-stage model. Specific suggestions for accomplishing this will be discussed in the following sections.

Stage I: Acquisition

The acquisition stage focuses on establishing a base of knowledge that is crucial for the following two stages. It is the knowledge of culture-ethnic/racial, religious, and sex differences that is so essential to the development of a rationale and/or a philosophy that is supportive of multiculturalism. It is only through a gathering of facts, generalizations, and specifics that relevant and meaningful content can be integrated into the curriculum. Often attitudes and behavior are generally affected through the acquisition of accurate and objective information. Therefore the gathering of information during this stage serves three basic purposes. First, it is a means through which an individual can begin to learn more about culture in general. It provides an opportunity for one to become more knowledgeable about his or her own cultural identity and, in so doing, discover how certain aspects of that culture have contributed to his or her values and lifestyle. Second, learning more about other cultures is important because it is through this information that an understanding of the differences that exist between and among people is gained. Third, establishing a knowledge base enables an individual to have the information necessary for developing the content that is used in Stage III. Success in the acquisition of knowledge is a requisite for Stage II. This does not mean, however, that one cannot develop a supportive rationale for multicultural education without a wide range of knowledge about diverse cultures. It is more likely that one will establish a philosophy for encouraging the implementation of education that is multicultural after an understanding of different cultures has been obtained. While Stage I does begin to prepare an individual for moving to Stage II and ultimately for becoming involved as described by Stage III, the degree to which one moves from one stage to another will also depend on the kinds of experiences an individual has had with people who are different. If a student in a preservice situation has had positive experiences with a member of an ethnic/racial group, the chances of that person quickly seeing the need for multicultural education will be good. Individuals who have either had no contact with people from other cultural groups or those who have had negative experiences will find it more difficult to see the value in this approach. For example, an African American who has lived a segregated lifestyle and who has experienced the terrors of racism will perhaps not become an advocate of multicultural education as quickly as one who taught in an integrated setting, has lived in a culturally diverse environment, and has had a variety of positive experiences through this involvement. Experiences are extremely valuable and play an important role in shaping attitudes and behavior.

Schools and colleges of education play a vital role in providing the teacher with the kinds of information that will be valuable in satisfying the requirements of Stage I. Much of this is done through the content of required courses; still more could be accomplished if students were encouraged to select courses that would supplement what they feel they need. In Chapter 3, the discussion on existing teacher education programs used as an illustration the program at the School of Education, the University of Michigan. In that program students were required to elect courses from a list of courses offered throughout the university that were multicultural either in focus or content. This approach allowed students to select the courses they felt would augment previously acquired information as well as introduce them to new and different facts. This approach also provided the students with an opportunity to select courses that were in accord with their interests as well as in their major and minor areas. In a teacher education program, it is much more practical to have teachers who are preparing to teach music or art explore cultural diversity from these points of view rather than from a purely historical one. This is not to say that music or art teachers do not need to look at the history of ethnic/racial groups in the United States. They also need to look at the history as it relates to their area of concentration. If teachers have a general background of knowledge and then proceed to examine those elements that are of particular interest to their subject area, they will be better prepared to integrate content when they are ready for the implementation stage. For some students in preservice education, the only exposure to the kinds of information they will need to teach multicultural curriculum will be obtained from the school or college of education they attend. Therefore it is crucial that the type of training provided is presented in such a way as to prepare the student adequately.

Inservice education provides another area through which teachers may receive assistance in multicultural education. This approach, while important and useful, has limitations. First, inservice education is usually short in duration and often does not allow the necessary time for the teacher to acquire all that is needed. However, if the experience is planned appropriately, much can be achieved even in a short period of time. What is important is that inservice education be structured so that it has some focus. Second, inservice education is generally not required. This could mean that not all of the faculty in a given school or district will benefit from even the best-planned program of inservice education. However, in spite of these shortcomings, inservice education is a vehicle for involving teachers in the process of making education multicultural. The advantage of inservice education is that those involved can apply what is learned to past experiences and readily adopt and adapt what they learn to their specific classroom situations. The students in preservice education do not have an opportunity to readily apply what they are learning. The situation is somewhat different for those who are student teaching, but even for these students, opportunities for implementation are limited.

The process of acquiring sufficient information to establish an adequate knowledge base is neverending, because it is almost totally impossible for one individual to know all that there is to know about culture and/or cultures. Because culture is not static but always developing and changing, we can at best learn only some of the fundamentals about other cultural groups. That is one of the most interesting aspects of multicultural education. Establishing a knowledge base is an essential aspect of preparing to teach a curriculum that is multicultural.

Stage II: Development

The acquisition stage was designed to form the basis for the two stages that follow, development and involvement. The assumption here is that if individuals are exposed to more information about their culture as well as the cultures of others, this exposure will encourage them to begin to see the importance of recognizing cultural diversity. As an individual moves through the process suggested by the model in Fig. 4.1, he or she is expected to develop a philosophy that will support diversity and also develop a rationale for teaching that will be consistent with the objectives of multicultural education. There are many aspects of the training model that are important to the successful implementation of this approach. However, the key to the entire process is the degree to which the individuals responsible for instruction believe in the value of multicultural education. Unless the teacher is convinced of the importance of teaching children about diversity and helping them to understand the implications of learning to live in a culturally pluralistic society, nothing else matters. The teacher is the most valuable link in the entire process. Surely the role of the teacher education institution should not be minimized but rather seen as essential to the education of the teacher. Whatever preparation a teacher goes through, it must be sufficient in helping that individual to assume the role of an advocate of multicultural education and in so doing develop the philosophy needed for becoming involved in its implementation.

In defining the essential dimensions a teacher needs in order to be effective in multicultural education, Thomas A. Arciniega suggests the following three orientations: personal, professional, and community. The personal orientation states that an effective teacher would demonstrate:

1. The belief that cultural diversity is a worthy goal.
2. A respect for the culturally different child and the culture he or she brings to school.
3. The conviction that the culture a minority child brings to school is worth preserving and enriching.
4. An awareness that cultural and linguistic differences are positive individual differences.
5. A commitment to enhance a minority child's positive self-image.
6. A positive self-concept of his/her ability to contribute to a TOC/ME program.*
7. A willingness to learn more about bicultural education.
8. A confidence in culturally different minority children and their ability to learn.
9. Flexibility in human relations
10. A capacity to contribute and share ideas.[21]

*A TOC/ME Program is an approach T.A. Arciniega refers to as Organized Centers for Multicultural Education.

For a teacher to achieve the level of competency in the ten areas defined by Arciniega will require information and knowledge. All the above competencies fall clearly in the development stage of the teacher preparation model. Teachers are more apt to believe that the acknowledgment of a respect for cultural diversity is important to the future of this country if they are given information to foster this attitude. Likewise, teachers who are aware of the importance of culture to the development of individuals are more likely to respect the cultures of all the children in their classrooms. As was discussed earlier in this chapter, an awareness of the need to attend to the individual differences of children is an instructional priority of multicultural education. Culture and language differences contribute to that which needs appropriate attitudinal and instructional responses. Teachers who view children as worthy human beings will structure the learning environment and experiences so as to reinforce positive self-images and at the same time foster learning. A teacher must have a positive orientation towards multicultural education if it is to be successful.

Carl Grant, in a discussion on the role of the teacher, sees the teacher as a "mediator of culture." This is an interesting concept and does not differ in intent from what Arciniega sees as being important for teachers. Grant recommends that teachers who are to become advocates of education that is multicultural must believe in showing respect for all people. Respect should be based on the fact that all people are human and no individual should be denied respect because of social, ethnic, cultural, or religious background.[22] The possibility of education that respects, acknowledges, and responds positively to ethnic cultural differences found in schools is predicated on the ability and willingness of teachers to support it.

Stage III: Involvement

Once a teacher has begun to establish a core of information about different cultures and develops an awareness of the value of respecting these differences, becoming involved in the implementation of multicultural instruction will be a natural step. The actual teaching of a multicultural curriculum requires a sufficient knowledge of diverse cultures, a willingness to teach about cultural differences, and the ability to develop the appropriate instructional techniques, strategies, and materials that will aid in the process. The discussion earlier in this chapter on instructional priorities stressed the value of teaching multicultural content in an integrated fashion, teaching about the ethnic and cultural experiences of the United States, and making individual and group differences the basis for planning instruction. Therefore the teaching strategies that are employed to facilitate the implementation of multicultural curriculum must adhere to these priorities. Chapter 5 will discuss in detail a process for developing an integrated curriculum; however, it must be kept in mind that an integrated approach is encouraged primarily, because if we are to accomplish the goals of multicultural education, it is important that the curriculum reflect cultural diversity as a natural dimension of the total society. If diversity and/or cultural differences are to be viewed as a natural and positive dimension of life in the United States, then careful attention should be given to them. Likewise, if a goal of multicultural education is to help individuals function effectively in a culturally pluralistic society, these skills must be developed comprehensively as learning occurs.

As the model in Fig. 4.1 illustrates, the teacher, through the teaching process, is primarily responsible for providing the content of instruction. This content, if the other two phases of the model have been experienced adequately, will be multicultural. In addition, the manner in which the teacher interacts with the students should reflect a respect for individual differences. The way a teacher feels about diversity will indirectly affect how students are perceived. Students will be expected to perform and to achieve in accord with their ability and not be limited by expectations that may be influenced by ethnic and cultural stereotypes. Teaching techniques that are employed in the implementation of a multicultural curriculum should be chosen and developed so as to enhance the learning of the respective content. These teaching techniques must also be consistent with the attitudes a teacher has about cultural differences in students.

Ethnic and cultural differences include language and gender differences, and it is extremely important that any program that seeks to prepare teachers for multicultural education give attention to these differences. Language is a crucial part of culture, and attempts to have children shed their first language must be discouraged. Careful attention must also be given to attempts to correct a child's speaking pattern. What is important with regard to language is that whatever language and speech a child has acquired be respected as a part of that individual. Exposure to the acquisition of an additional language and or correct usage of an existing language must be done in ways that are compatible with multicultural education.

Careful attention much also be given to gender. Far too often, classroom instruction and behavior reinforces sexist behavior and thought. Multicultural instruction can help to rid society of sexism if teachers clearly understand their own attitudes about gender and work to create an atmosphere of equality as it pertains to males and females. Many of the attitudes and behavior that produce sexual harassment have their early beginnings in educational environments. Schools and teachers can do much to prevent sexist behavior. Success can be determined by the knowledge children gain through content that is integrated with multicultural concepts and facts. If implemented effectively, the interactions between children in the classroom and throughout the school should reflect an understanding of and appreciation for differences. The process of multicultural education should begin with the very earliest experiences a child has with school and must become an integral part of every aspect of the educational environment.

The model as presented has several advantages. First, it is applicable to existing curricular structures of most teacher-training institutions and therefore easy to manage. Second, it offers structure to both preservice and inservice programs with guidance for individual orientations as well. Third, the model is fluid, open-ended, and allows for continued growth. Fourth, it provides a minimal amount of structure so that creative responses are encouraged. Through effective teacher education whether it be preservice or inservice, multicultural education can become a reality. However, the preparation of teachers cannot be accomplished effectively in a haphazard fashion. Planning must take place if the preparation is to be successful. The model offered in Fig. 4.1 is one way of planning for an effective multicultural teacher preparation program.

Imperatives for Multicultural Teacher Preparation

Earlier in this chapter we discussed three instructional priorities for preparing teachers to teach a multicultural curriculum. Priorities were general in nature and should serve to guide the development of a program. In addition to these priorities, there are some specific experiences that teachers will find beneficial. Therefore the following imperatives are offered as specific areas of concern:

1. There is a need for teachers to be involved in experiences that will allow them to examine their own cultures and to have an understanding of the importance of cultures, including ethnic/minority backgrounds, in the development of individuals.
2. Teachers need opportunities that will expose them to the diversity of the United States, with emphasis on those groups that are pervasively represented in this country.
3. Teachers need experiences that will encourage the development of positive attitudes about ethnic/cultural diversity, thereby establishing a philosophy consistent with the objectives of multicultural education.
4. Teachers need to be involved in situations that will provide opportunities for them to have direct contact with individuals who differ from them.
5. Teachers need to understand the importance of language in culture and the implications bilingualism has for both learner and teacher.
6. Teachers should be familiar with a second language and the culture from which the language emanates.

7. Teachers should have an opportunity to thoroughly explore the impact of reducing racist and sexist attitudes and behavior through the implementation of multicultural education.

These seven imperatives incorporate much of the intent of the priorities and also encompasses Stages I and II of the teacher preparation model. The following three imperatives represent specifics that are consistent with the implications of Stage III:

8. Teachers need to be instructed as to how to design, implement, and evaluate instructional materials appropriate for multicultural instruction.
9. Teachers must acquire the ability to analyze, evaluate, and select for use existing and commercial instructional materials for their relevancy to multicultural objectives.
10. Emphasis must be placed on guiding teachers to develop teaching techniques that will allow for culturally individualized teaching/learning environments.

If education is to help prepare children to live effectively in a society that is culturally diverse, then the preparation of the teacher is of the utmost importance. It is the teacher who must facilitate the curriculum and the learning environment so that it is multicultural. All aspects of teacher education, preservice and inservice, must provide the most effective preparation possible. Multicultural teacher preparation is what is needed to restructure education so that it does indeed prepare individuals who not only can live comfortably in a pluralistic environment but who can also contribute to the maintenance of a democratic society.

Notes

1. Lawrence Stenhouse, *Culture and Education* (New York: Weybright and Talley, 1967), p. 67.
2. Wilbur B. Brookover and Edsel L. Erickson, *Society and Schools and Learning* (Boston: Allyn and Bacon, 1969).

3. Charlotte Epstein, *Intergroup Relations for the Classroom Teacher* (Boston: Houghton Mifflin, 1968), p. 58.
4. J. Kenneth Morland, "The Development of Racial Bias in Young Children," in *Teaching Social Studies to Culturally Different Children,* ed. James A. Banks and William W. Joyce (Reading, MA: Addison-Wesley, 1971), p. 31.
5. Jean D. Grambs and John C. Carr, *Black Image Education Copes with Color* (Dubuque, IA: William C. Brown, 1972), p. 152.
6. Kenneth B. Clark, *Prejudice and Your Child* (Boston: Beacon, 1955).
7. Mary Ellen Goodman, *Race Awareness in Young Children* (London: Collier-Macmillan, 1952).
8. Bruno Lasker, *Race Attitudes in Children* (New York: New American Library, 1970).
9. Gwendolyn C. Baker, "The Role of the School in Transmitting the Culture of All Learners in a Free and Democratic Society," in *Educational Leadership 36* (November 1978): 135.
10. William R. Hazard and Madelon D. Stent, "Cultural Pluralism and Schooling: Some Preliminary Observations" in *Cultural Pluralism in Education: A Mandate for Change*, ed. Madelon D. Stent, William R. Hazard, and Harry N. Rivlin (New York: Appleton-Century-Crofts, 1973), p. 20.
11. B. Othanel Smith, Saul B. Cohen, and Arthur Pearl, *Teacher for the Real World* (Washington, D.C.: American Association for Teacher Education, 1969), pp. 1–3.
12. Delores E. Cross and Emilye Fields, "Influence of Individual Differences on Instructional Theories," in *Theories for Teaching,* ed. Lindley J. Stiles (New York: Dodd, Mead and Company, 1974), p. 118.
13. Don Hamachek, "Characteristics of Good Teachers and Implications for Teacher Education," in *Learning to Teach in the Elementary School,* ed. Hal D. Funk and Robert T. Olberg (New York: Dodd, Mead, 1972), p. 24.
14. Molefi Kete Asante, "Afrocentric Curriculum," *Educational Leadership 49* (December/January 1992): 28–31.

15. William E. Sedlacek and Glenwood C. Brooks, Jr., *Racism in American Education: A Model for Change* (Chicago: Nelson-Hall, 1976), p. 5.
16. Gwendolyn C. Baker, "Multicultural Imperatives for Curriculum Development in Teacher Education," in *Journal of Research and Development in Education 11, no. 1* (1977): 73.
17. Ibid., p. 74.
18. Ibid.
19. James A. Banks, "The Implications of Multicultural Education for Teacher Education," in *Pluralism and the American Teacher: Issues and Case Studies,* ed. Frank H. Klassen and Donna M. Gollnick (Washington, D.C.: American Association for Colleges of Teacher Education, 1977), p. 25.
20. Geneva Gay, "Curriculum for Multicultural Teacher Education," in *Pluralism and the American Teacher: Issues and Case Studies,* ed. Frank H. Klassen and Donna M. Gollnick (Washington, D.C.: American Association for Colleges of Teacher Education, 1977), p. 33.
21. Thomas A. Arciniega, "The Challenge of Multicultural Education for Teacher Educators," *Journal of Research and Development in Education 11, no. 1* (Athens, Georgia, Fall 1977): 67.
22. Carl A. Grant, "The Mediator of Culture: A Teacher's Role Revisited," *Journal of Research and Development in Education 11, no. 1* (Fall 1977): 109–13.

5
Developing Multicultural Curricula

Principle VI: Multicultural education should begin with the background of the students for whom the process is intended.

Principle VII: The development of multicultural education should take place over an extended period of time.

The need for an undergirding policy that reinforces the need for multicultural education was discussed in Chapter 3. The discussion in this chapter will proceed on the assumption that what is suggested here will be considered after policy has been established and implementation has begun in the school district and/or the institution. Chapter 4 discussed the importance of individuals developing a rationale for teaching multicultural education. Such a philosophy, it was pointed out, is much easier to establish once an understanding of what is to be achieved is clear. In other words, the goals of the approach should be well defined.

A Philosophy

School districts and institutions of higher learning need to articulate individual philosophies embracing the objectives of multicultural education. Once this step has been accomplished, curricula can be developed and relevant decisions made on the basis of the direction obtained from a supporting philosophy. A well-defined philosophy is stressed by Edmund C. Short, who states that a "decided-upon curriculum is the only way to guarantee that aimless, useless, or undesirable learning do not waste the time of pupils and teachers and the resources supporting the schools."[1] Curriculum changes require a direction, and the decisions that must be made when developing curricula need to be made within the confines of an existing philosophy. Developing curriculum that is multicultural can be achieved once the direction has been established. A philosophy that supports multicultural education, as was discussed earlier, is not necessarily a separate statement, but rather whole educational philosophy that integrates the goals of multicultural education throughout. According to Short, "when explicit choices have been made about philosophy, purposes, and objectives, the remaining choices about what shall be taught and how to do it are more easily made within the established framework of ideas."[2]

Ultimately it is the classroom teacher who makes the final decisions about what is to be taught and how to teach it. However, the "what" can be ensured if the teacher is provided with a guiding philosophy. A curriculum guide that has been developed on the basis of a well-defined philosophy can provide this kind of guarantee. "The curriculum represents a framework for justifiable choices on the part of the teacher and in keeping with the school's philosophy." [3] Decisions about content are made with respect to what has been prescribed by the educational philosophy of the district or institution. The process of how the curriculum will be developed should also be planned around stated objectives. Even though teachers may have guidelines to follow, they generally will determine classroom process and instructional methods independently of the overall planned content and process.

Content and Process

The curriculum of most schools is not as organized or as defined as perhaps it should be. In order to avoid wasteful and disjointed efforts in curriculum planning, planners should take into account the fact that a relationship must exist between what is planned and what may emerge. In some recent work done by Gail McCutcheon, it was revealed that curriculum planning in local schools often operates at different levels, thus leading to disjointed and unharmonious programs. The result is a curriculum that resembles an emerging crazy-quilt rather than the planned patchwork quilt. However, even a crazy-quilt (or an emergent curriculum) can have unity if it is carefully designed.[4] To avoid an irregular and incoherent curriculum, careful attention must be given to the content as well as to the process of curriculum development.

In this context, content is "the compendium of information which comprises the learning material for a particular course or a given grade."[5] Curriculum planning should not provide all of what is to be transferred to the student, but it should provide the general nature of what is to be taught. An effective way for achieving this is to provide fundamental concepts for instruction. This method establishes an outline for content; the teacher is free to embellish the concepts at will. The degree to which concepts are then elaborated on and explored will depend largely on what information the teacher has on the subject on hand. If teachers have established a broad knowledge base, as was discussed in Chapter 3, then it is quite possible that the concepts will be developed with multicultural understanding included. For example, what could be developed from a basic concept in music, such as "Jazz is a form of music unique to the United States"? If a teacher knows that (1) West African music contributed to the development of blues, (2) blues played an important part in the development of jazz, and (3) jazz is influenced by the geographic region it is played in, then the original concept will begin to take on a multicultural approach. This approach is multicultural because the involvement of African Americans and of other ethnic and cultural groups in the development of this form of music will be studied. Provisions for ensuring content that is multicultural must be made by those involved in planning curriculum.

Process differs from content in that it gives the structure in which the content resides. Again, once curriculum planners are sure of what they want to achieve, then planning can be done in an atmosphere of clarity. In planning and organizing for multicultural instruction, an orderly method for achieving goals must be developed. Every process must have a constructive underlying scheme that provides order and direction.[6] In organizing a school's curriculum, decisions need to be made for arranging learning experiences in some kind of sequence so that one experience builds on another. For example, young children could be taught the value of differences by examining different kinds of differences; in this way, they will better understand diversity before they concentrate on specific ethnic differences. This type of progression should be well defined in the curriculum. Curriculum guides should not be limited to providing sequential steps but should attend to scope as well. Scope can be attended to quite adequately by including other organizing elements, such as fundamental concepts, generalizations, and modes of inquiry to be developed in all disciplines and/or subject areas. Returning to the earlier example of sequence, scope can be provided by presenting fundamental concepts and generalizations relating to diversity in science, mathematics, social studies, and other subject areas.[7]

When organizing for multicultural instruction, it is best to develop curriculum only after a well-defined philosophy exists. A curriculum design that provides an orderly method for achieving its goals—a process—should also contain the fundamentals for developing relevant content. What is to be taught and when it is to be taught should be stated in general terms. The responsibility for implementation rests in the hands of those providing the instruction.

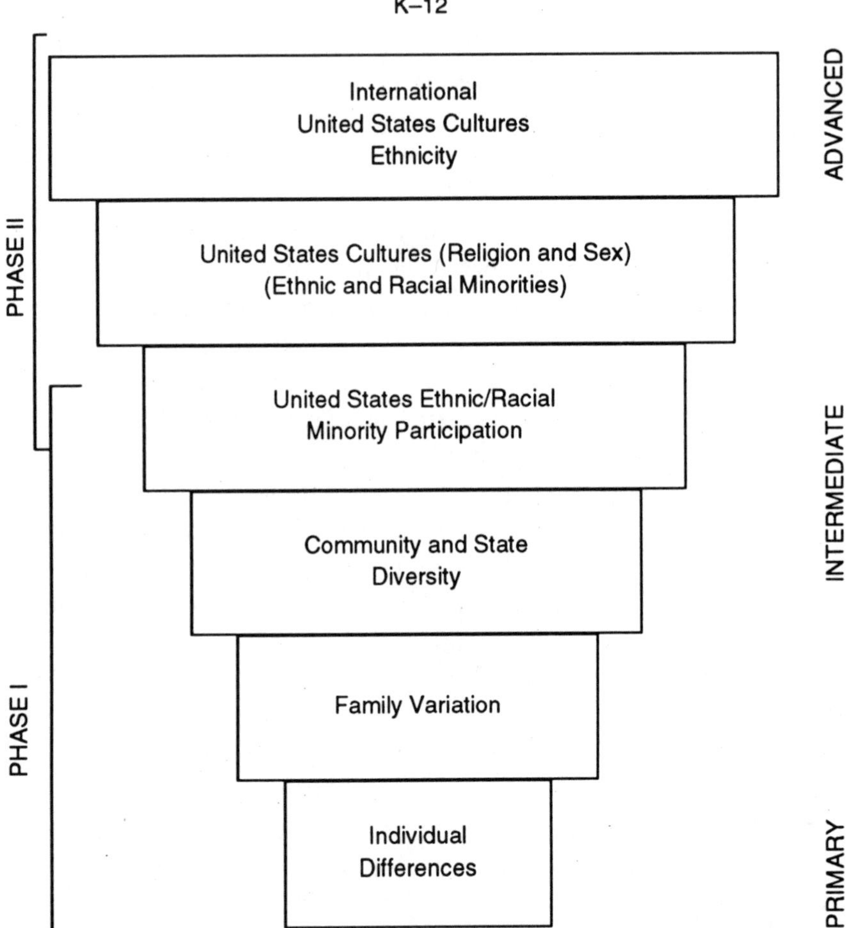

Figure 5.1 A Model for Developing a Multicultural Curriculum

Source: G. C. Baker, "The Role of the School in Transmitting the Culture of All Learners in a Free and Democratic Society, "*Educational Leadership*, vol. 36, no. 2 (November 1978), p. 135.

A Curriculum Model

An approach to developing multicultural curriculum is presented in Fig. 5.1. The model suggests that planning be done by giving attention to two basic phases of what may be taught. In Phase I, which includes the primary grades and the earliest grades of the intermediate level, the content should be concerned with exploring diversity in general as it relates to the individual, the family, and the community, both local and state. Attention to ethnic and racial groups and to minority representation should be given after basic concepts have been introduced. Phase II begins with a study of ethnic and racial groups in the United States. This phase examines the participation of minorities in the development of the United States and builds on the basic concepts presented in Phase I. In Phase II, students who are at the intermediate level begin to explore the various cultural groups in this country; in addition to ethnic and racial groups, they begin to study other cultural groups, such as those determined by religious beliefs, sex, and other distinguishing characteristics. Phase I is also the period during which the importance of ethnicity in general is considered in relation to the larger cultural groups. International/global education is introduced in terms of its relationship to ethnicity and culture, but the study of other countries will have been included in the curriculum at a much earlier point. Generally, the study of other countries will be introduced early in the primary grades. Dividing the approach into these two basic segments helps to provide a general approach to planning content. Approaching the development of curriculum in this manner can provide some direction for determining a process.

Individual Differences

An exploration of individual differences should begin with the earliest experiences a child may have in school. It is important that all of the learning experiences illustrate the basic concept that all people differ from one another. It is not enough to tell this to children; examples must be given in order to help them understand how all living things differ one from the other. How these fundamental concepts are taught is more important at this stage than at any other. What is taught—the content—in these early learning experiences provides the foundation on which the rest of the curriculum will be built. It is important to stress differences before attention is given to similarities because it is much easier for individuals to identify similarities than to acknowledge differences. The intent in stressing differences is to make children feel comfortable with themselves and with others. What may seem like very simple concepts are often complex and should be taught over and over again in a variety of ways. For example, "All living things are different from one another" can be taught in units of study about plants and animals. The examples used in this stage should be simple and the exotic introduced only after the differences in what is already familiar to the child have been presented. At the beginning, it will be easy for children to recognize the differences in domestic pets and plants; young children will recognize and understand that cats and dogs vary in size and color. At the same time, they will also be able to understand that cats and dogs have some things in common with one another. Children should be taught fundamental concepts such as the following:

- Each kind of animal is different from all other kinds.
- Each kind of animal has its own way of life.
- Each is especially suited to the place where it lives and to the food it eats.[8]

These basic concepts can form the fundamentals for learning activities that demonstrate diversity. The same approach can be used with plants and the generalizations, then transferred to people. These same examples can serve to point out the similarities that also exist. Teaching about individual differences should be done on an ongoing basis. These concepts need to be included in all subject areas and integrated throughout the classroom experiences. It is important to teach about differences in a subtle manner. Children learn much that is negative about people and about diversity in very discreet ways. Positive learning can and should occur under the same kinds of conditions. Teaching about individual differences can form the foundation for a multicultural curriculum.

Family Variations

Once young children have learned to understand and appreciate individual differences, other kinds of variations may be introduced.

Fundamental understandings about different kinds of families— their size, composition, and responsibilities— are important. Deliberate attempts to dispel the notion of the "model" family must be made. Children need to know that while there may be some families that have both a mother and a father, there are others that may have only one parent and in some cases two of one sex. The effect that divorce and death have on family structure should be discussed. The variety in the size of families is something that is important to explore. For example, the extended family, if viewed from a cultural context, is a viable family structure and should not be considered unique or deviant. Learning about the various kinds and types of families presents a wonderful opportunity to dispel myths about sex roles. Children need to understand roles and their purpose in a family and, through this basic understanding, can be helped to see the relationship between what needs to be done in a household and who does it. They need to be helped to understand that a role and/or task should be filled or completed by the person who can do it best or is available. As illustrated in Fig 5.1, building on the understanding of individual differences to learn about family variations helps to prepare children for understanding diversity in the larger community as well.

Community and State Diversity

Helping children to recognize and to acknowledge forms of diversity in their respective communities will provide an understanding for an exploration of the diversity within the society. A study of diversity in the local community, town, and/or city can be accomplished through all subjects studied in both the primary and intermediate levels. The more heterogeneous a community is, the greater the opportunities there will be for learning about diversity. However, even the more homogeneous communities can provide numerous examples. Diversity in the community can be seen in housing styles, housing patterns, religious structures, shopping arrangements, restaurants, and forms of recreation; the possibilities are many. Perhaps the most logical subject through which to explore community and state diversity is social studies. However, the possibilities for creative study of diversity through science, art, music, math, and other subject areas should not be overlooked. Food variations are often used to point out the more obvious kinds of differences among people. If food is looked at from a scientific approach, a study of food and eating patterns can form a useful and interesting study.

Once children are helped to understand diversity in the first three realms as presented in the model, a more concentrated study of ethnic and racial groups is appropriate. A study of minority participation in the development of the United States will not only be appropriate at this stage but may be achieved more effectively with young children. If children feel positive about differences and are disposed toward understanding and accepting diversity in general, they should then be ready for an objective study of ethnic and racial differences.

United States Ethnic/Racial Minority Participation

In studying the racial and ethnic composition of the United States, emphasis should be placed on the participation of these various groups in the development of the nation. Generally, attention to ethnic and racial diversity is presented in the context in which these groups have contributed, but this approach can become so fragmented by bits and pieces of irrelevant information that the impact of the different groups' involvement is lost. It must be kept in mind that although multicultural education stresses the importance of creating the kind of environment that allows individuals the freedom to maintain a variety of cultures, it also encourages support of a common culture. Therefore, careful attention must be given to ensure the reinforcement of this basic idea whenever possible. This can be accomplished through the study of ethnic and racial groups, if emphasis is placed upon their participation as a group in the development of the nation rather than on individual contributions alone. This is not to say that contributions made by individuals of various ethnic groups are not important. However, it is more meaningful if these contributions can be acknowledged within a larger frame of reference. For example, to know that Nat Love, an African-American cowboy, won three contests in the Deadwood Rodeo to earn the title of "Deadwood Dick" is interesting but, in itself, not that important. However, to learn this fact within the context of the role of African Americans in the development of western history has much more impact. This is highlighted by William Lore Katz in writing about the participation of African-Americans in western history:

> Many had been brought West as bondsmen and were cowboys before they became free men. Almost a third of the trail crews that drove cattle up the Chisholm Trail after the Civil War were Negroes. In 1878 one of the greatest migrations to reach the West was made up of thousands of ragged Negroes fleeing Southern oppression and seeking new opportunity in Kansas.[9]

A further well-known illustration is the involvement of the Chinese in the building of the Transcontinental Railroad. Chinese immigrants provided most of the labor for building the Pacific portion of this railroad. Again, this information takes on a greater significance when studied within the context of the effects of immigration legislation on the economic development of this country.[10]

Fig. 5.1 suggests that the study of ethnic and racial diversity begins to take place at the end of Phase I and serves to introduce the more concentrated study of these groups in Phase II. When students have learned to understand diversity and are able to build on this understanding through further learning about ethnic and racial diversity, it will be possible to extend this knowledge to the broader context of cultures.

United States Cultures (Ethnic and Racial Minorities)

The focal point of multicultural education should be the larger cultural groups in the United States. At this point in the curriculum, the impact of ethnic and racial experiences on individuals in these cultures will be felt. The interactions within and between groups is important. Differences in response will be further explained by the unique experiences various groups have had in the development of this country. It is necessary for students to examine the influences that ethnicity and minority status have had on religious groups, and vice versa. To further examine the effects of ethnicity on the cultures of both men and women will provide basic information that is necessary for understanding why men and women may respond in a variety of ways to the same issue. Chapter 2 pointed out that the number of cultural groups included in this particular concept of multicultural education will be determined by the application of the definition of culture presented in that chapter. In addition to religion and sex, it was suggested that the physically disabled, the aged, the poor, and youth cultures also be included. Understanding the interactions and the interrelatedness of these various forms of diversity within larger cultural groups will help to prepare individuals for a greater appreciation of diversity not only in this country but in the world at large.

International/Global, United States Cultures, Ethnicity

International/global education is generally dispersed, to some degree, throughout the primary, intermediate, and advanced grade levels. However, in the more advanced levels it is presented with an emphasis on foreign affairs and/or international foreign policy. In a multicultural curriculum, international education may be expanded in such a way as to provide the establishment of bridges between other countries and United States ethnic populations. For example, links that exist between some African nations and African Americans in this country, between Japan and Japanese Americans, and between Latin American countries and Spanish-speaking populations should be established. Little attention need be given to how weak or how strong these connections may be. The important fact is that there are certain ties that must be understood if an international perspective is to help students understand more completely cultural diversity in the United States.

An overall approach to curriculum planning and design is needed, but some attention to concurrent efforts towards achieving multicultural education must also be given. A process for providing side-by-side instruction can be valuable. Once the process has been developed, the content can emerge from the existing overall design. Implementation of multicultural instruction can then take place in two different ways, with each method satisfying a particular need. The overall design provides direction and structure for a period of years and for the entire school experience. A process that provides for instruction that can take place on a concurrent basis and one that is supplemental to the overall design is needed for more immediate implementation.

A curriculum designed on the basis of the model presented here can provide the ingredients for a multicultural curriculum. A planned curriculum should provide the structure that is needed for an orderly process to occur. It should also include the fundamental concepts that are to be introduced. This objective can be achieved when a commitment to the goals of multicultural education are clear and supported by a well-defined philosophy.

It is essential to build the development of curriculum on the background of the students. A curriculum that provides for a sequential approach to an examination of diversity over a period of years may have a better opportunity of achieving the goals of multicultural education than one that is haphazard in its approach. An unwavering commitment to multicultural education, a supporting philosophy, and a well-organized plan for developing a multicultural curriculum will ensure success.

Notes

1. Edmund C. Short and George D. Marconnit, *Contemporary Thought on Public School Curriculum* (Dubuque, IA: William C. Brown, 1968), p. 150.
2. Ibid., p. 151.
3. Ibid.

4. Gail McCutcheon, "The Curriculum: Patchwork or Crazy Quilt?" *Education Leadership* 36 (November 1978): 114.
5. Short and Marconnit, *Contemporary Thought on Public School Curriculum*, p. 131.
6. Ibid.
7. Ibid., p. 315.
8. Lorus J. Milne and Margery Milne, "Animals," *The World Book Encyclopedia*, vol. 1 (Chicago: Field Enterprises Educational Corporation, 1976), p. 446.
9. William Lore Katz, *Teacher's Guide to American Negro History* (Chicago: Quadrangle Books, 1968), pp. 119–26.
10. James A. Banks, *Teaching Strategies for Ethnic Studies*, 2nd ed. (Boston: Allyn and Bacon, 1979), pp. 301–16.

6
Implementation

Principle VIII: The instructional component of multicultural education must be integrated throughout the curriculum.

Discussion in the preceding chapters centered around the planning necessary for the implementation of multicultural instruction. This chapter includes a section concerned with ways through which teachers can begin to initiate multicultural instruction. The full integration of multicultural concepts and approaches takes time, and there are several ways to achieve full implementation. The balance of this chapter presents one method for accomplishing this. A section on unit preparation has also been included.

The instructional priorities for educating teachers, presented in Chapter 4, included a priority that stressed the importance of integrating multicultural content throughout the curriculum. The principle as stated above also focuses on the importance of making sure that the instructional aspects not be segregated into separate units or lessons of instruction but that integration is the key. The earlier discussion also suggested that often racism and sexism are so subtly interwoven throughout a curriculum that they may not be obvious. However, the effects of this are not difficult to detect. Therefore, if direct efforts are made to reduce the effects of curricula that foster racist and sexist attitudes and behavior, the results may be as effective. This chapter will focus on describing the process through which multicultural content may be taught in an integrated manner.

Sedlacek and Brooks, in their discussions on what can be done to change racist behavior, argue for an integrated approach to help achieve the goals they have identified. They suggest the following strategy:

> Integrate minority and racism-related content in the curriculum. Rather than set up a "Black Week," integrate an ongoing program on the contributions, feelings, and lifestyles of minorities in the curriculum. Also, the facts about racism, both individual and institutional, should be presented in context.[1]

In a discussion on the "polycultural curriculum," Robert L. Williams stresses the similarities between that approach and the curriculum that is multicultural. Williams feels that they both embrace the following ideals: a state of equal, mutually supportive coexistence between ethnocultural groups, and one planet of people of diverse physical and cultural characteristics. Basic to the acceptance of these ideas is the belief that every person who respects his or her ethnocultural identity should extend the same respect to people of other cultures. Williams also supports the notion that this type of curriculum should be integrated into a school's total educational effort.[2] Total educational effort, in this context, speaks to more than curriculum or type of instructional content. The process suggested here is one that should include the total educational environment, because if education is to become multicultural, the total environment must reflect this approach. No aspect can be overlooked because it is the entire educational setting in which a child functions that influences how the child thinks and behaves. Therefore, attention will be given to ways in which the school setting as well as classroom instruction can become multicultural.

The school's responsibility goes beyond academic achievement. The school must also assume the responsibility for helping students develop the skills necessary for learning to live successfully in a culturally pluralistic society. Myles W. Rodehaver and his colleagues express their belief about how the school should teach culture:

> The school then must teach the cultural elements of the society in which the school functions; and if ethnocentrism is to be avoided, the school must also teach the rudiments of other cultures. Culture has previously been defined as the learned and the shared behavior of human beings in groups. Culture presupposes association and interaction, but it involves cooperative understanding as well. Since abilities and experiences vary, individual perceptions will vary also, thus giving rise to difficulties in learning about and sharing experiences and behavior. It is the school's responsibility to provide the sharing experiences that result in cooperative understanding. Through the teaching of such skills as language, the school helps the individual to absorb the culture of his society, transmitting to him the social heritage of traditions, knowledge, belief, values and attitudes. Through activities that foster association the school helps the individual to acquire the skills essential for personal adjustment to the groups. Thus the school, along with other institutions, socializes the individual.[3]

It is the intent of this discussion to provide some of the elements teachers will need to reduce and/or to eliminate the difficulties that could arise from learning and sharing cultural information, backgrounds, and experiences. The strategies and techniques that will be suggested in this chapter should guide students through learning experiences that will help them acquire the skills essential for living harmoniously in a country and world that are filled with diversity. The process suggested here for integrating multicultural content into the schools involves the integration of relevant content into an existing monoculturally oriented curriculum. The ideal way to establish a multicultural curriculum would be to start with a curriculum that has already been infused with multicultural content. While the latter approach is more desirable, adapting the existing curriculum may take a shorter period of time and ultimately gain more support because the process will be less involved. The process for implementation of a multicultural curriculum has been divided into three stages. The first stage is labeled "initiating," the second "involving," and the third "integrating." Each stage will be described and examples will be given to illustrate the process of implementation at both the elementary and secondary levels. Charts to help simplify the suggested activity in the initiating stage are included for school and classroom environments only.

Initiating: Stage I

The three stages involved in the implementation of a multicultural curriculum on the elementary and secondary levels are presented in Charts 6.1 and 6.2. These two charts give an overview of the progression and display the cumulative effect of moving from the initiating stage to the final stage of integrating.

CHART 6.1
Stages for the Implementation of a Multicultural Curriculum (Elementary Level)

SUBJECT AREA	STAGE I INITIATING	STAGE II INVOLVING	STAGE III INTEGRATING
School Environment			
Classroom Environment			
• Language Arts			
Reading	X	X	X
Spelling/Writing			X
Speaking/Listening	X	X	X
• Mathematics			X
• Social Studies		X	X
• Science			X
• Music			
• Art		X	X
• Physical Education			

CHART 6.2
Stages for the Implementation of a Multicultural Curriculum (Secondary Level)

SUBJECT AREA	STAGE I INITIATING	STAGE II INVOLVING	STAGE III INTEGRATING
School Environment			
Classroom Environment			
UNITED STATES HISTORY I*			
• Before 1492–1763	X	X	X
• 1763–1775		X	X
• 1775–1860			X
• 1860–1900			X
UNITED STATES HISTORY II			
• 1900–1945	X	X	X
• 1945–1961		X	X
• 1961–1974			X
• 1974–1980			X
Bibliography	X	X	X
Required Reading		X	X
Audiovisual Aids	X	X	X
Resource People			
Research Projects			
Other–Trips			

*United States History is used as an example in this chart. The implementation process would be the same for any subject area.

Each chart is subdivided into three major sections; each section is concerned with a different aspect of the school environment. Charts 6.3 and 6.4 were designed to elaborate on the general information presented in Charts 6.1 and 6.2. Chart 6.3 identifies several areas in elementary and secondary schools where action may be taken to create a multicultural environment. Starting at this point will involve primarily the nonteaching staff. It is this group of individuals who are crucial to the development of an approach that will make the entire educational environment multicultural. The ideas of involvement that are listed in Chart 6.3 have implications for the principal, secretaries, clerks, chef, and in some instances the faculty who have responsibility for extracurricular activities.

CHART 6.3
Initiating Classroom Environments
(Elementary-Secondary)

AREA	ACTION
Staffing Patterns	Faculty and staff must include minorities and women at all levels.
Bulletin Boards and Displays	Pictorial representations and language on bulletin boards must reflect cultural diversity.
Announcements (Public Address System)	Announcements should be free of sexist and racist terminology and bilingual if appropriate.
Printed Materials for Distribution	Flyers, brochures, newspapers, and all other printed matter must depict cultural diversity through both pictorial and language content.
Food Service	Snack bars, luncheon menus, and other forms of food service must respond to the cultural eating patterns of the students.
Social Activities	Sexist and racist policies and practices must be eliminated.
Extracurricular Activities	No club or organization will discriminate on any basis.
Athletics Clubs/Organizations Assemblies	All assemblies must be planned to include content and speakers appropriate for all students.

School Environments

Staffing Patterns

Chapter 3 devoted considerable discussion to the need for making sure that the staff and faculty of schools reflected as much different ethnic/racial and gender representation as possible. The importance of having as much diversity as possible at all levels of responsibility is

CHART 6.4
Initiating Classroom Environments
(Elementary-Secondary)

AREA	ACTION
Bulletin Boards	Pictorial displays must include pictures that portray diversity.
Seating Arrangements	Students should have the freedom to sit where they would like, but caution must be taken to avoid racist and sexist seating patterns.
Audiovisual Aids	Books, films, filmstrips, slides, charts, and all other forms of audiovisual aids must be multicultural.
Resource People	Deliberate attempts must be made to ensure the inclusion of minorities and women as resource people in non-traditional roles.
Field Trips	Field trips should be planned so as to expose students to forms of diversity that they might not otherwise have the opportunity to experience.
Holidays	No student should be discriminated against for observing religious holidays and/or for not participating in those observed by the school.

stressed. Too often, when minorities and women are not represented in schools except as secretaries, food-service workers, and custodians, the limitations of minorities and women are reinforced. The importance of ensuring the adequate involvement of minorities and women is to provide role models for all students. Providing role models is one reason for the involvement of minorities and women, but the contribution they can bring to the administration of the school and to the instruction and counseling of students is extremely valuable.

Bulletin Boards and Displays

All schools, elementary and/or secondary, have a variety of bulletin boards in central offices, in the cafeteria, and in the hallways. These bulletins boards must not only provide information for students and teachers but also serve as instructional devices. Students, parents, faculty, and staff receive all kinds of indirect messages from these boards. To restrict the pictorial display of people on bulletin boards to those of one sex and/or one ethnic or cultural group certainly tells one kind of story. To confine the language used in these displays to English, especially in schools where children are bilingual, immediately denies the full participation of the student who is bilingual and further communicates to all students the attitude of the school toward the understanding and acceptance of language differences. Bulletin boards in schools that have homogeneous populations need to be concerned about integrating their displays as much as those buildings whose student populations are more diverse. It is not as common to see Christmas trees and religious displays in schools today, but a word of caution about the practice must be given. Unless a school can very delicately handle the display of the symbolic nature of the holidays so as not to offend any one group, it is suggested that Christmas decorations and other forms of religious displays not be included. There are groups of people who do not observe Halloween, Valentine's Day, and other similar holidays. Parades in which children show off costumes and parties where children exchange valentines should not be held unless adequate arrangements can be made for those students whose beliefs do not allow participation. An excellent example of how to handle the observance of Halloween is the action taken by a teacher in an elementary school in Flint, Michigan. This third-grade teacher was well aware that there were several students in her class who did not celebrate Halloween because of their religious beliefs. The teacher organized a set of activities around the theme "autumn celebrations." The suggestion here is not to eliminate all holiday observances for the sake of a few but to encourage responses that recognize the differences that children bring to school.

Announcements

Most schools communicate with teachers and students through a public address system. Often announcements are made without much concern for the language that is used. Generally there is more sexism than racism involved in the making of announcements through the elimination of the pronoun "she" and/or the making of direct references only to male students. Careful attention should be given to what is announced with regard to the celebration of holidays. Alternative plans should be developed to accommodate those students who do not observe certain holidays. The public address system is an excellent way of sharing information about certain holidays that are not celebrated by most students, with the intent to broaden the background of those students who are not involved and also to create an environment of support and understanding for those who are.

Printed Materials

The suggestions for how bulletin boards and displays can be made multicultural also apply to materials that schools print for distribution to students, faculty, staff, and parents. Care must be taken to ensure that all announcements are free of racist and sexist language. A recent advertisement announcing a career fair carried the following heading: "Decide Now Whether You Want to Be Doctor, Lawyer, or Indian

Chief." The individuals who designed the announcement had no sensitivity to what it means to be an Indian chief; they certainly did not set out to create a racist announcement, but the result was just that. This is an example of what must be avoided; it is hoped that through the process of multicultural education, it will be. Equally damaging is to see notices to parents in a predominantly African-American school with sketches of children who appear to be nonminority. It is better to omit sketches and/or pictures if there are none available that are appropriate.

Food Service

Food service is difficult enough to plan in and of itself because of nonculturally related individual needs and desires. However, if schools are going to become multicultural, the approach to planning menus for lunches, parties, and other occasions will need to be sensitive to the kinds of food different people eat. This does not imply that every meal must include ethnic dishes suitable for all groups represented in the student body, but it does mean that attempts to satisfy some of these needs should be made at least on a weekly basis. Some schools approach this goal by offering, in addition to the regular menu, one ethnic dish per day. Again this serves to introduce different kinds of foods to those not familiar with them and helps to make the students of that ethnic group feel more a part of the group. To include ethnic foods in the menus for parties, coffee hours, and dinners for parents may be accomplished with more ease because the parents can play a role in helping to provide what is needed. The pride that this kind of participation from parents can develop may also result in more parental involvement and support for the educational program of the school.

Social Activities

Social activity can be an area where students experience a great deal of isolation and rejection. Generally parties and other types of social activity do not take into account the kinds of music, dancing, and games that minorities are familiar with. The kind of music that is selected for students to dance to is crucial to whether or not all the students enjoy the event. In some instances it can mean whether or not they attend the party. Plans should include definite attempts to play a variety of music, to provide for different forms of dancing, and to provide opportunities for students to engage in other forms of social activity. A sure way to provide for this type of diversity of activity is to include representatives from as many different ethnic/racial groups as there are in the school on the committee to help organize the event.

Athletics

Title IX of the Education Amendments of 1972 has contributed a great deal to the elimination of sexism in athletics. But there is still much more to be accomplished. Because Title IX does exist, this discussion will not include much on sexism in athletics. There is still a need for groups like cheerleading teams to be composed of males and females and to include representatives from minority groups as well. There also is a need to plan strategies that will include minority students and women in certain types of sports where they were previously not encouraged to participate. For minority students this has meant not participating in tennis, swimming, and skiing, primarily because they have not had access to facilities outside of the school environment that promote the development of these skills.

Clubs and Organizations

School policy can control the organization of groups that may have a tendency to exclude by making it very clear what the policy is before a group is endorsed by the school. Special attention will need to be given to the types of groups that are organized for the purpose of planning for class activities such as senior trips. There should be several options for students to select from that will accommodate their interests and financial situations. All students may not want to go to Europe but may find travel to Spain or Africa rewarding. Still others may find it more financially comfortable to travel to New York City or Washington, D.C. Students should have choices that will encourage their participation rather than discourage it.

Assemblies

Assemblies are another important learning activity that can serve to further the goals of multicultural education. In order for this to occur, each assembly should be planned in such a way so as to meet the needs of all students in one way or another. Panels should be organized to include minorities, males, and females. Films should be chosen because they are instructional and should be previewed to make sure the content will offend no individual or group. It is often helpful to plan assemblies for the school year in much the same way that a classroom teacher plans a course or teaching unit for the year. A plan encompassing the entire year can reflect an honest attempt to respond to the needs of all of the students and provide new information about cultural diversity that will further the development of their knowledge in this area.

School environments can offer much in the way of lending support for the development of a multicultural curriculum. Establishing a supportive environment for education that is to be multicultural will make the job of the classroom teacher easier and instruction at the classroom level more effective.

Classroom Environments

Charts 6.1 and 6.2 focus on the classroom environment in elementary and secondary schools, respectively. Much like the in-school environment, there are several areas in the classroom that can contribute to the development of a multicultural curriculum. In addition to the elements of the environment that can be used to assist in initiating the approach, certain types of general activities can also go a long way toward strengthening the efforts to help make the instruction and the learning experiences of the student multicultural.

Bulletin Boards

Chart 6.4 suggests that bulletin boards must include pictures and language that portray diversity. Not very long ago, it was almost im-

There are several areas in the classroom that can contribute to the development of a multicultural curriculum.

possible to discover magazine pictures that would assist in this effort. Fortunately, today many pictorial representations, including pictures, photographs, and commercially designed picture sets, can be obtained to make this step a relatively simple task. The design of multicultural bulletin boards must be sensitive to displays that will depict interaction among and between groups as well as acknowledge the existence of more than one ethnic/racial group or gender. A bulletin board, particularly in the primary grades, that presents children of different sexes and different ethnic/racial groups doing things together is encouraged. A display that confines the pictorial representations to one sex and/or to two groups, each in separate kinds of activities, will not convey the same message as one that shows people working and/or playing together. Bulletin boards created from student works are strongly encouraged. Often student artwork can be stimulated from reading a poem or book or showing a film that is multicultural. Students should be encouraged to discuss the activity and to express their feelings about the experience. If the work selected as the stimulus for this activity is multicultural in content, the discussion that follows should be guided so as to reinforce the multicultural nature of the experience. The artwork that will result from this activity should be suitable for helping to reinforce the multicultural learning experience and for developing a bulletin board that displays what was learned.

Seating Arrangements

Seating arrangements can also contribute to helping children feel comfortable in a classroom and at the same time allow them to experience differences that exist among and between people. Too often children are allowed to seat themselves according to established friendships, and this usually creates a seating arrangement that can also be sexist. Care should be taken to create an environment that at times allows students to select where they will sit, but there should also be other times when the teacher arranges the seating to avoid sexism and racism and to help children become acquainted with each other. This can be done formally through seat assignment on a weekly or monthly basis and/or through grouping to accomplish a team approach to an activity. Whatever technique is used, it should be done to make seating arrangements that help create a multicultural classroom environment.

Audiovisual Aids

Perhaps one of the most exciting ways a teacher can plan to make classroom activities multicultural is the selection of audiovisual aids. This process can be exciting because it is a means through which two things can be accomplished. First, it encourages the teacher to seek out deliberately materials that are multicultural and in so doing increase his or her sensitivity to the need for evaluating instructional materials. Second, the teacher becomes more knowledgeable about the kinds of materials that are available. Also, through reading children's books and previewing films, filmstrips, picture charts, slides, and other forms of audiovisual aids, the teacher will expand his or her knowledge base about other cultural groups. Third, through the selection of the best available multicultural material, the classroom becomes alive with material that will help to support learning experiences about differences. If a teacher includes books about a variety of children, lifestyles, and cultures in the classroom library, book corner, or interest center, this in itself conveys a message to the students about the acceptability of cultural diversity. Once the selections are sanctioned and appear in an integrated manner in the classroom, students will partake. Creating corners where children can read and view filmstrips or slides that are multicultural will teach them about diversity and help reinforce reading and observation skills. An extremely effective approach is to have the teacher read a book to the children that will teach about another cultural group or about a situation or experience that concerns another culture. The type and length of book will depend on the grade level of the children and on what is to be accomplished.

Reading to children for ten- or fifteen-minute periods is a good way to begin the day and an excellent strategy for settling the class down before moving to another activity or class or to dismissal. Reading to children and encouraging them to listen is also an effective strategy for aiding in the development of student reading skills. An important aspect for integrating multicultural education into the curriculum is to do it in such a way that content is learned at the same time skills are being developed.

Resource People

There are many situations when parents or other people who represent a particular profession or individuals who have a special knowledge about a subject are invited into the classroom to talk with the students. The teacher should pay special attention to make sure that there is a great deal of diversity among those who serve as resources to a class. Care must be taken, for example, to locate a male nurse when young children are learning about career choices. Likewise, special effort must be made to invite a female telephone installer or a minority or female physician, dentist, or banker to talk to the class. If it is not possible to accomplish this through the actual appearance of individuals in the school, then films, filmstrips, videos, and picture charts may have to substitute. There may be occasions when a teacher will have to prepare a slide collection that will achieve the same approach. A teacher in a community where there was little ethnic/racial diversity spent part of one summer visiting an urban area where there was a great deal of diversity and developed several sets of slides that included pictures of all kinds of people performing all types of tasks and being involved in different kinds of professions. This teacher wanted to develop a multicultural curriculum and took advantage of a course in photography to put together a multicultural slide presentation on careers, thus initiating the approach in the classroom and acquiring course credit and a degree of expertise all at the same time. Teachers will need to make deliberate attempts to ensure the inclusion of minorities and women as resources, especially in nontraditional roles.

Field Trips

Field trips can contribute toward creating an environment that is multicultural. A trip itself can be the contributing factor and/or the people who guide the children on the tour can help to teach the students a lesson. For example, one teacher who planned a trip to the post office in a town where there was only one minority postal worker specially requested that this individual be assigned to guide the second grade class of all white children through the post office. This same situation probably would never occur in large urban areas where there are many minorities working in post offices, but for this particular class the trip was a multicultural experience. This same approach can be used, depending on what exists in the community and on the needs of the children, to create a multicultural experience. The other aspect of planning field trips that foster a multicultural experience is to plan trips to places that will expose the students to a variety of forms of diversity. The subject that is being studied will affect what may be needed. A trip to a minority college could have several advantages for minority and nonminority students alike. Trips to religious edifices can go a long way toward helping children to understand differences in the way people worship. Trips to museums, fairs, and exhibits that expose children to information about specific cultural groups have unlimited opportunities for helping to move in the direction of developing a multicultural curriculum. Field trips should be planned so as to expose students to forms of diversity that they might not otherwise have the opportunity to experience. If the form of diversity has the tendency to convey negative approaches, then special attention must be taken to instruct students as to the cause of the situation. For example, if in an exploration of housing, the trip includes a visit to a dilapidated section of a city and it appears that the area is inhabited by only one or two ethnic groups, the economic, social, and political dimensions of the situation will need to be examined thoroughly before the trip is made and explained after the site has been visited. If racist attitudes and behavior have contributed to the situation and to the plight of the people, this should be pointed out and discussed as objectively as is possible.

Holidays

Holidays were discussed very briefly under the heading of school environments. However, there is more recognition and observance of holidays in total school environments and communities than ever before. If the observance of these holidays is handled appropriately, discussions and learnings can occur that can enhance the multicultural curriculum. In a school community where these observances are not shared by all, some children will elect to observe special days and therefore be absent from class. In a multicultural classroom setting, students are not penalized for observing special days and a truly multicultural curriculum would take advantage of a holiday to further expose other students to its meaning. This is a wonderful opportunity to invite parents in to work with the students in presenting the meaning of the celebration. In far too many schools, certain holidays are celebrated that automatically exclude some students. The celebration of these holidays should be conducted in such a way so as to make the celebration a learning situation for all students. The occasion should be observed in a manner that does not offend or discriminate against any student. Some schools have eliminated the celebration of Christmas and celebrate "winter holidays" instead; these then can include learning about a variety of holidays that occur during the winter months. Other schools extend this approach throughout the year and thereby incorporate a variety of different kinds of observances and coordinate classroom celebrations with schoolwide functions, such as assemblies. Still, though rather rarely, some schools have disregarded the celebration of any holiday in schools, including birthdays. Birthday celebrations are not observed by all people and the way these are acknowledged in schools should be attended to. Pledging allegiance to the flag of the United States does not necessarily fall under the heading of holidays, but attention is called to the fact that not all cultural, religious, ethnic, or racial groups participate in this practice. To insist on this practice in school can cause a great deal of difficulty for some children. Care needs to be taken when consideration is given to including this activity in the daily routine of the classroom. Students must be allowed the freedom to observe their holidays without fear of punishment. Schools should take great care when setting policy about the observance of holidays if the educational environment is to be multicultural.

Elementary Academic Content

The third section of Charts 6.1 and 6.2 suggests that steps toward initiating a multicultural curriculum should also be taken with regard to academic content. These charts suggest that the efforts to include relevant multicultural content begin only in a few areas at the initiating stage. The reason for this is primarily the time it may take teachers to become familiar enough with the kinds of information needed and the ways to introduce the content effectively. For example, it is suggested that efforts to integrate multicultural content at the elementary level be made in two areas perhaps in the first semester or during the first few weeks. The speed at which the integration of content is achieved should be determined by the school system through its plan of implementation, the individual school, and/or the teacher. Generally full integration will take two to three years to achieve.

When teachers are planning to initiate a multicultural approach to reading, the following steps are suggested:

1. If textbook usage is required, then care should be taken to select a textbook that it multicultural.
2. Once the textbook is selected, multicultural supplementary material should be used to augment the material presented in the book.
3. If textbook usage is not required, teachers can design reading programs around materials that are multicultural, such as trade books obtained from school libraries and other sources.

Plans for involving speaking and listening activities in the initial stages of integrating should involve those steps discussed under audiovisual aids. For easy reference and to include other suggestions, the following list is offered:

1. Select books for children to use in the classroom that represent diverse cultures and/or lifestyles.
2. Select books to read on a daily basis to children that will teach about cultural diversity and/or a variety of multicultural experiences.
3. Arrange learning corners that contain filmstrips, videos, and slides that are multicultural.
4. Record multicultural stories and poems on tapes and place them in listening corners for children to use independently.
5. Select only multicultural films, filmstrips, videos, and slides for use in classroom instruction.
6. Through records, resource persons, and/or the teacher, the opportunity to teach a second language is available. Expose students to simple phrases of at least one other language.

Once an activity has been initiated by the classroom teacher, the stage is set for the creation of a multicultural learning environment. More effort can be exerted at the initiating stage, but the steps suggested in this discussion represent the minimal amount of integration that should be accomplished in the implementation of a multicultural curriculum on the elementary classroom level.

Secondary Academic Content

For demonstration purposes only, the subject of history has been selected to show how information that is multicultural can be integrated into either the content of a history text, if required, or into a teacher-prepared history course. A later section in this chapter will include instructions that teachers may find useful in constructing teacher-prepared and teacher-planned units of instruction when developing multicultural curriculum independent of a textbook.

Some history textbooks have begun to integrate information about the involvement of minorities, but most are not as completely integrated as they could be. Therefore the process suggested here makes possible the inclusion of more multicultural content and allows the teacher the freedom to include it when and where he or she feels it would be most appropriate. Chart 6.2 proposes that the initiating stage begin with the inclusion of multicultural content in just one period of a history course outline per semester. This approach will allow the teacher to identify the kinds of information that might be included. The outline presented in Chart 6.2 contains larger historical segments than most teachers would use, but again the large historical periods are included here only as examples. When a teacher is preparing to integrate multicultural content, it is suggested that some time be given to reading books and/or textbooks that focus either on minorities in a historical context or on a single minority group. Since most teachers do not have a great deal of time to do research, a simple way to acquire large amounts of information in a short period of time is to read recommended books that have been written for young children. A couple of hours in an elementary school library reading about the history of a particular minority group will provide more information than one needs to make an initial step toward the integration of multicultural content. Care must be given to selecting those books that have been recommended as bias-free materials. Teachers will also find that a great deal of information can be readily acquired through the reading of introductory adult-level books on ethnic groups, such as the *Ethnic Groups in American Life* series published by Prentice-Hall that includes the title *Japanese Americans* by Harry Kitano. It is suggested that a teacher begin to integrate the involvement of only one or two ethnic/cultural groups at this stage. Confining the initial step to one or two groups will simplify the process and provide ample time for developing the strategies necessary for presenting the content. If, for example, a teacher decides to focus first on integrating content about African Americans, elementary textbooks similar to those suggested below can provide what is needed:

Basil Davidson. *A Guide to African History*. New York: Doubleday, 1965.

Milton Finkelstein, Hon. Jawn A. Sandifer, and Elfreda S. Wright. *Minorities: USA.* New York, Chicago, Dallas: Globe, 1971.

Jane Hurley, and Doris McGee Haynes. *Afro-Americans, Then and Now.* Westchester, IL: Benefic Press, 1969.

Milton Meltzer and August Meier. *Time of Trial, Time of Hope: The Negro in America, 1919–1941*. New York: Doubleday, 1966.

John J. Patrick. *The Progress on the Afro-American.* Westchester, IL.: Benefic Press, 1970.

There is no shortage of materials at whatever level is needed to help teachers adequately prepare to introduce objective and accurate content about the participation of African Americans in the development of the United States. Information on other ethnic groups is becoming more available. A source for succinct, factual content about many ethnic groups is *Teaching Strategies for Ethnic Studies,* 2nd ed., by James A. Banks (Boston: Allyn & Bacon, 1979). This book is highly recommended for the teacher who is just beginning to introduce multicultural material because it is organized so as to provide the reader with factual content that can easily be integrated into an existing history-course outline. This source can also be helpful for the teacher who may need help with strategy and techniques.

In addition to initiating the integration of multicultural content, Stage I encourages the teacher to compile a bibliography for students that will include appropriate supplemental materials. This is as important as the earlier suggestion for elementary teachers to include books on various cultures in the classroom library. It is important because such inclusion by the teacher is the sign of approval, and students will have a tendency to use the material more readily when it is recommended by the teacher. The selection of audiovisual aids to help teach the course is another important technique at this stage. Films and videotapes are excellent for presenting supplementary material. The book by Banks is also helpful because it contains excellent annotated bibliographies and lists of films and filmstrips about ethnic groups. In summary, the teacher beginning to integrate multicultural content in any subject area should consider the following:

1. Select at least one segment of the course each semester that can serve as the focal point to include information about a group that has not previously been included.
2. Select only one or two groups to begin with. This will eliminate the need for a lot of research and allow time for developing appropriate instructional strategies.
3. Use resource material to gain introductory information that is bias-free.
4. Suggest relevant supplementary materials in students' bibliographies.
5. Use as many multiculturally oriented audiovisual aids as possible.

Involving: Stage II

Each of the stages builds on what has occurred in the previous stage. Stage II in the implementation of a multicultural curriculum on both the secondary and elementary levels should include two to three additional subject areas. The primary reason for taking the process step-by-step is to allow time for the teacher to identify and locate the appropriate materials and information and to develop instructional strategy. It is assumed that during this process support will be available from curriculum consultants in the school district and through inservice education provided at the school level.

Elementary Academic Education

In the previous stage, reading and speaking/listening activities served as the focal points for the initial integrating effort. In Stage II two other academic areas are added to help make the integration of content more involved. This stage could begin as early as the second or third month of the school year or be delayed until the beginning of the second semester. Social studies and art are two areas that could logically follow in the process. These two areas are suggested primarily because of the ease with which multicultural material can be integrated into them. At this point, only general steps are discussed; more specific suggestions on how to handle multicultural material will be given in Chapters 7 through 12.

In the elementary school, social studies usually consumes much of the time and instructional effort. Some of this is due to the fact that many other subjects are related to the teaching of social studies, i.e., music, reading language-arts activities, and art. Therefore, the suggestion has been made to focus on social studies and art in Stage II. The social studies unit, whether it is taught through the use of a textbook or through a unit prepared by the teacher and/or students, is most suitable for the integration of multicultural concepts and information because of the nature of social studies. There is no topic under the heading of social studies that cannot be involved in helping to teach multicultural content, because social studies is teaching about people and the ways they think, live, and behave. When one is preparing to focus on involving social studies in the implementation of a multicultural curriculum, it is suggested to begin with only one unit topic. It may also be helpful to confine the integration of content to one or two ethnic groups, to begin with. If the efforts in Stage I resulted in students absorbing information and content on a variety of groups during reading and speaking/listening activities, then it may be easier for the teacher to confine the social studies integration to one or two ethnic groups. If in the initiation of Stage I all of the effort included information on only one ethnic or cultural group, then it would be profitable to select different groups for the social studies curriculum so as to provide more diversity. Again, it is suggested that the teacher seek resource material that is introductory in nature (e.g., by using children's references) so as to quickly establish a knowledge base about the group or groups to be included. Again, too, *Teaching Strategies for Ethnic Studies* by Banks will prove to be extremely helpful at this point.

Because the involvement of art in social studies activity can provide reinforcement of concepts and learning experiences, a strong emphasis on art activity at this stage is encouraged. For example, a social studies unit on shelter could be expanded to include learning about different kinds of houses and housing patterns, which could include the historical development of housing. Through the study of this topic, a study of the concept of the ghetto could lead to an exploration of types of ghettos in the United States; this could lead to learning about barrios, Indian reservations, and other types of neighborhoods and sections of cities that are inhabited by individual ethnic groups. While this exploration of housing could be general, the focus could also be confined to learning more about Mexican-Americans and/or Native Americans. The construction of dioramas to depict the relationship of geographic location to type of shelter could be an art activity. Another project could be a mural showing the development of housing in the United States. Field trips to museums, churches, and shops in an ethnic neighborhood could serve as the catalyst for students to work in chalk or watercolor to create their impressions of what they see.

There is no end to the possibilities that can come from integrating multicultural content into social studies and art. It may be helpful to remember the following when plans are made to move from Stage I to Stage II:

1. Select only one topic or unit in social studies to focus on integrating multicultural content.
2. Confine the inclusion of material to that of one or two ethnic groups that have not be previously included in Stage I activity.
3. Try to relate the art activity at this stage to what is being studied in social studies.

Secondary Academic Content

Becoming more involved in the integration of multicultural content in the secondary subject areas basically means expanding the approach used in Stage I to an additional area in the curriculum outline. This approach would result in having information about ethnic groups included for a longer historical time period. Several things could happen at this stage. First, the teacher could decide to continue with a focus on the one or two ethnic groups that were introduced in Stage I or begin to focus on yet another group. However, in the case of history, it might be more practical to continue with the original one or two groups until they have been integrated throughout and to begin to add more groups on a semester or yearly basis. How one proceeds will depend largely on how the material will be presented and on the needs of the students. It is hoped that the responses of the students and the classroom interaction will encourage and create yet other ways of including multicultural content that were not necessarily planned for by the teacher. The focus here should be on what the teacher can do to help restructure the curriculum so that it is multicultural. The way through which English, social studies, music, mathematics, and other subjects taught in the secondary schools are integrated will be similar to the process suggested for history but will also be somewhat different, depending on the subject and how it is structured to be taught.

An additional effort at this point to involve the whole curriculum more could be made in the required reading. In Stage I, the suggestion for integration was limited to including relevant reading materials on the students' bibliographies. In Stage II, the strategy is to build on the activity by specifically requiring students to read materials that are related to the groups included in the course. By the time the areas in Stage II have been effectively integrated into the content of the course and into the instructional strategies of the teacher, the implementation of a multicultural curriculum will have been achieved at a 50-percent level of involvement. Specifically, what is to be accomplished in Stage II is as follows:

1. Two additional periods in history and/or segments of a course outline are to be included in the integration process.
2. Depending on the approach of the teacher and the needs of the students, the ethnic groups included in Stage I will continue to be included and/or other groups will be added at this time.
3. Students will be required to read relevant material that will expand on the information formally presented in the course. Do not overlook the use of newspapers and other media for augmenting textbook reading. Selected commercially produced film and movies as well as television shows can be extremely helpful.

Integrating: Stage III

By the time a teacher reaches Stage III, the final stage, sources will have been discovered that will make this cumulative approach effective and easier to implement. The first two stages provide for a gradual initiation of efforts to involve content and teaching strategies toward a multicultural curriculum. Once the process to restructure the curriculum has begun to meet the demands of multicultural education, the teacher and the students have become involved. Progressing from being minimally involved to becoming totally involved takes the process to the point of working for complete integration of the curriculum. Ideally, complete integration could be achieved at the end of one year, but it is more realistic to expect to achieve this at the end of the second year. In some cases, it may take three years to successfully complete the process. As was stated earlier, the length of time it will take may depend on the support systems and resources available to the teacher. It will also depend upon how committed and interested the teacher is in helping to move to full implementation.

Elementary Academic Content

In the final stage of implementation, the remaining academic subject areas become the focal point for the integration of ethnic/cultural content. Chart 6.1 suggests that writing/spelling, mathematics, science, and music become involved. The addition of these four areas may appear to be a lot to manage but if the teacher has planned well, much of what will be needed to include these areas will have been discovered through searches for information to use in Stages I and II. For example, in searching for content to include in social studies and/or in a reading activity, materials such as poems, stories, books on myths, and fables may be discovered that can be used to stimulate writing activity that focuses on cultural differences. Encouraging children to write stories and poems about themselves, their families, and their experiences is a multicultural activity because it is an opportunity for them to express their own feelings and to share with others something about themselves.

A sensitive teacher will be able to develop the techniques that will be helpful in using all kinds of writing experiences to support efforts toward making the curriculum more multicultural. Spelling becomes multicultural when children learn to spell words they need; some words may be culturally oriented. If a spelling text is used, careful attention will need to be given to the selection of a multicultural text. Racist and sexist ideas can be spread through illustrations used in the presentation of spelling lessons in a textbook as easily as they can be by a nonmulticultural reader. Pictorial representations are equally important, and attention should be given to what the pictures in a spelling book are teaching. Ideally, a multicultural approach to spelling is one that is structured around the needs of the children in the classroom and not around the textbook. Spelling is also an excellent opportunity to reinforce the teaching of other languages, which was suggested as a possible activity under Stage I in the area of speaking/listening. A bilingual approach to spelling may be more appropriate in some schools than in others but is strongly encouraged in every classroom. If a teacher is not bilingual, he or she can become so by taking courses, listening to records, learning phrases from teachers who are bilingual, and/or learning from students and parents.

Mathematics is not as culturally free as most teachers believe. Because of the nature of mathematics, the techniques for approaching it will need to focus on the historical development of mathematics, the application and importance of mathematics for all students, and the types of examples used to teach mathematics. Children can be encouraged to learn arithmetic, algebra, geometry, and other forms of mathematics if in the early stages of learning, basic concepts are taught through examples they can relate to. This situation is particularly true for minorities and females. When the examples in a textbook refer only to males and are not culturally relevant to all students, there may be little motivation to learn. A story problem that a child can identify with can go a long way toward helping to teach a mathematical concept. Teachers may discover that even if a multicultural text is available, they will need to supplement it with material prepared to make the learning experiences more culturally relevant. That is why Chapter 9, on the teaching of math, has been added to the revised edition of this book.

Making the teaching of science multicultural can be achieved in much the same way as for social studies. Generally, science is taught from a textbook and/or from units prepared by teachers. If a textbook is used, the teacher should begin by selecting a science text that will lend itself to the integration of multicultural content. This may be more feasible if the unit is developed by the teacher and the text used as one of the resources. Introducing a scientist from an ethnic group that children are not familiar with is one method of integrating multicultural content. Another method could be a scientific exploration on why people are physically different. Integrating multicultural content into the teaching of science may be easier to accomplish if the units are prepared by teachers and/or in collaboration with students. The material presented in Chapter 11 will demonstrate more specifically how this may be achieved.

Steps to include music in a multicultural curriculum can be most enjoyable and should present little difficulty. Music is derived from the cultural experiences of people, and children can be exposed to all kinds of music through hearing records, dancing, singing, learning about instruments, attending concerts, and a host of similar kinds of experiences. The important thing to keep in mind is to make sure that a variety of music from several ethnic/cultural groups is presented. It is also very important to refrain from placing values on specific kinds of music. For example, to refer to the music of Beethoven or Bach as "good music" teaches students that music that is not similar is not good. Children need to be exposed to as many different kinds of music as possible so as to better understand the music and the culture from which it comes. However, to increase their experiences with different forms of music will also prepare them for learning how to enjoy the music of more than one culture.

The final stage accomplishes the goal of restructuring the curriculum so that it is multicultural. In planning for full integration in Stage III, the following suggestions should be helpful:

1. If textbooks are to be used, they must be selected with multicultural content in mind.
2. If textbooks are used to teach writing/spelling, mathematics, science, and music, the teacher will need to supplement them with relevant material.
3. In each subject area, the teacher should select only one unit or section through which multicultural content can be presented. Expansion into the remainder of the unit and/or subject area should follow as information is available.

4. Opportunities to help children become bilingual can be coordinated with the activity presented in speaking and listening.

Secondary Academic Content

Achieving full integration (Stage III) on the secondary level requires continuing the same type of activity that occurred in Stage II. By the time Stage III has been reached, all sections of the course outline should include ethnic content on several different groups. By this time, the technique for effectively integrating multicultural content into a course in an effective manner should be familiar. Caution should be taken so that once this stage has been reached, the teacher does not feel the restructuring process has been completed. What has been accomplished will need to be enriched and modified as the course continues to be taught. The content will change depending on the needs of the students and on how much additional information the teacher is able to obtain. Stage III also allows for the inclusion of all other kinds of learning activity promoted by the course. For example, term papers, reports, and research projects should be assigned to include some exploration into the involvement of other groups in what is being studied. In English classes, this could mean a comparison of the poetry written by individuals from two different ethnic groups at a particular period in history. It might also mean a comparison of poetry written by women of different cultural groups in a specific time frame. The crucial point to remember is that Stage III is not a termination stage but rather a stage that indicates all phases of the course and/or subject have been imbued in some way with multicultural content. The challenge now becomes how to make the course even more multicultural. Plans for activity at this level might take the following into account:

1. All aspects of the course should contain content that is multicultural.

2. All activity associated with the teaching of the course should include a focus on locating, analyzing, and evaluating information that will contribute to make the course multicultural.

The discussion of stages for the implementation of a multicultural curriculum has included the elementary and secondary levels. No specific mention of the junior high level and/or middle school was included because the suggestions given for the other levels, elementary and secondary, can be modified to meet the needs of intermediate-level schools.

Enriching

Continuing to include multicultural materials should be thought of as enriching the curriculum. Enriching the curriculum was not included as the fourth stage because it was a process of expansion and simply a means of building on what was suggested for the other three stages.

The discussion in the chapter did not stress the involvement of special-subject teachers in the restructuring process but this does not mean they should not be involved. In fact, it is hoped that as music, art, physical education, and other teachers who assist the regular classroom teacher on the elementary level become available, they too will be involved in the process. The classroom teacher should make an effort to plan with the other teachers to ensure the continuation of the restructuring process in classes taught by special-area teachers. Close cooperation, achieved through planning with the school librarian, can provide all that is needed in the identification of appropriate teaching materials.

Cooperation at both the elementary and secondary levels with other classroom teachers will allow for an exchange of information and ideas. The process of implementing a multicultural curriculum can be exciting when it is done in an environment that encourages collaboration.

Preparing a Unit

It is rarely possible to identify commercially prepared materials that are appropriate for multicultural instruction. One of the most effective methods teachers may use in the teaching of multicultural content is to develop their own units of study. Steps for the creation of teacher-prepared units are presented in this section. The specific examples given should aid in the development of various components.

Too often the classroom teacher has been encouraged to rely on commercially prepared units of instruction. Commercially prepared units or textbooks do save time and offer valuable information, but they have limitations. It is almost impossible for a textbook on any subject to provide what is needed to teach a specific subject to a particular classroom. The information contained in the textbook is usually general in nature and restricts what teachers are able to present to students. As was pointed out in the previous chapter, textbooks often do not include multicultural content, and when included, it is not necessarily relevant to the students in a given school or community. Textbooks can serve as excellent resources; however, to confine the teaching of a subject to the use of a single textbook limits the learning experiences of students and often does not provide what the teacher needs to make the material interesting or truly multicultural.

Advantages of Teacher-Prepared Units

Learning to prepare teaching units can be a helpful tool for the teaching of any subject at any grade level. There are several advantages of teaching units prepared by teachers. First, units prepared by teachers provide an opportunity for them to structure the learning experiences around the students' backgrounds and to respond to students' individual needs. The greater degree of individualization is consistent with the discussion on instructional priorities in Chapter 4. One of the three priorities offered for consideration suggested that individual differences serve as the basis for planning and organizing multicultural instruction. Therefore, a unit of instruction that is prepared by the teacher can be organized so that the content of the unit and the teaching strategies meet the individual needs of the class. A second advantage of a teacher-prepared unit is that it provides the opportunity for the teacher to integrate multicultural content that is pertinent to the class. To include content about ethnic/cultural groups to which the class cannot in some way relate will have less meaning than information that is relevant to students' experiences. Another advantage of a teacher-prepared unit is that the teacher can control the focus of the unit of instruction as well as the length of time the unit is to be taught. All units do not need to be lengthy, and a unit that is prepared by the teacher allows the teacher the flexibility to control the content and length of study. A fourth advantage of a teacher-prepared unit is that it encourages and requires the teacher to become more involved in the instructional content. For most teachers, this may present a challenge and provide for more enjoyment in the classroom. Many teachers become bored by the use of commercially prepared materials. However, teachers who become involved in what they are teaching by designing their own units of instruction do not need to watch the clock.

Types of Units

There are at least three basic types of instructional units that require considerable input and preparation by teachers. The first, planned solely by the teacher, may be called the "the teacher-prepared unit." This is usually a unit of instruction planned around a specific theme or subject, for a particular group of children, and for a definite period of time. The students receive the instruction and generally contribute little to the planning and preparation of the unit. This is not the ideal way to plan instruction for the classroom, but a unit of this type serves the purpose of this discussion in two ways. First, if a teacher is interested in acquiring techniques for learning how to control what is to be taught in his or her classroom, the teacher should develop his or her techniques first through learning how to construct a unit. It is easier to learn how to organize the teacher-prepared unit because the teacher does not need to react to the suggestions of others. A teacher needs only to be concerned with the information that should go into the unit and the most effective way to teach the content. Second, when a teacher is learning how to integrate multicultural content into classroom instruction, the teacher-prepared unit allows her or him to select the ethnic/cultural content to be included. The teacher also decides where the multicultural content will be included and how the information will be presented. For these two reasons, the material included in the latter section of this chapter will focus on helping the teacher organize the teacher-prepared unit and suggest ways through which this process can aid in making the instructional content multicultural.

A second type of unit that requires a good deal of input from the teacher but also provides for input from students may be called "teacher-student prepared unit." In the preparation of this kind of unit, the teacher generally selects the topic but works with the students in selecting the content. The students suggest ways through which they can learn what it is they feel they need to know about the subject. The teacher contributes much in the way of providing resources and maintains about 75 percent of the control of the development of the unit. Many teachers prefer this kind of approach to planning a unit because it allows for student input, satisfies student needs, and places responsibility for motivation more on the student than the teacher. It thus achieves a greater degree of individualization. In the teacher-student prepared unit, the integration of multicultural content may depend more on the teacher than on the student because the knowledge base of the teacher may be broader in this area. Once a teacher has mastered the ability to organize the teacher-student prepared unit, it may be easier to use this style of developing instructional materials.

A third type of unit, the "student-prepared unit," greatly reduces the contribution of the teacher in planning but depends heavily on the teacher for guidance and direction. This approach allows students to decide what it is they want to study, how they will approach it, and how long they want to spend on the exploration of the topic. This type of unit planning is generally done in classroom environments that are more open and have less structure to them than is the case in classrooms where the two other types of unit planning take place. For the students to be in control of planning their own learning experiences does not mean the teacher is not involved. What it does mean is that the teacher's responsibility shifts from one of "planning" to one of "guiding." In the development of a unit of instruction by students on any level, the teacher must be totally aware of what each student is pursuing so that the teacher can provide resources and ensure the integration and exploration of multicultural content. This approach may be more comfortable for those teachers whose teaching style involves a more informal approach to classroom instruction.

The integration of multicultural content into the curriculum can be achieved by any one of these three styles of development. However, because the first style introduced, "the teacher-prepared unit," has the advantage of being easier for most teachers to learn how to develop, detailed attention will be given to how this type of unit may be created. A unit prepared by the teacher also provides more opportunities for teachers to initiate, involve, and integrate content that is multiculturally relevant.

The Teacher-Prepared Unit

A unit of instruction prepared solely by the teacher will usually have a good deal of structure. Generally it will consist of several distinct sections, each contributing to the development of the instructional module. It is suggested that an instructional unit contain each of the following:

1. Goals and objectives
2. A content outline
3. A set of behavioral objectives
4. Generalizations
5. Activities (lessons)
6. Resources

In this section, the words *goals* and *objectives* will be used interchangeably and will be distinguished later from behavioral objectives. To some teachers, stating goals and/or objectives will seem like a waste of time, and they may prefer to move on to more meaningful activity in the construction of a unit. Nevertheless, stating goals is perhaps one of the most important aspects of preparing a unit. It is important to take the time to write out why the unit is to be taught. Roger F. Mager, in his work on helping teachers understand the value of transmitting skills and knowledge through the preparation of instructional objectives, writes the following:

> Once an instructor decides he will teach his students something, several kinds of activity are necessary on his part if he is to succeed. He must first decide upon the goals he intends to reach at the end of his course or program. He must then select procedures, content, and methods that are relevant to the objectives; cause the student to interact with appropriate subject matter in accordance with principles of learning; and, finally, measure or evaluate the student's performance according to the objectives or goals originally selected.[4]

Mager is emphasizing in this statement the need for a teacher to be clear about the reasons the unit is to be taught. It is helpful to take the time to write out the goal or goals of the unit. According to Richard W. Burns, "Goals are statements of broad, general outcomes of instruction and they do not state or convey meaning in a behavioral sense—they do not tell what the learner is to do at the end of instruction."[5] For the purpose of this discussion, a study of Washington, D.C., has been selected as the topic of the sample unit.

The teacher should recognize that goals and/or overall objectives are not meant to explain and/or predict specific instructional aims of a unit but rather give general outcomes of the instruction. Therefore, the task of constructing a goal statement for a unit on Washington, D.C., becomes less complicated.

Burns offers the following definition for goals, pointing out that they are:

- Broad, encompassing terms.
- Sometimes expressed from the learner's point of view.
- Sometimes expressed from the teacher's point of view.
- When listed, usually few in number.
- Not expressed in behavioral terms.[6]

Keeping in mind that goals are stated in general terms, we may use words and phrases that reflect this when constructing a goal statement or an overall objective for a unit. The words and phrases in the following list may be used in creating goals and objectives:

- To have a greater appreciation.
- To better understand.
- To be able to enjoy.
- To develop respect for.
- To have a greater degree of sensitivity.

An appropriate goal statement for a unit of study on Washington, D.C., could be stated in any of three ways:

- To aid students in developing an appreciation for the District of Columbia.
- To help students better understand the history and development of Washington, D.C.
- To help students gain a respect for the uniqueness of the District of Columbia.

The three goals stated here are not only broad in scope, but there is nothing about them that would indicate the study of the unit is to include a multicultural approach. The third goal statement is perhaps the closest to a multiculturally stated goal and is a good lead-in to the development of a fourth goal that could make this set of goals multicultural. A fourth multicultural goal statement could thus be written in the following way:

- To help students understand the role and contributions of different ethnic groups in the development of the District of Columbia.

The list of goal statements could continue with an additional statement that would further strengthen the multicultural intent of the unit on Washington, D.C.:

- To help students appreciate the ethnic/racial composition of the city.

All of the preceeding are general in scope and cannot be measured for achieved outcomes as a behavioral objective could be. Taking the time to formulate goal statements for a unit of study is a necessary first step in constructing a teacher-prepared unit.

Content Outline

The next step in the preparation of the unit is to make some decisions as to what will be included in the study. In this case, what will be included in the study of Washington, D.C.? How much is to be included will depend on the amount of time that can be allotted. Suppose, for example, the unit will be studied for a period of eight weeks. The content outline is a description of what the unit will include; it is helpful if it is organized in outline form. Before the outline can be organized, the teacher will need to have as much information about Washington, D.C. as possible. Having a grasp of the history and development of the District and its current posture geographically, politically, socially, economically, and culturally can provide the teacher with what is needed to construct an outline spanning eight weeks of study.

As was suggested earlier, a quick and effective means for gaining a lot of information on any subject in a short amount of time is to use resources that have been prepared for children at the elementary level. This kind of resource material also presents information in such a way as to suggest a content outline for the teacher to use. Another excellent source for helping the teacher construct an outline is an encyclopedia. Most encyclopedias summarize a section of information on a specific subject in outline form, and this presents an excellent opportunity for the teacher to modify the outline or abstract what is pertinent for his or her use and in a very short period put together a comprehensive outline.

The following outline, **A**, was constructed by the latter method and, except for the one reference to ethnic groups in Section V, the content is not multicultural. However, the examples in the second outline, **B**, suggest ways of modifying outline **A** to ensure that it will be more multicultural in its approach.

CONTENT OUTLINE **A**
A STUDY OF WASHINGTON, D.C.

I. A View of the City
   A. Northwest Section
   B. Northwest Section
   C. Southeast Section
   D. Southwest Section
   E. Metropolitan Area

II. The History of the City
   A. Washington Chosen as Capital
   B. Early Days
   C. Growth and Development
   D. Recent Developments

III. The Economy
   A. Federal Government
   B. Private Business
   C. Transportation
   D. Communication

IV. Local Government

V. The People
   A. Ethnic Groups
   B. Housing
   C. Education
   D. Social Problems
   E. Cultural Life and Recreation[7]

As was stated earlier, this outline includes information about the city of Washington that could be taught from a point of view that would not necessarily be multicultural. However, with some modifications, the teacher can redesign the outline to include relevant information that can be integrated and help make the unit multicultural. The degree to which the outline can be multicultural will depend upon how much information the teacher has available. It is important at this point to stress that the teacher can begin to initiate the integration of multicultural content only when the information is known. Therefore, a teacher will need to establish the all-important knowledge base about the subject that is to be studied before plans can be made to make the unit multicultural. For example, if a teacher is unaware of the involvement of Benjamin Bannecker, an African-American astronomer, in the design of the city of Washington, the class could very well study the city without ever learning about his contribution. However, when this kind of information is familiar to the teacher, then the second type of outline, **B**, can be designed. The same applies to the manner in which Section I of this outline has been redesigned to include other areas that will contribute to multiculturalism.

CONTENT OUTLINE **B**

I. A View of the City
    A. Design of the City
        1. Geographic location
        2. Designers/Engineers
            a. Pierre Charles L'Enfant
            b. Benjamin Bannecker
    B. Sections of the City
        1. Northwest
            a. Largest section
            b. Diplomatic influence (international)
            c. Five of the largest universities
            d. Adams-Morgan area

2. Northeast
   a. Location of Museums (those of particular relevance for this study, i.e., ethnic-specific and the Women's Museum)
   b. Catholic University
   c. African American population (largest)
   d. Other ethnic populations
3. Southeast
   a. Depressed areas
   b. Capitol Hill area
   c. Ethnic populations
4. Southwest
   a. Smallest section
   b. Urban renewal program

V. The People
   A. Ethnic Populations
      1. African-American
      2. Spanish-speaking
      3. White ethnic populations
      4. Others
   B. Housing
      1. Patterns
      2. Urban renewal
      3. Economics
      4. Regentrification
   C. Education
      1. Governing bodies
      2. Curriculum
      3. Achievement
      4. Economics

When students begin to learn about the sections of the city, information such as the international diplomatic influence exerted in the District can help to make them more aware of the ethnic/cultural diversity of the people who have this influence.

A discussion of the origins of and the differences between the five universities that are located in the northwest section can highlight the importance of Howard University and the University of the District of Columbia for the education of African Americans and other ethnic groups. Adams-Morgan in the northwest section is an area that is definitely ethnically diverse and contains a large Spanish-speaking population. As students continue to explore the sections of the city, it will be important for them to know that the northeast section contains the largest African-American population. The location of the Catholic University adds yet additional information that is culturally related. The fact that the southeast section contains both a wealthy area, near the location of the Capitol, that is largely inhabited by whites and a large, less affluent area that is predominantly African American is information that students will need in order to explore the causes of these conditions and to understand the implications they have for people in these areas and for the city of Washington. This section could be modified further to include additional multicultural content; the extent to which this can be done will depend on the knowledge and ability of the teacher.

Section V in Outline **B** has been modified to suggest ways of integrating content about Washington's people—how they live and how they are educated—that also contributes to making the unit multicultural. One relevant point for a multicultural unit of study is that Washington, D.C. has the largest African-American population of any major city in the United States and has elected its first African-American woman mayor. Students should be helped to understand the reasons why the city is more than 70 percent African American and how demographics affect the lives of those living in Washington. The growing Spanish-speaking population has implications for city planning; also, the contributions of this population to the diversity of the city cannot go overlooked. The remainder of Section V includes possible areas that will lead to the study of other dimensions of the unit directly involving multicultural content. Only modifications of Sections I and V have been included in Outline **B** to suggest ways of making

Whether creating a unit on Washington, D.C., or New York City, the teacher needs to state goals and objectives, construct an outline, and determine a specific learning outcome.

the unit of study, presented in Outline **A**, multicultural. The other sections of the unit could and should be modified in similar fashion to ensure that multicultural content will be integrated throughout.

This unit is one that can be taught to students living in and around the District of Columbia and/or in any section of the country. However, the discussion of behavioral objectives, generalizations, and activities will show examples that are particularly relevant to students residing in the area.

Once the goals and objectives have been stated and the content outline constructed, the next step is to determine the specific learning behavior that is expected as an outcome of the study of the unit. Learning how to state behavioral objectives and how to help students achieve them forms the basis of planning for the types of learning activities that will come later.

Behavioral Objectives

A main characteristic of goals is that they are general in scope. The examples previously given for the unit on the District of Columbia follow this pattern; they are general goals and are in no way measurable. Behavioral objectives are the opposite in that they are specific and describe outcomes that can be measured.

Burns describes terminal behavioral objectives as "relatively specific statements of learning outcomes expressed from the learner's point of view and telling what the learner is to do at the end of instruction." [8] Some of his examples include:

- The learner is to know the names of fifty states so that he or she can list them (from memory) in any order.
- The learner is to develop skill in the use of the word processor so that he or she can produce a two-page essay using correct style and spelling.

In other words, terminal behavioral objectives are

- specific rather than broad.
- always expressed from the learner's point of view.
- statements which include a description of the behaviors of the learner or what he [or she] is able to do as result of or at the end of instruction.[9]

Keeping these examples and Burns's definition of behavioral objectives in mind, the following objectives would be appropriate for the unit of study on Washington, D.C.:

- The student will be able to label and identify on a map the four major sections of the city.
- The student will be able to write a one-page history of the city, including the date when it became the capital of the United States.
- The student will be able to write the names of the individuals who have been mayors and include the dates of their terms.

Each of these behavioral objectives is specific and represents behavior that can be measured. The three examples given above were developed from Outline **A** and are not necessarily multicultural. To add to the list to make it more multicultural in content, the following behavioral objectives would be appropriate:

- The student will be able, in one page, to identify Benjamin Bannecker and described his contributions to the development of the city.
- The student will be able to list at least three ethnic groups living in the city and give their approximate percentages within the population.
- The student will be able to identify two universities in the city that contribute greatly to the education of African Americans.
- The student will be able to give the name and background of the first African-American woman mayor of the city.

These behavioral objectives are primarily multicultural. A complete list of behavioral objectives for this unit would include the integration of multicultural objectives so as to reflect the integration of multicultural content throughout the entire unit of study. After the teacher has formulated a complete list of behavioral objectives for the entire unit, it is appropriate to develop plans for organizing the instruction through various types of learning experiences and activities. This is best accomplished when the teacher is able to decide what is to be taught for each section on the outline. Some teachers will find it easier if a group of generalizations and behavioral objectives forms the basis of instruction for a week. Other teachers will be more comfortable doing this on a daily basis. Whatever method is selected, it must be organized so that all of the generalizations and behavioral objectives flow from the outline.

Generalizations

The key to a successful unit of study will depend on how well organized the plans are for the exploration of the topic. When a teacher is clear about why it is important to study the topic, is specific about the content, and is definite as about student outcomes, the unit is on its way to being well-organized. In order to continue the development of the unit and to ensure that the students will have certain kinds of learning experiences, the content will need to be further organized, and further generalizations will need to be formulated.

According to James A. Banks, "A key goal of ethnic studies should be to help students develop decision-making and social action skills."[10] Because of the relationship between ethnic studies and multicultural education, this goal is incorporated in the objectives and goals of multicultural education. One way to achieve these goals and objectives is to organize instruction from a conceptual point of view—that is, to limit the teaching of a unit to the discovery and discussion of factual information that could ultimately help students learn to make good decisions and choices. What is needed is a method of combining facts and concepts so that the instruction is organized around broader forms of knowledge. Generalizations serve this purpose well. Banks defines generalizations in the following way:

> A generalization contains two or more concepts and states the relationship between them. Like empirical facts, generalizations are scientific statements which can be tested and verified with data. Generalizations are very useful tools in instruction because they can be used to summarize a large mass of facts and to show the relationship between higher-level concepts which students have mastered. Like concepts generalizations vary greatly in their level of inclusiveness; there are low-level generalizations, which are little more than summary statements, and there are very high-level generalizations, which are universal in applicability.[11]

Banks stresses the usefulness of generalizations because they are broad in scope, group together sets of facts, and demonstrate the relationship between concepts. When a unit is being organized, the teacher will need to formulate generalizations that will serve to guide classroom instruction. In addition to serving as the organizing factors for the content of the unit, generalizations will also influence the methods the teacher chooses. Deciding the kind of learning experiences that students and/or an individual student may need in order to grasp information more efficiently will influence the kinds of activities that are planned for the classroom. Banks makes a distinction between several levels of generalizations and suggests that teachers can benefit by planning around high-level generalizations and then selecting lower-level statements, as needed, to relate to the specific content being used. The following illustrations used by Banks help to illustrate differences in generalizations and should be useful to the teacher in preparing to develop this section of the unit:

Fact: Chinese immigrants who came to San Francisco in the 1800s established the huikuan.
Lower-Level Generalization: Chinese immigrants in America established various forms of social organizations.
Intermediate-Level Generalization: All groups immigrating to the United States have established social organizations.
Highest-Level, or Universal, Generalization: In all human societies, forms of social organizations emerge to satisfy the needs of individuals and groups.[12]

This illustration demonstrates the process of developing a generalization focused on one ethnic group. The breadth of the highest-level generalization provides opportunities for students to learn facts and concepts that are part of the broader statement.

Using once again the sample units on the study of Washington, D.C., and Banks's illustration, we can use Section V of Outline **B** to illustrate further the development of a generalization:

Fact: African Americans comprise 70 percent of the population of Washington, D.C.
Lower-Level Generalization: The African American population is unevenly distributed in the four major sections of the city.
Intermediate Level Generalizations: Socioeconomic factors control the housing patterns in cities.

Highest-Level, or Universal, Generalization: The economic, political, and social structure of a city is influenced by its ethnic composition.

The universal generalization allows students to learn both general facts and concepts and specific facts and concepts about Washington, D.C. A generalization of this type is all that may be needed for a specific section of the content outline. This statement will help the teacher develop the appropriate instructional methods. The number of generalizations a teacher will use with a specific unit will depend on how the unit is organized and how the teacher structures the generalizations. The level of the students involved in the instruction will also determine how abstract and complex the generalization will be. Caution must be taken when formulating generalizations for young children so that efforts to reduce complexity do not substitute facts for the generalized form the statement should take. After the list is completed, the teacher can then plan specific learning activities.

Activities

The activities planned in this part of the unit are the actual teaching strategies and techniques that the teacher will use to help teach the generalizations. The methods and learning experiences the teacher selects will be consistent with his or her teaching style and should meet student needs. The methods should be pedagogically sound and, if this principle is adhered to, the activities should reflect a variety of approaches. According to Calhoun C. Collier and his colleagues, the planning of learning experiences should include:

> Planning should reflect knowledge and application of principles of learning. Pupils are more likely to participate actively in activities that are comfortable and satisfy one of more needs. Since a wide range of human variabilities—intellectual, social, physical, and cultural characteristics; interest; attitude; natural drive; motivation—exist within a group of youngsters, plans should provide for learning at different rates and in a variety of styles.[13]

Behavioral objectives and generalizations provide the structure from which learning experiences are planned. It may be helpful at this point for the teacher to organize the learning experiences and activities by the week and finally by the day in accordance with the generalizations. This can be accomplished in several ways. One way to organize is in outline form, including the generalization(s) and the behavioral objective(s) that will be focused on that week. The following is an example of what an outline of the plan for the first two days of a week might look like:

UNIT OF STUDY
WASHINGTON, D.C.

Week I

I. Generalization(s): (list)

II. Behavioral Objectives: (list)

III. Activities:

  A. Monday

    1. Initiate the unit by constructing a bulletin board with the class from newspaper articles and pictures about the city.
    2. Discuss with children the content of the bulletin board and relate this to the overall design and location of the city, e.g., the location of various events in the city.

  B. Tuesday

    1. Introduce the film *Washington, D.C. Today* by reviewing the discussion that was held the previous day.
    2. Ask the class to identify one specific landmark shown in the film in at least two different sections of the city.

This type of planning allows the teacher to do detailed planning for the week on a daily basis. In continuing to plan for the unit, the teacher should make a plan for each one of the eight weeks and should include the culminating activity. It is helpful to leave space on one of the margins to develop a system that will help indicate when audiovisual aids have been ordered and the dates confirmed. The system used under item B-1 indicates the date the film was ordered, and the check mark shows that the film was confirmed. The line under the check serves to tell the teacher that the necessary audiovisual equipment was ordered and will be available.

Another helpful way to organize the unit is to develop a grid. Organizing by using a grid can provide an overview of the unit's activity and also identify by number the specific generalizations and behavioral objectives on the grid that are the focus for a particular week or day. If the generalizations and behavioral objectives have been developed by the teacher as previously suggested, then these can be numbered or assigned letters. The corresponding numbers and letters can be included in the grid as shown in Chart 6.5. If the grid plan is used, then a daily lesson plan should be developed by the teacher as needed. Note that the same method of indicating when audiovisual aids have been ordered is used in the grid presented in Chart 6.5

These are two of the many ways a teacher may select to organize a unit. The method of organizing should be comfortable for the teacher to use and serve to support the overall structure of the unit.

The information presented in this chapter can be of assistance to teachers who are interested in the integration of ethnic and cultural content into the existing curriculum. Successful units can be developed if teachers are definite about the topic of study they want to present. They need to be sure about the reasons they want to teach this topic, their goals and objectives for doing so, and the extent to which they want to explore the subject. Once this planning has been achieved, it will be necessary to formulate generalizations that will serve to give direction to the organizing of learning activities. Successful implementation of a multicultural curriculum will depend a great deal on how well multiculturalism is integrated throughout all the activities of the school.

Part III of this book presents teaching strategies in several subject areas that were designed according to this method. These areas include mathematics, science, and language arts among others.

CHART 6.5
Unit of Study
Washington, D. C.

MONDAY	TUESDAY	WEDNESDAY	THURSDAY	FRIDAY
9/7 1*, A and B** Construct D. C. bulletin board Class discussion	9/8 Film: "Washington, D. C. Today"	9/9 Write paragraphs summarizing film	9/10 Complete paragraphs Illustrate summaries using watercolors	9/11 Complete artwork
9/14	9/15	9/16	9/17	9/18
9/21	9/22	9/23	9/24	9/25
9/28	9/29	9/30	10/1	10/2

* The numeral 1 represents the generalization that is being focused on in Week 1.
** The letters A and B represent the behavioral objectives being focused on in Week 1.

Notes

1. William E. Sedlacek and Glenwood C. Brooks, Jr., *Racism in American Education: A Model for Change* (Chicago: Nelson-Hall, 1976), p. 103.
2. Robert L. Williams, *Cross Cultural Education: Teaching Toward a Planetary Perspective* (Washington, D.C.: National Education Association, 1977), p. 10.
3. Ann Richardson Gayles, *Instructional Planning in the Secondary School,* Myles W. Rodehaver, William B. Axtell, and Richard E. Cross, "The Responsibility of the School." (New York: David, McKay, 1973), p. 118.
4. Roger F. Mager, *Preparing Instructional Objectives* (Belmont, CA: Fearon Publishers, 1961), p. 1.
5. Richard W. Burns, *New Approaches to Behavioral Objectives* (Dubuque, IA: Wm. C. Brown Publishers, 1972), p. 3.
6. Ibid., p. 3.
7. *World Book Encyclopedia,* vol. 21 (Chicago: Field Enterprises Education Corporation, 1976), pp. 62–71.
8. Richard W. Burns, *New Approaches to Behavioral Objectives,* p. 3.
9. Ibid., p. 9.
10. James A. Banks, *Teaching Strategies for Ethnic Studies,* 2nd ed. (Boston: Allyn and Bacon, 1979), p. 38.
11. Ibid., p. 40.
12. Ibid.
13. Calhoun C. Collier, W. Roberts Houston, Robert R. Schmatz, and William J. Walsh, *Modern Elementary Education: Teaching and Learning* (New York: MacMillan, 1976), p. 168.

Part III

Instruction

7
Generalizations and Teaching Strategies for Art

Introduction

Art is a valuable subject through which people can learn about their histories, values, and beliefs. The work of the artist helps us to understand and to learn more about those who differ from us. Almost everyone enjoys some form of art, and thus teaching and learning through art can be a very pleasant experience. Children love to create, and through the creation of an object of art much learning about the self and others can take place. Jo Miles Schuman in her book on multicultural art projects, *Art From Many Hands,* expresses her feelings about the value of art for learning about others in this way:

> I also hope that in a world where differences in culture and ethnicity sometimes bring conflict, learning about cultural differences in arts and crafts can help students appreciate and respect one another. In America's communities and classrooms, where children of several ethnic backgrounds often live and work together, these arts can be a language of understanding.[1]

Art comes in many forms and says something different to each of us. No two people see the same thing in a work of art, but basic principles and understandings about people and the way they live can be gained by many individuals from the same examples of artistic expression.

The two units presented in this chapter on art were selected because the nature of the topic lends itself to learning about how other people live and think. The topics also allow the art specialist or the classroom teacher to take a comprehensive approach to the subject and to include examples of art from several different ethnic/racial and cultural groups. A study of folk art is an interesting area that should permit the student to develop a greater appreciation for the cultural values and beliefs of people who have had little or no formal training and who create what they like. Masks are yet another form of art through which much can be learned about culture.

The suggested lessons in this chapter can be taught by the art specialist in schools where most of the art is taught in this manner or in the classroom by the classroom teacher. An ideal arrangement would be a collaborative approach by both the specialist and the classroom teacher in the same learning environment. Regardless as to who does the teaching, these lessons and other multicultural art lessons prepared by the teacher will go a long way towards helping students to understand and appreciate diversity.

Folk Art

Suggested Content Outline

A. Folk Art Defined

B. Types of Folk Art
   1. Painting
   2. Sculpture
   3. Other
      a. Household Objects
      b. Scrimshaw

C. Folk Artists from United States Cultures
   1. Asian and Pacific Islanders
   2. African Americans
   3. Puerto Rican Americans
   4. Mexican Americans
   5. Native Americans

Generalizations:

I. Folk art is the artistic expression of people who generally are not trained to be artists.

II. Painting and sculpture are two kinds of folk art that are used to display the lifestyle and thoughts of a group of people during a certain period and from a particular geographic region.

III. The religious views, social behavior, and political attitudes of ethnic/cultural groups are often expressed through folk art.

Generalization I: Folk art is the artistic expression of people who generally are not trained to be artists.

Level: Primary

Objectives:

1. To help students understand what folk art is.
2. To develop an appreciation for folk art.
3. To help students become aware of the different kinds of folk art, including folk dolls.
4. To motivate students to create a folk doll.

Teaching Strategy:

1. Discuss with students different kinds of art forms such as painting, sculpture, and weaving. Continue the discussion by

introducing the word *folk*. Help the students to grasp the meaning of the word and introduce the term "folk art." Lead the students to understand that folk art is created by people who generally are not trained artists. Folk art has no rules.

2. Show the class several pictures of folk art in books, such as *How to Know American Folk Art* by Ruth Andrews and *Beyond Necessity: Art in the Folk Tradition* by Kenneth L. Ames. Make a list of as many different kinds of folk art as the class can suggest; be sure to include folk dolls.
3. Share with the class the many different kinds of folk dolls that can be made. A good resource is *Making American Folk Art Dolls* by Gini Rogowski and Gene Deweese.
4. Encourage the students to suggest other ways that dolls can be made, and make a list of the kinds of materials needed.
5. Have students bring in as many of the materials on the list for making dolls as they have at home, such as scraps of material, yarn, odd socks, clothespins, buttons, and ribbon.
6. Conclude this lesson by reviewing the concept of folk art. Plan with the class for an art session during which they will create their own folk dolls and thereby become folk artists.

Resources

Kenneth L. Ames. *Beyond Necessity: Art in the Folk Tradition.* New York. W.W. Norton and Company, 1977.

Ruth Andrews. *How to Know American Folk Art.* New York: E.P. Dutton, 1977.

Gini Rogowski and Gene Deweese. Making *American Folk Art Dolls.* Radnor, PA: Chilton, 1975.

Level: Intermediate

1. To introduce to the class the concept of folk art.
2. To develop an appreciation for folk art.
3. To help students become aware of various kinds of folk art, including quilts.

Teaching Strategy

1. Begin this lesson by playing a game. Have the students choose partners and together list as many different kinds of art as they can think of in five minutes. The winners will be those with the most forms on their list. If the term *folk art* or a type of folk art, such as weather vanes or scrimshaw, appears on the list, continue the lesson by having the students develop a definition of folk art. If there is no reference to folk art, then the term will need to be introduced. Help the class to grasp the idea that folk art is similar to "homemade or homegrown," versus more formal expressions of art.
2. With the class list on the chalkboard the different kinds of artwork that are considered folk art; include quilt making.
3. Using the book *Once Upon a Quilt* by Celine Blanchard Mahler, tell or read to the class the story of the quilt. Reinforce the idea presented by Marguerite Ickis, the author of *The Standard Book of Quilt Making,* that "the story of the quilt is the record of the human family."
4. Show pictures of various quilt patterns from *Once Upon a Quilt: The Standard Book of Quilt Making and Collecting,* and other books or pictures that are available. Discuss with the class how the pattern of a quilt may tell a story about the lives of the people who made it. For example, the log-cabin pattern indicates a certain lifestyle.
5. Have each student in the class use crayons to design a pattern for a quilt square on a piece of 8 1/2" x 11" manila paper. It will describe some aspect of the way they live, think, or behave. Assemble the designs on a bulletin board so they form a paper quilt. If the class is interested, discuss plans for making the quilt out of material. This would be an excellent project and allow the students to work on their individual pieces in their spare time or during other art periods. The quilt could be displayed in the school, given to

a family through a drawing process, or raffled off at a school Folk Art Fair that would feature other kinds of folk art by the school community.

Resources

Lenice Ingram Bacon. *American Patchwork Quilts.* New York: Bonanza Books, 1980.

Marguerite Ickis. *The Standard Book of Quilt Making and Collecting.* New York: Dover, 1949.

Celine Blanchard Mahler. *Once Upon a Quilt: The Standard Book of Quilt Making and Collecting.* New York: Van Nostrand Reinhold, 1973.

Level: Advanced

Objectives

1. To aid students in understanding that folk art has been used by people in very practical ways.
2. To assist students in developing appreciation for the simple and functional beauty of folk art.
3. To encourage students to use a folk art form that expresses their feelings about themselves and their environment.

Teaching

1. This lesson could be used as an introductory lesson to a unit on folk art. It is designed to expose students to a wide variety of American folk art. *The Bird, The Banner and Uncle Sam* by Elinor Lander Horwitz provides an excellent overview of folk, painting, and sculpture by portraying images of American life. *A Carrot for a Nose* by M. J. Gladstone identifies a number of folk art forms in everyday use such as weather vanes, gate designs, whirligigs,

gravestones, and trade signs. Examples of folk painting and sculpture in the United States should be shown to the students. These may be found in books identified in the listed resources. Some of the qualities of folk art should be pointed out.

- Folk art is created by men or women who are largely self-taught.
- Folk art often takes a useful form, such as household items, weather vanes, gravestones, trade signs, and quilts.
- This art form tends to be decorative and designed to enhance the beauty of its surroundings.
- Folk painting often displays a homespun quality. Fruits, flowers, pets, and animals are often included. The work may be whimsical and even amusing.
- Folk art can be complex without being pretentious.
- Folk art tends to be straightforward in its presentation. There are no overlays from art-school training.

2. Following the showing of examples of folk art, the teacher should encourage students to identify other examples from selected books that demonstrate the above characteristics.
3. Continue the lesson by having the students share their examples with each other.
4. A discussion should follow, bringing to memory household items and community signs and murals that identify folk art in the students' environment. Conclude the lesson by having the students create an original design for a useful household item complete with decoration—a weather vane, a trade sign, or another form of folk art. The student may wish to do a self-portrait and include his or her pet.

Resources

Sandra Brant and Elissa Cullman. *Small Folk, a Celebration of Childhood in America.* New York: E.P. Dutton in association with American Museum of Folk Art, 1980.

M. J. Gladstone. *A Carrot for a Nose: The Form of Folk Sculpture on America's City Streets and Country Roads.* New York: Charles Scribner's Sons, 1974.
Elinor Lander Horwitz. *The Bird, The Banner and Uncle Sam: Images of America in Folk and Popular Art.* Philadelphia and New York: J.B. Lippincott, 1976.
Karen M. Jones. *From A to Z: A Folk Art Alphabet.* New York: Mayflower Books, 1978.

Generalization II: Painting and sculpture are two kinds of folk art that are used to display the lifestyle and thoughts of groups of people during a certain period and from a particular geographic region.

Level: Primary

Objectives:

1. To aid students in the exploration of painting as a kind of folk art.
2. To help students discover that much can be learned about the way people lived in the past by observing folk art paintings.
3. To stimulate the desire to paint a mural that will show something about the way the students live now.

Teaching Strategy:

1. Review the characteristics of folk art. Help students identify aspects of the way people live, including the natural environment which could influence the way they paint.
2. Discuss with the class their immediate environment and list the conditions such as terrain, weather, and type of community that might influence the kinds of pictures they would paint.

3. Using the book *Contemporary American Folk Artists* by Elinor Horwitz, show paintings by several of the artists whose work is included, and identify how the painting describes the way or the place the artist lives. This book also contains pictures of the artists, and this may help the students to identify other reasons for the type of story the paintings tell. For example, the work of an African-American woman who lives in the Southeast will be different from the work of a Mexican-American male who lives in the Southwest.
4. Tell the class that they are to become folk painters. Review the list of the conditions of their natural environment that might influence their paintings. Organize the class for painting a mural that will depict their surroundings and the adjustments they have made to it. Have small groups of students be responsible for certain aspects of the mural, e.g., snow, ice, trees, and people.
5. Use the mural for a follow-up lesson by having each student write a story about what is going on in the mural.

Resources

J. T. Ericson. *Folk Art in America.* New York: Mayflower Books, 1979.

Elinor Horwitz. *Contemporary American Folk Artists.* New York: J.B. Lippincott, 1975.

Level: Intermediate

Objectives:

1. To introduce some aspects of Eskimo (Inuit) culture to the class.
2. To help the students understand the relationship between the lifestyle of a group of people and their art.

Teaching Strategy

1. The teacher, after reading the following passage about Eskimos, should rephrase and share it with the class.

> The Eskimos believed powerful spirits controlled nature. They also believed people and animals had souls that lived in another world after a person or animal died. The Eskimos followed rules to please these spirits and souls. If they ignored the rules, Eskimos thought the spirits and souls would punish them by causing sickness or other misfortune. The Eskimos believed in several spirits, including spirits of the wind, the weather, the sun, and the moon. Perhaps the most important spirit was the sea goddess, Sedna, who lived at the bottom of the ocean and controlled

Art is a valuable subject through which people learn about their histories, values, and beliefs.

the seals, whales, and other sea animals. The Eskimos believed that if they did not please Sedna she might drive away the animals. To please her, they followed certain rules regarding sea animals. In part of Alaska, for example, the Eskimos saved the bladders of seals they killed. Then during a special ceremony each year, they threw the bladders into the sea.[2]

2. Read *Sedna: An Eskimo Myth* by Beverly Brodsky McDermott to the class. Discuss the story and relate it to the information already presented to the class about the beliefs of Eskimos and the manner in which these beliefs influenced the way they lived.
3. Present the name "Inuit" as the name Eskimos call themselves. *Inuit* means "people," and much of the art of the Eskimo is referred to as Inuit art. Inuit stone sculpture is often done by ordinary people. The Eskimos made their sculpture from materials in their environment, such as whalebone and soapstone. Small sculptured pieces were often used as toys by the children.
4. Arrange to have the students carve a sculpture from a piece of artificial sandstone. This process is described in detail in *Art From Many Hands* by Jo Miles Schuman. If it is not possible to obtain the materials suggested in this book, have the students carve shapes of animals from pieces of soap, using blunt scissors.
5. Plan to display the artwork under a caption such as "Folk Art of the Eskimos" or "Inuit Sculpture—Art of the People."

Resources

Shirley Glubok. *The Art of the Eskimo*. New York: Harper and Row, 1954.

Beverly Brodsky McDermott. *Sedna, An Eskimo Myth.* New York: Viking Press, 1975.

Jo Miles Schuman. *Art from Many Hands: Multicultural Art Projects for Home and School.* Englewood Cliffs, N.J.: Prentice-Hall, 1981.

Level: Advanced

Objectives:

1. To introduce students to examples of folk painting and sculpture from three different geographical regions of the United States.
2. To aid students in understanding that folk painting and sculpture reflect the lifestyle and thoughts of groups of people during different periods and in geographic regions.
3. To encourage students to express themselves through folk painting in the style of a geographic region or historic period.

Teaching Strategy:

1. This lesson should be used after the class has discussed American folk art in general and the students have a clear understanding of some qualities characterizing folk art. Identify and collect resources available in your area for folk art representative of different ethnic and cultural groups. Bring as wide a selection of books as possible to class for use in the lesson. See list of resources for possible works.
2. If possible, have students visit local museums and places where folk painting and sculpture may be collected to see what local folk artists have created.
3. Arrange to have students interview older people to identify former craftspeople in the community and types of useful items made by hand. Encourage students to interview their grandparents or other older family members to see what

family portraits may have been painted (other than professional ones) and what family heirlooms may have been made and by whom.

4. Show students examples of painting and sculpture created by different folk artists from three different geographic regions. For example, contemporary works by black artists may be found in collections featuring African-American artists—e.g., Meta Vaux Warrick Fuller's bronze "Water Bay" in the National Archives in Washington, D.C. There are excellent examples of mural paintings by black artists in New York, Chicago, and Detroit.
5. Discuss with the students what factors might have influenced the development of a particular painting or sculpture style. Emphasize factors such as geographical setting (e.g., influence of mountains and rivers). Urban areas, such as New York or Detroit, stimulated a different style than the rural mesas of the Southwest.

Resources:

Tom Armstrong. *Two Hundred Years of American Sculpture.* David R. Godine in conjunction with the Whitney Museum, 1976.

Robert Bishop. *Treasures of American Folk Art.* New York: Harry N. Abrams and the Museum of American Folk Art, 1979.

Frederick J. Dockstader. *Indian Art in North American Arts and Crafts.* Greenwich, CT: New York Graphic Society, 1961.

Middleton Harris. *The Black Book.* New York: Random House, 1974.

W. M. Hawley. *Chinese Folk Designs.* New York: Dover Publications, 1949.

Henry J. Kauffman. *Pennsylvania Dutch American Folk Art.* New York: Dover Publications, 1946.

Jean Lipman. *American Folk Art in Wood, Metal and Stone.* Magnolia, MA: Peter Smith, 1948.

Jean Lipman and Tom Armstrong. *American Folk Painters of Three Centuries.* New York: Hudson Hills Press in conjunction with the Whitney Museum of American Art.

Generalization III:** **The religious views, social behavior, and political attitudes of ethnic/cultural groups are often expressed through folk art.

Level: Primary

Objectives:

1. To illustrate, through the history of kites, how religious beliefs contributed to the development of a type of Chinese folk art.
2. To motivate the students to construct a kite.

Teaching Strategy:

1. Initiate a discussion on who might have invented the kite and for what purpose. After the students have exhausted the possibilities, introduce the fact that the Chinese invented the kite many years ago. They will be interested in knowing that the art of kite flying arose as an amusement and as an outgrowth of religion. The making of kites became a folk art. The history of the kite is told in an interesting manner in the book *Chinese Kites* by David F. Jue. This book also contains a description of how to make kites.
2. Discuss the possible uses of kites and the manner in which their design reflects use and possibly the beliefs of the kite maker. For example, a kite used for fishing will differ in design and construction from a kite used as a scarecrow or one used in parades.
3. Show the class pictures of kites made by the Chinese, and compare these to kites made by the Japanese, as found in the book.
4. Have the class decide whether they would like to make one large kite, e.g., a centipede type of kite, or work in pairs to

construct smaller types of kites. (Kite-making is an excellent project for children in upper levels and younger children to work together on.)

5. When the kites have been completed, plan a mock festival similar to the festival described in the book by Jue, and entertain the school with the flying of the kites.

Resources:

David F. Jue. *Chinese Kites: How to Make and Fly Them.* Rutland, VT: Charles E. Tuttle, 1967.

Tal Streeter. *The Art of the Japanese Kite.* New York: Weatherhill, 1974.

Level: Intermediate

Objectives:

1. To help students understand that much can be learned about the religious views of people through their folk art.
2. To introduce the work of folk artists to students.
3. To develop an appreciation for African-American folk painting.

Teaching Strategy:

1. Begin the discussion of folk painting by reviewing the definition of folk art the class has developed in previous lessons. Discuss the kinds of things that could be included in the work of folk painters that would tell how they lived and thought. Include in the discussion the way the ethnic, racial, or cultural group the artist belongs to might influence the painting.

2. Introduce the works of Clementine Hunter and Horace Pippin as two popular African American folk artists. Show Hunter's painting *The Funeral on Cane River* and Horace Pippin's painting *Christmas Morning Breakfast* to the class. These paintings can be found in *Two Centuries of Black American Art* by David C. Driskell. Have the class identify the African-American aspects of both works and list some of the characteristics that the painters have in common. Stress the strong religious beliefs that are obvious in both works.
3. Have the students divide into groups of four and select one of the following topics to gather information on: the life of Clementine Hunter, the life of Horace Pippin, works and lives of other African-American folk painters, or African-American religious folk paintings. To aid this process, the teacher could work with the librarian prior to the lesson to gather as many resources as possible for the students to use for this assignment. Assemble all of the resources in one place in the library or in the classroom. Once gathered, the information should be shared with the class in brief reports.
4. The lesson could appropriately be followed with one or two class sessions during which each student would paint a picture of something he or she felt strongly about. All of the students' paintings can then be displayed in an appropriate place for the school to enjoy.

Resources:

Robert Bishop. *Folk Painters of America.* New York: E.P. Dutton, 1979.

David Driskell. *Two Centuries of Black American Art.* New York: Alfred A. Knopf and Los Angeles County Museum of Art, 1976.

Anita Schorsch and Martin Greif. *The Morning Stars Sang: The Bible in Popular and Folk Art.* New York: Universe Books, 1978.

Joshua C. Taylor. *America As Art.* New York: Harper & Row, 1976.

Level: Advanced

Objectives:

1. To help the students to recognize social behavior, political attitudes, and religious views in folk art.
2. To help students express a political or religious attitude in a work of folk art of their own creation.

Teaching Strategy:

1. Begin the lesson through discussion by identifying some basic religious themes. These could include understanding of creation, fertility, birth and death, good and evil, love and hate, power and helplessness. List these themes on a chalkboard or on a sheet of newsprint under the heading "Religious Themes." Under the heading "Political Themes," list the categories drawn out in the discussion. These should include freedom and bondage, human rights, forms of government, such as democracy or dictatorship, and other themes. If time permits, develop a list of social behaviors that evolve from the religious and social themes. For example, rituals dealing with birth could include baptism and/or christening. Funerals would be a social behavior relating to death. Riots would be a social behavior related to bondage and hate. Parades and marches would relate to human rights and freedom.
2. From the list of resources and others that may be found, the teacher should gather as many examples of folk art as are available for use by the students. Remember to look around the students' immediate environment for local examples. Wall murals and graffiti should not be overlooked.
3. From the resources available, have students locate paintings, sculpture, and other folk art expressions, such as Hopi kachinas and totem poles of the Northwest Indians. Have students arrange an informal display of these works and add

labels identifying the themes discussed previously and listed on the blackboard.

4. Encourage students to select one theme from the group discussed and incorporate that theme into a drawing or painting. Number 2 pencils, pen and ink, oil crayons, magic markers, or watercolors provide the easiest media for general classroom use. Students may combine media for greater interest and multidimensional expression.

Resources:

Bard Bailor. *They Put on Masks.* New York: Charles Scribner's, 1974.
Shirley Glubok. *The Art of the North American Indian.* New York: Harper & Row, 1964.
See also those listed for the previous lessons.

Masks

Suggested Content Outline

A. Purpose of Masks
   1. Protection
   2. Disguise

B. Kinds of Masks
   1. Ceremonial
   2. Theatrical
   3. Burial and Death
   4. Festival of Masks

C. Masks of Ethnic/Cultural Groups in the United States

D. Masks of Other Countries
   1. African
   2. Chinese
   3. Japanese
   4. Greek
   5. Egyptian

Generalizations:

I. Masks are worn to disguise or protect the face for one purpose or another.

II. Masks worn by ethnic/cultural groups in the United States often reflect their beliefs and values.

III. The wearing of masks by people throughout the world has played an important role in the perpetuation of cultural rites and traditions.

Generalization I: Masks are worn to disguise or protect the face for one purpose or another.

Level: Primary

Objectives:

1. To aid students in understanding the various uses of masks.
2. To encourage students to design a mask that is used for a particular purpose.

Teaching Strategy:

1. This activity could serve as an introductory lesson for this unit. With the class, begin to list many different kinds of situations where people would use masks. Separate masks into two categories: those that are used for protection and those that are used for disguise.
2. Present a brief history of masks from the material found in *Mask Magic* by Carolyn Meyer. Discuss the various kinds of masks included in this book, and if necessary, add to the list the class has developed.

3. Have each student select a type of mask he or she is interested in and, with colored chalk and manila paper, draw the environment in which someone would wear the mask. The drawings should include some depiction of the mask wearer and the setting in which the mask is worn. For example, one student might draw a scene in an operating room showing a doctor or nurse wearing a mask. Another might draw a picture of a welder in a shop and still another of someone attending a masquerade ball.
4. Once the drawings are completed, have the students find out more information on the type of mask they have chosen to study and in a follow-up lesson encourage them to design and make a replica of the mask.
5. Arrange and/or assemble the masks on a bulletin board or in a case. The following format could make an interesting caption for a bulletin board:

Masks are used for protection

African masks are used for many purposes

Some masks are used for disguise

Kachina masks are worn by Hopi dancers

Spirit masks are worn in several cultures

Resources:

Carolyn Meyer. *Mask Magic*. New York: Harcourt Brace Jovanovich, 1978.

Level: Intermediate

Objectives:

1. To assist the class in developing a system for categorizing the uses of masks.
2. To explore masks used in African cultures.
3. To help the students understand the importance of wearing masks in some cultures.

Teaching Strategy:

1. Have each student complete on a strip of construction paper the following sentence: Masks are worn ______. Once these are finished, have students read their sentences to the class and, when finished, place them on a bulletin board according to the function of the mask as described by their sentences. Once the class has completed this activity, the statements should be grouped according to at least two basic categories: those that are worn for protection and these that are worn to disguise. Other names for these categories could revolve around masks that are worn for health purposes and for fun. The general idea is to help the class become aware of the various functions of masks.
2. Focus the remainder of the lesson on examining the reasons for mask-wearing in African cultures. Using the resources listed, plus others, have the students, working in groups of two or three, share resources and see how many different purposes masks have been used for in these cultures and compare the purposes with those of masks in the United States.
3. Encourage each student to design a mask they would wear for a specific purpose if they lived in Africa and were a member of a specific African tribe. These masks could be designed from brown art paper, paper bags, or construction paper, or similar materials. If there is sufficient time, the

students can make a more elaborate mask from papier mâché. An excellent description of how to make a mask in papier mâché is contained in *Art From Many Hands* by Jo Miles Schuman.

4. This learning experience would be enhanced if a class trip could be made to a local museum that has a collection of African masks.

Resources:

Penelope Naylor. *Black Images: The Art of West Africa.* Garden City, N.Y.: Doubleday 1973.

Jo Miles Schuman. *Art From Many Hands: Multicultural Art Projects for Home and School.* Englewood Cliffs, NJ.: Prentice-Hall, 1980.

Level: Advanced

Objectives:

1. To assist students in identifying times and occasions when masks are worn.
2. To encourage students in understanding that a variety of motives exist for wearing masks.

Teaching Strategy:

1. This lesson is designed to introduce the subject of masks and to provide an overview of what groups in the United States continue to wear masks, when they are worn, and how masks cover and protect the wearer or transform that wearer into something or someone other than the existing person. Begin the class discussion by inviting students to share the times and places they have worn masks or have seen others wear them. These might include parties, Halloween dramatic presentations, dances, and others. Ask why the wearer was

utilizing the mask. Continue by asking students if they can identify times and places where invisible masks were worn to protect or disguise the wearer. Examples would be a mask of confidence when one is frightened or a mask of happiness to hide depression and/or sadness.

2. Continue by asking the student to list three places where that student goes on a regular basis, such as home, school, work, gym, or place of religious worship. Have the student list one activity he or she engages in besides the places previously listed. Examples could be home—dinner, school—class discussion, and so forth. Continue by having the student identify a feeling experienced while carrying out the activity in a given place, for example, school—class discussion (fear of being thought dull or dense). Continue by having the student add a third list of words that represent a "look" or mask that could be worn to disguise a feeling of vulnerability.
3. Provide the students with paper, pencils, crayons, white glue, and old magazines. Have students lightly draw an outline of a face on the paper. Students should then select one complete set of words in Step 2. Now have students select pictures and words from magazines to create a collage depicting the feelings evoked by the set of words selected. Encourage students to tear magazine pictures so that only parts of images are used. Some images can be overlapped. Space should be left for texture and line to be added between others. Students should select one color of crayon that will integrate the composition and fill in the spaces around the paper images with color. Add facial features such as eyes, nose, and mouth that express mask characteristics that disguise or protect the basic feeling expressed in the images.

Resources:

Byrd Baylor. *They Put on Masks.* New York: Charles Scribner's Sons, 1974.

Eugene Bischoff and Kay Bischoff. *Kachina Dolls Cut and Color.* Albuquerque, NM: Eukabi Publishers, 1950.
Kari Hunt and Bernice Wells Carlson. *Masks and Mask Makers.* Nashville: Abingdon Press, 1961.
Shari Lewis and Lillian Oppenheimer. *Folding Paper Masks.* New York: E.P. Dutton, 1965.

Generalization II: Masks worn by ethnic/cultural groups in the United States often reflect their beliefs and values.

Level: Primary

Objectives:

1. To help students understand that many Native American groups wear masks that reflect their beliefs and values.
2. To aid the students in the identification of several groups of Native Americans and the places they live.
3. To introduce the concept of totem poles and what they represent.

Teaching Strategy:

1. Using a large outline map of the United States, begin by having the students name as many different groups of Native Americans as they can think of and help them locate the areas of the United States in which they live.
2. Read to the class *They Put on Masks* by Byrd Baylor. During the reading of the book, as a different group is mentioned, locate where that group of Native Americans live on the map and indicate by labeling the area with the name of the group. Some of the groups included in the book are Apache, Pueblo, Hopi, Zuni, Yaqui, Navajo, Iroquois, Kwakitui, and Eskimos. Have one-half of the students listen for the kinds of things that masks were made of and the other half of the class

listen for the reasons people wore the masks. At the conclusion of the reading, review the names and places where the groups lived, the purpose of the masks for each group, and the material the masks were made of.

3. Discuss reasons mentioned in the book for constructing totem poles. Have each student design a mask or symbol on brown paper 8 1/2" x 11" or smaller to be added to a totem pole for a reason the class decides. The designs should reflect the purpose—that is, the beliefs and values—the totem is to depict. Place the designs end-to-end to form two to three two-dimensional totem poles on the wall of the classroom.

Resources:

Byrd Baylor. *They Put on Masks.* New York: Charles Scribner's Sons, 1974.

Level: Intermediate

Objectives:

1. To expose students to a variety of kinds of masks and their different uses.
2. To explore the importance of the theatrical masks used in Chinese and Japanese cultures.
3. To motivate the class to develop skits in which they may wear the theatrical masks they construct.

Teaching Strategy:

1. The book *Mask Magic* by Carolyn Meyer contains a description of several different kinds of masks, e.g., theatrical masks, spirit masks, kachina masks, carnival masks, portrait masks, and others. Introduce these different kinds of masks to the class. Discuss the uses of the masks and identify,

where possible, how the use and the construction of masks relates to the values and beliefs of particular groups of people that use them.

2. Focus on the use and construction of theatrical masks. Share with the class the fact that the ancient Greeks used masks in plays to express different kinds of emotions. The Chinese also use masks in drama productions, as do the Japanese. The Japanese have a type of play called *Noh* in which masks are worn to represent emotions.
3. With the class, list several emotions that could be represented by a mask. Once this list is completed, have the students create a brief skit or skits that would use the emotions they have listed.
4. Have the students select one emotion to illustrate. Using large narrow pieces of colored construction paper and a variety of materials such as colored chalk, crayons, paste, foil, and yarn, make a mask to represent the emotion selected.
5. Wearing the masks, dramatize the original skit or skits made up by the class, or make up several others so that all of the students in the class have an opportunity to participate.

Resources:

Carolyn Meyer. *Mask Magic.* New York: Harcourt Brace Jovanovich, 1978.

Level: Advanced

Objectives:

1. To help students understand that some ethnic and cultural groups in the United States still use masks for serious religious and cultural purposes.

2. To help students understand how those masks reflect the beliefs and values of their creators and users.

Teaching Strategy:

1. This lesson will focus on Native American masks, since these groups not only use a variety of masks but use them in a way that clearly reflects beliefs and values. Byrd Baylor's *They Put on Masks,* illustrated by Jerry Ingram, provides an excellent overview of Native American masks and how they relate to the group's values. Read to the students the following passage from the book. Then show illustrations of the masks from the book, pointing out items mentioned in the passage.

They made their masks of
wood
and deerskin
and seashells
and cornhusks
and horsehair
and bones

Yes,
and they made them of
magic
and dreams
and the oldest dark secrets
of life.

They made masks of
beads
and string
and ivory
and turquoise
and flowers

Yes,
and they made them of
wishes
and hunger
and thirst
and they even made them
of prayers.[3]

Follow the reading with a discussion of items students are familiar with in expressing religious beliefs and values. These might include religious symbols used in ceremonies and special clothing worn by priests, ministers, or rabbis. Have students note that masks are *not* used in these groups but that special robes, caps, and other clothing are utilized. Point out the use of hoods by the Ku Klux Klan and have students discuss how people from that group might be expressing themselves through the use of masks.

2. Help students identify three groups of Native Americans that use masks. Have students suggest the beliefs and values they think may be reflected in the masks. Compare their suggestions with factual information about the meaning of these masks. For example, for Northwest Coast Indians, masks honor clan ancestors by showing respect for birds, animals, and sea creatures and also represent heroes of stories. Indians of the Southwest, such as the Apache and Hopi, stress the value of rain in their masks, since their livelihood depends on rainwater in that desert area. Utilizing the Native American tradition of expressing beliefs and values through the wearing of masks, each student should create a papier mâché mask based on his or her own beliefs and values. Either plasticine or crushed newspaper can serve as a base. Features should be built up on an exaggerated form before the newspaper strips are dipped in papier mâché and applied. The masks could be painted, then adorned with feathers, shells, beads, and other items. The student should work to express a belief or value relevant to his or her own beliefs, values and life view. Refer to Native American masks for guidance here.

Resources:

Byrd Baylor. *They Put on Masks.* New York: Charles Scribner's Sons, 1974.

Eugene Bischoff and Kay Bischoff. *Kachina Dolls Cut and Color.* Albuquerque, NM: Eukabi, 1950.

Kari Hunt and Bernice Wells Carlson. *Masks and Mask Makers.* Nashville: Abingdon Press, 1961.

Shari Lewis and Lillian Oppenheimer. *Folding Paper Masks.* New York: E.P. Dutton, 1965.

Generalization III: The wearing of masks by people throughout the world has played an important role in the perpetuation of cultural rites and traditions.

Level: Primary

Objectives:

1. To aid students in understanding the use of masks in some African cultures.
2. To reinforce the importance of mask wearing in carrying out the rites and traditions of cultural groups.

Teaching Strategy:

1. Using a variety of resources including those suggested, show the students pictures of the kinds of masks that are used in some African cultures. Discuss the various types of ceremonies at which the masks are worn and what they represent. Attention should be given to the way the masks are constructed. Some African masks have skirts and/or are decorated with shells, cloth, metal pieces, gems, and other objects. Discuss the meaning of this type of adornment. The color, as well as the materials the masks are made from, often is symbolic of the meaning of the mask.
2. Continue the discussion by focusing on one or two reasons for wearing masks such as the meaning of the butterfly mask worn by West Africans in Upper Volta. The butterfly mask and its story are described in *Black Images: The Art of West Africa* by Penelope Naylor.
3. Have the students design a butterfly mask by using a combination of papers and decorating it with cloth, yarn, crayon, paint, and other materials. Display the butterfly masks around a bulletin board that contains a brief story of the butterfly mask. Or, the students might present a brief

assembly program telling about the uses of masks in African cultures, culminating the presentation with the butterfly story and the students wearing the masks they have made.

Resources:

Penelope Naylor. *Black Images.* New York: Doubleday, 1973.
Christine Price. *Dancing Masks of Africa.* New York: Charles Scribner's Sons, 1975.

Level: Intermediate

Objectives:

1. To help students understand the meaning of the Kachina dancer in Pueblo Indian culture.
2. To explore the role of the Kachina dancer in the perpetuation of Pueblo cultural traditions.
3. To study the type of mask the Kachina dancer wears.
4. To introduce students to a female Native American artist.

Teaching Strategy:

1. The Kachina dancer and masks are described in the book *Mask Magic* by Carolyn Meyer. Share with the students the meaning of the Kachina dancer in the Pueblo Indian culture. Discuss the importance of the dancer to the perpetuation of a particular tradition. Have the students examine the style of masks the dancer wears. Help them associate the bright colors and decorations of the mask with the friendly nature of the Pueblo gods.
2. Discuss with the class the kinds of decorations they might use on a mask to indicate a friendly nature. Using paper bags that will fit the head comfortably, have the students design a

mask using the bag. Use crayon or colored chalk and encourage students to use lines and colors that will give the masks a friendly look.

3. Introduce to the class the artist Pablita Velarde, whose paintings often are of Kachina dancers. A story about Pablita Velarde can be found in *American Indian Contributors* by Ruth Franchere. This very skillful artist paints to show how Pueblo Indians live, work, and worship. The class should be made aware of how some of the people who lived in her pueblo of Santa Clara felt about women artists and their work. Many negative feelings were expressed toward Pablita Velarde and her work. After she became a famous artist and won numerous awards, many of the people who had criticized and resented her for painting recognized her skill and accepted her as an artist.

Resources:

Ruth Franchere. *American Indian Contributors.* New York: Thomas Y. Crowell, 1970.

Carolyn Meyer. *Mask Magic.* New York: Harcourt Brace Jovanovich, 1978.

Barton Wright. *Hopi Kachinas: The Complete Guide to Collecting Kachina Dolls.* Flagstaff, AZ.: Northland Press, 1977.

Level: Advanced

Objectives:

1. To give students an overview of different types of masks worn throughout the world.
2. To help students experience and understand that cultural rites and traditions are transmitted through the wearing of masks.

Teaching Strategy:

1. An excellent overview of masks and their role in many countries is provided by Kari Hunt and Bernice Wells Carlson in *Masks and Mask Makers.* In class discussion, invite students to share their knowledge of the use of masks in other countries. Some examples might be modern European merry-making festivals, masks made in the Far East and worn by dancers and in theatrical performances, masks for the dead in Africa, and masks for protection used by warriors. After students have shared their knowledge and experiences, the teacher should embellish that information with further examples. Visual illustrations should be utilized whenever possible.
2. Following the overview, teacher and students should list on the chalkboard or newsprint cultural rites and traditions expressed through mask wearing. Countries and cultures utilizing masks for the purpose of perpetuating these should be added. Particular notice should be given to traditions that groups in the United States practice. Another example is the merry-making festivals in modern Europe that express anger toward political figures and/or personal enemies through the use of masks. The counterpart of that in the United States is the Mardi Gras.
3. Have the students select one cultural rite or tradition. The student should list the rite or tradition at the top of the page. The student should then identify an activity to perpetuate that rite or tradition. For example, students may identify the tradition of honoring children by gift-giving at the celebration of Christmas. In this case, the example of the use of masks is Santa Claus. Another rite or tradition with a religious/educational dimension would be the use of Kachina masks by dancers to honor their children, give gifts, and teach about religious values.

4. The student should proceed to make a sketch with pencil (No. 2 softness), pen and ink, or magic markers of persons wearing appropriate masks and other costumes to carry out the rite or celebration. If students do not wish to choose from known traditions, they should be encouraged to create a new celebration with new mask and costume form.

Resources:

Byrd Baylor. *They Put on Masks.* New York: Charles Scribner's Sons, 1974.

Eugene Bischoff and Kay Bischoff. *Kachina Dolls Cut and Color.* Albuquerque, NM: Eukabi, 1950.

Kari Hunt and Bernice Wells Carlson. *Masks and Mask Makers.* Nashville: Abingdon, 1961.

Shari Lewis and Lillian Oppenheimer. *Folding Paper Masks.* New York: E.P. Dutton, 1965.

Notes

1. Jo Miles Schuman, *Art From Many Hands: Multicultural Arts Project for Home and School* (Englewood Cliffs, NJ: Prentice Hall, 1981).
2. *The World Book Encyclopedia* (Chicago: Field Enterprises, 1976), p. 28.
3. Byrd Baylor, *They Put on Masks* (New York: Charles Scribner's Sons, 1974).

8
Generalizations and Teaching Strategies for Language Arts

Introduction

Language arts presents many opportunities for designing instruction that is multicultural. There is no other subject area as pervasive as language, and because of its nature, appropriate instruction can be provided for in a variety of ways. Speaking, listening, reading, and writing are involved in every activity that occurs in an instructional setting and therefore offer numerous possibilities for introducing and integrating multicultural content.

This chapter will contain material that may serve to help teachers begin to organize language arts instruction so it will be multicultural. Folklore and poetry have been selected as examples of areas of study that can be integrated effectively with multicultural content. Both topics are unique in that all groups of people, at one time or another, express themselves through poetry and through various forms of folklore. Each area offers excellent opportunities for comparing and contrasting these specific forms of literature for a variety of ethnic and cultural groups.

Folklore

Suggested Content Outline

I. The Origin of Folklore

II. Kinds of Folklore
   A. Myths
   B. Fables
   C. Legends
   D. Folktales
   E. Fairy Tales
   F. Riddles and Rhymes

III. Folklore in the United States
   A. Asian and Pacific Islander
   B. African-American
   C. Native-American
   E. Other American Folklore

IV. Folklore of Other Countries

Generalizations:

I. Folklore is made up of various forms of stories, written or oral, that have been passed from one generation to another.

II. Each kind of folklore is designed to describe or to explain different aspects of life and living things.

III. Different ethnic/racial groups in the United States have their own folklore that helps to partially explain their beliefs, values, and customs.

Generalization I: Folklore is made up of stories, written or oral, that have been passed from one generation to another.

Level: Primary

Objectives:

1. To help students understand the nature of folklore.
2. To help students understand that a folktale is one form of folklore.
3. To convey that many folktales come to the United States from other countries.

Teaching Strategy:

1. Introduce the story *Anansi the Spider: A Tale from the Ashanti,* by Gerald McDermott, by reviewing with students the names of the continents. Using a map of the world, point out the continent of Africa as the place of origin of this folktale. The students should be made aware that there are many countries on the continent of Africa and that this folktale is from Ghana, a West African country, the area from which the ancestors of African Americans come.
2. Before the story is read to the students, discuss with them the different kinds of folklore, folktales as stories that have been handed down through the years, and various ways that stories can be preserved both in oral and written form.
3. Have the students listen carefully for the theme of the folktale and ask them to remember the names of three of the characters and their contributions to the tale.
4. After the reading of the story, help the students to understand the purpose of the tale and the similarities and differences between this tale and others with which they are familiar.
5. Encourage the students to suggest ways of helping to preserve a story and lead them to examine the possibility of passing tales from one generation to another through drawings.

6. Review the characters of the story, list their names on the chalkboard, and discuss the contributions of each one. Have the children select their favorite character, and draw the character, using colored chalk or construction paper, in such a way as to illustrate the function of the character in the story.
7. Design a bulletin board using the drawings, and group the characters in the sequence in which they appear in the tale. This will allow for each review of the tale, thereby reinforcing the possibility of preserving a story through drawings.

Resources:

Elphinstone Dayrell. *Why the Sun and The Moon Live in the Sky.* Boston: Houghton Mifflin, 1968.

Gerald McDermott. *Anansi The Spider.* New York: Holt, Rinehart & Winston, 1972.

______. *Arrow to the Sun: A Pueblo Indian Tale.* New York: Viking, 1974.

______. *The Stonecutter: A Japanese Folktale.* New York: Viking, 1975.

Diana Wolkstein. *8,000 Stones: A Chinese Folktale.* New York: Doubleday, 1972.

Level: Intermediate

Objectives:

To help students understand that:

1. There are many different kinds of folklore.
2. A legend differs from other forms of folklore in several ways.

Teaching Strategy:

1. Explore with the students the various types of folklore, and focus on comparing and contrasting at least three of the different kinds, e.g., myths, legends, and fables. For example, students will need to know that myths deal with gods and goddesses and attempt to explain the great forces of nature; legends are sometimes partly true and often put human beings together with supernatural creatures; fables are usually about animals and end with a moral.
2. Show the filmstrip *John Henry*, from the *American Folklore Series II,* as an example of a legend. Point out the fact that this legend is enjoyed by all but is one that many African Americans consider as a part of their literary heritage because John Henry is an African American. Discuss the characteristics of legends that are evident in this example. Make a list of the characteristics and show the filmstrip a second time for the purpose of having the students look for additional characteristics to add to the list.
3. Divide the class into small groups of four or five and have each group identify a portion of the legend that illustrates one of the characteristics on the list. Encourage each group to pantomime the portion selected and have the remainder of the class guess which characteristic the dramatization is portraying.

Resources:

Verna Aardema. *Why Mosquitos Buzz in People's Ears.* New York: Dial, 1975.

John Bierhart. *The Ring in the Prairie: A Shawnee Legend.* New York: Dial, 1970

Ann Cromwell. *Shadow on the Pueblo: A Yaqui Indian Legend.* Champaign, IL: Garrard, 1972.

Harold W. Felton. *John Henry and His Hammer.* New York: Albert A. Knopf, 1950.
Ezra Keats. *John Henry: An American Legend.* New York: Pantheon, 1965.
Filmstrip: *John Henry, American Folklore Series II.* Santa Monica, CA: BFA Educational Media.

Level: Advanced

Objectives:

1. To help students understand and make distinctions between different kinds of folklore.
2. To help students appreciate folklore by creating their own.

Teaching Strategy:

1. Discuss three different types of folklore: myths, legends, and fables. List distinguishing features of each. For example, myths involve gods and goddesses and usually serve to explain a phenomenon in nature. Fables usually involve animals and end with a moral. Legends may have some basis in truth but are larger than life. Ask students to offer examples of each type and explain their choice of classification.
2. Have a student (or students) read aloud a myth such as "The Man in the Moon" in *Folktales of China* by Wolfram Eberhard. Discuss the features that make it a myth. Explore with the class how the tale might be retold to become a legend or what lines might be added to create a fable.
3. In a short-term exercise, divide the class into three groups to write modern day folklore. Each group would represent a specific type of folklore. Supply a title to each group. Some examples are: (1) myth—"Why Fish Swim Upstream," (2)

legend—"Ferdinand the Fearless Fish," and (3) Fable—"The Kind Fish and the Wicked Alligator."
4. On completion of this task, have a reporter from each group read what was written. Let the class decide whether each type of folklore meets the listed criteria.

Resources:

Mason J. Brewer. *American Negro Folklore.* New York: Quadrangle/New York Times, 1968.
Richard M. Dorson. *African Folklore.* New York: Doubleday/Anchor, 1972.
Wolfram Eberhard. *Folktales of China.* Chicago: University of Chicago Press, 1965.
Vladimir Hulpach. *American Indian Tales and Legends.* London: Golden Pleasure, 1965.

Generalization II: Each kind of folklore is designed to describe or to explain different aspects of life and living things.

Level: Primary

Objectives:

1. To help students understand that legends generally attempt to explain an aspect of nature.
2. To encourage the students to write creatively.

Teaching Strategy:

1. Begin by having students list natural occurrences that might warrant an explanation, e.g., wind, sun, etc.
2. Before showing the filmstrip *How Fire Came to Earth,* explain to the class that this is a Native American legend

attempting to explain how fire came to earth. Ask the children to look for explanations of other natural occurrences in the story. Stress how close the Native American is to nature and discuss possible reasons for this.

3. Following the viewing of the filmstrip, have the students discuss the purpose of the story and identify the relationship of each animal to the explanation. Continue with the identification of explanations for the origin of the physical characteristics of other animals in the filmstrip.
4. Have students individually select an animal not mentioned in the story and have them develop stories about the possible contribution that animal might have made to the bringing of fire to earth. Ask students to include a brief explanation as to the effects on a physical characteristic of the animal.
5. Once the stories are completed, they may be shared with the class and with children in other classes.

Resources:

Filmstrip: *American Indian Folk Legends,* Educational Enrichment Materials. New York: New York Times.

Level: Intermediate

Objectives:

To help students understand that:

1. Myths often deal with gods and goddesses to help explain forces of nature.
2. There are many different kinds of mythology that have emerged from a variety of ethnic/cultural groups.

Teaching Strategy:

1. Read *Sedna: An Eskimo Myth* by Beverly Brodsky McDermott to the class and have the class identify the main

difference between this story and other nonmyth story types. The class should be guided to discover that a spiritual being is used to help explain the purpose of the story.
2. Continue by showing the filmstrip *Myths* to further explain the characteristics of myths by discussing Greek mythology. Help the students to compare the differences between Greek mythology and the Eskimo myth *Sedna*.
3. Review the story of *Sedna* and divide the myth into five or six sections. Have the students choose the section of the story that is their favorite and encourage them to work in small groups to decide how they might illustrate their part of the story on a section of a large mural. This would begin a larger project that would continue for several days.
4. Invite several classes to attend a short program. Present the completed mural, with a representative from each group telling the part of the story that group has illustrated.

Resources:

Cottie Burland. *North American Indian Mythology.* New York: Hamlyn, 1965.

Beverly Brodsky McDermott. *Sedna: An Eskimo Myth.* New York: Viking, 1975.

Geoffrey Parinder. *African Mythology.* New York: Hamlyn, 1967.

Filmstrip: *Myths: Literature for Children Series.* Series 3. Verdugo City, CA: Pied Piper Productions.

Level: Advanced

Objectives:

1. To help students understand that folklore often serves to explain natural occurrences or other events.
2. To help students appreciate similarities and differences between the folklore of various ethnic or cultural groups.

Teaching Strategy:

1. Read or have students read aloud a few versions of world and human creation while the rest of the class reads along. Good examples are "The Cheyenne Account of How the World Was Made" from *Literature of the American Indian* by Thomas Sanders and Walter Peek; sections of "The Creator," e.g., "Creating the Earth," from *African Mythology* by Geoffrey Parrinder; and "Why There Are Cripples on Earth" from *Folktales of China* by Wolfram Eberhard.
2. Explain that these myths represent different versions of the world's creation. List some similarities and differences among them. One similarity is that the earth comes from nothing or from wasteland. A difference involves the three versions of human creation. Briefly clarify any vocabulary that is unique to a particular ethnic group, e.g., the forces of yin and yang.
3. Cite examples to show that folklore is often used to explain all kinds of natural phenomena, from rainbows and butterflies to skin color. One example is "Why the Rabbit has a Short Tail" in *American Negro Folktales* by J. Mason Brewer. List other examples that the students may think of, e.g., Prometheus bringing fire to earth or Atlas holding up the world.
4. Note that today with our scientific knowledge and advanced technology, we know many of the answers to "why" and "how," or we know how to find those answers. Ask students to take a moment to pretend that we do not. For a few moments, let them ponder a question like, Why do some people have red hair? or Why are no two snowflakes alike? Compare their answers.

Resources:

J. Mason Brewer. *American Negro Folklore.* New York: Quadrangle/New York Times, 1968.

Richard M. Dorson. *American Negro Folktales.* Greenwich, CT: Fawcett, 1968.
Wolfram Eberhard. *Folktales of China.* Chicago: University of Chicago Press, 1965.
Geoffrey Parrinder. *African Mythology.* New York: Hamlyn, 1967.
Thomas Sanders and Walter Peek. *Literature of the American Indian.* New York: Glencoe, 1973.

Generalization III: Different ethnic/racial groups in the United States have their own folklore that helps to partially explain their beliefs, values, and customs.

Level: Primary

Objectives:

1. To help students learn to appreciate folklore of different ethnic and cultural groups.
2. To increase the students' level of awareness of the kinds of folklore that exist.

Teaching Strategy:

1. This lesson may be introduced by asking students to recall the titles of folklore with which they are familiar and by identifying the ethnic/cultural groups that the stories came from.
2. Have the class listen to the recording of a traditional Puerto Rican folktale, "Perez and Martina," read by Pura Belpre. Follow the first listening session with a discussion of the story, including the characters, the plot, and the ending.
3. Discuss what it takes for a storyteller to make a story interesting. Replay the recording, having the students listen very carefully for the techniques the storyteller uses to make the listening enjoyable.

4. Make a list on chart paper of the various ways the storyteller uses his or her voice to make listening to the story enjoyable.
5. Make a list on chart paper of the various ways the storyteller uses his or her voice to tell the story, e.g., pitch, volume, and pace.
6. Have the class select one or two of their favorite folktales, myths, or legends. Review the stories and, with the aid of a tape recorder, record one or two of the stories and involve several children in the retelling.
7. Play the story back for the students to listen to and have them identify the storytelling techniques used by each of their classmates.
8. Record a second story involving different students, and encourage them to include techniques that may have been omitted in the first taping.

Resources:

Recordings:
"Perez and Martina." New York: CMS Records.
"American Indian Stories for Children," vol. 1. New York: CMS Records.
"Hopi Tales." New York: Folkways Records and Service Corp.

Level: Intermediate

Objectives:

1. To help students appreciate folklore of different ethnic and cultural groups.
2. To expose students to a variety of folklore from different ethnic/cultural groups.

Teaching Strategy:

1. Prior to the introduction of this lesson, instruct the class at least a week in advance to visit the library and select and read a story (folklore, myth, fable, or legend) that represents a specific ethnic culture. Once the story has been read, encourage each student to draw a picture representing the story and add it to a bulletin board designed for this purpose.
2. Introduce this lesson by having the students develop a class list of the different ethnic groups that were represented in the reading. Discuss those characteristics that appear to be unique in several of the stories because of the ethnic/cultural environments they come from. This discussion may be extended to an identification and a location of the country from which the ancestors of the ethnic groups originated. The pictures drawn by the students could be used to help illustrate the characteristics.
3. Read to the class *The Riddle of the Drum,* a folktale from Mexico by Verna Aardema. Follow the reading by helping students identify the characteristics of the story that are related to the culture of Mexico. List on the board the Spanish words that were used in the tale and discuss their meaning in English.
4. This lesson may be continued for several days by introducing a story each day from a different ethnic group. Another excellent tale to read orally to the class is *I Am Your Misfortune* by Marguerite Rudolph. This interesting Lithuanian folktale will help to extend the students' knowledge of folklore and provide an opportunity for the students to compare the cultural characteristics of this tale with those identified in *The Riddle of the Drum* and other stories.
5. The viewing of the Native American folktale "Loon's Necklace" will provide an additional experience for the

students to compare and contrast the characteristics that make this story different from the stories of other ethnic groups.

Resources:

Verna Aardema. *The Riddle of the Drum: A Tale from Tizapan, Mexico.* New York: Four Winds Press, 1979.
Judith Ish Kishor. *Tales From the Wise Men of Israel.* New York: J. B. Lippincott, 1962.
Marguerite Rudolph. *I Am Your Misfortune: A Lithuanian Folktale.* New York: Seabury, 1968.
Clarence Westphal. *Folktales of Korea.* Minneapolis: T.S. Denison, 1970.
Filmstrip: *Loon's Necklace, an Indian Tale.* Chicago: Encyclopedia Brittanica Educational Corporation.

Level: Advanced

Objectives:

1. To help students describe some characteristics and experiences of different ethnic and cultural groups based on a knowledge of their folklore.
2. To help students appreciate folklore of different ethnic and cultural groups.

Teaching Strategy:

1. Have students read through "Brer Rabbit's Cool Air Swing" from *Folklore in America* by Tristram Coffin and Hennig Cohen and quickly identify the United States ethnic groups from which this story probably originated.
2. Discuss the reasons that this tale is similar to other African-American folktales, e.g., probable geographical location of

the characters, language patterns, the fact that this is probably a rural as opposed to an urban setting, the presence and the role of "Mr. Man."

3. Explain that Brer Rabbit is a popular character in African folklore and that he always has the same relationship to the wolf or the fox. To understand that relationship more clearly, read another short tale, like "Rabbit and Fox Go Fishing" in *American Negro Folktales* by Richard Dorson. Ask children to explain why a rabbit (a common animal) who consistently outsmarts a fox (traditionally the superior animal) would be so popular in African-American slave culture. Give a summary of a similar tale, "John the Bear and the Pateroll," also in *American Negro Folktales*. Show that Brer Rabbit and John are essentially the same character.
4. Emphasize that although we can never make assumptions that will apply to everyone in any ethnic or cultural group, we can learn much through folklore. For example, from "Brer Rabbit" and similar tales, we know that it was important for some slaves to think of themselves as superior to their masters. From other African-American folklore, we learn that many blacks felt that they had a practical and personal friendship with God. From Native Americans' folklore, we learn that nature was a dominant force in their lives. Ask students to list some of the important beliefs or practices that they think would be included in folklore about their own individual ethnic or culture groups. Discuss these.

Resources:

Cottie Burland. *North American Indian Mythology.* Hamlyn publishing Group, 1970.

Tristram P. Coffin and Hennig Cohen. *Folklore in America.* New York: Doubleday, 1966.

William J. Faulkner. *The Days When the Animals Talked.* Chicago: Follett, 1977.

Julius Lester. *Black Folktales.* New York: Grove Press, 1969.[1]
Americo Paredes. *Folktales of Mexico.* Chicago: University of Chicago Press, 1970.

Poetry

Suggested Content Outline

I. What Is Poetry
  A. History
  B. Form

II. Types of Poetry
  A. Lyric
  B. Narrative
  C. Dramatic

III. Poetry of the United States
  A. Asian and Pacific Islander
  B. African-American
  C. Hispanic
  D. Native American
  E. Other American Poetry

IV. Poetry of Other Countries

Generalizations:

I. Poetry is one of the oldest forms of literature used by all people to express thought.
II. Poetry can generally be grouped into two basic categories, lyrical and narrative.
III. Ethnic and cultural experiences are often expressed through poetry.

Generalization I: Poetry is one of the oldest forms of literature used by all people to express thought.

Level: Primary

Objectives:

1. To aid students in understanding that poetry has been used to express feelings and thought for many years.
2. To help the students develop an appreciation for poetry.
3. To encourage students to express themselves in poetic form.

Teaching Strategy:

1. This lesson could be used as an introductory lesson to a unit on poetry because it is designed to expose the students to various kinds and types of short verse. *The First Book of Short Verse* by Coralie Howard is a useful book to read for the purpose of introducing students to various forms of poetry. This book also contains poetry written by people of all ages and from several ethnic and cultural groups. The following list suggests poems that may be read to the class; it also contains information to share and discuss:

   - Poems that are examples of *free verse* written by very young children: "Drowsyhead At Night," "Night By The First," "City Nights," "Grow and Grow," and "Mountains."
   - An example of *tanka,* a form of Japanese poetry that consists of five lines: "Tanka."
   - Poems written by Indian children: "Silence in Camp" and "Locust Song."
   - An example of *cinquain,* an American form of poetry that resembles the Japanese tanka: "The Grand Canyon."
   - Poems written by African-American poets: "The Unknown Color" and "Mexican Market Women."
   - Examples of *haiku,* a form of Japanese poetry that consists of seventeen syllables in three lines (5-7-5): "Poppies," "Foxes Playing," "Fiddler Crabs," and "The Heron."

- Very old poems: "Shadows" (200 years), "Song For a Dance" (400 years), and "The Maltese Dog" (1900 years).

2. Follow the reading of these poems and others by having the students talk about the kinds of thoughts, feelings, and objects that the poems were about. Encourage them to develop a list of things they would like to write a poem about.
3. Continue the lesson by discussing how a poet uses words to describe an object, a feeling, or a thought, and have the class give examples.
4. Select an object such as a tree, an animal, or a musical instrument, and work with the class to develop a short poem.
5. This lesson may be continued by having the class individually illustrate the class poem on geometrically shaped pieces of construction paper that can be mounted and displayed around a copy of the poem on the bulletin board.

Resources:

Gladys L. Adshead and Annis Duff. *An Inheritance of Poetry.* Cambridge, MA: Houghton Mifflin, 1948.

Louis Bogan and William Jay Smith. *The Golden Journey.* Chicago: Reilly, 1965.

Helen Ferris. *Favorite Poems Old and New.* New York: Doubleday, 1957.

Coralie Howard. *The First Book of Short Verse.* New York: Franklin Watts, 1964.

Level: Intermediate

Objectives:

1. To introduce the students to a contemporary poet, Gwendolyn Brooks.

Speaking, listening, reading, and writing are involved in every activity that occurs in an instructional setting and therefore offer numerous possibilities for introducing and integrating multicultural content.

2. To reinforce the fact that poetry is the oldest form of literature.

Teaching Strategy:

1. This lesson should be used after the class has discussed poetry in general and the students have a clear understanding as to how long poetry has been used as a form of expression. Select several poems from *Bronzeville Boys and Girls* by Gwendolyn Brooks to read to the class: Read the selected poems before the poet is introduced. Select a variety of poems on different subjects and have the children try to describe the kind of person the poet is, e.g., lives in the city, likes children, is from a large family, enjoys food. Each poem should generate at least one characteristic of the poet.

2. Introduce the poet by first giving a biographical sketch and relate this information to the characteristics the class has identified. Continue by reading additional poems by Brooks.
3. Discuss with the class how the poetry of Brooks might have been different if she had lived in different times. Use as an example "The Admiration of Willie," which talks about planes, cars, and trains.
4. Prepare small folded slips of paper having the titles of poems by Brooks. Have the children select a slip of paper and create a poem using the title to stimulate the writing.
5. Follow with a period when each student can compare his or her poem with the one bearing the same title as that written by Brooks. Have each student share the comparisons with the class. This may be done orally or in writing or in a combination of these.

Resources:

Gwendolyn Brooks. *A Street in Bronzeville.* New York: Harper, 1945.

———. *Bronzeville Boys and Girls.* New York: Harper, 1956.

———. *Selected Poems.* New York: Harper and Row, 1963.

Level: Advanced

Objectives:

1. To reinforce the fact that poetry is one of the oldest forms of literature.
2. To offer examples of some of the earliest types of poetry.

Teaching Strategy:

1. Observe that poetry is one of the oldest forms of literature and ask students to name some of the oldest poetry they are

familiar with. Point out that while poets were writing in Greece, Rome, and other European locales, other poets were chanting and dancing to poetry in the Americas.

2. Begin a discussion of Native American poetry by noting that there is no single kind of Indian poetry. There are hundreds of tribes in the United States alone and many others in Canada and the other Americas. Each tribe has its own set of practices and language patterns. For a listing of some tribes, see *American Indian Authors* by Natachee Momaday.
3. Describe and list general characteristics of Indian poetry:

   - Poetry was passed from generation to generation orally through chants, songs, and prayers. Poets not only sang the poetry but danced it.
   - Poems were often about life events, such as love, sickness, death, harvest, and battle.
   - The poetry involved the personification of the forces of nature, e.g., Earth Mother, Wind Spirit.
   - Rhyme did not appear to be popular in early Native American poetry. The poetic "feeling" came from the repetition of phrases.
   - Many times the poems did not tell a complete story, but rather summarized or highlighted the stories that were familiar to everyone in the tribe.

4. Read or have students read three or four English translations of Native American poetry. Some examples are "Rain Song," "Song of the Skyloom," "The War God's Horse Song," and "Prayer Spoken While Presenting an Infant to the Sun," all in *American Indian Prose and Poetry* by Margaret Astrov. Another good example is "Songs in the Garden of the House God," in George Cronyn's *American Indian Poetry*. Where possible, identify the tribe and its geographical location along with the title given to the poem.
5. There are many things that these poems tell us about the culture of each. Have the students identify some of them.

6. This lesson may be followed by group research projects on different practices. The research might include a trip to the museum.

Resources:

Margot Astrov, ed. *American Indian Prose and Poetry.* Gloucester, MA: Peter Smith, 1970.
George W. Cronyn, ed. *American Indian Poetry.* New York: Liveright, 1962.
Charlotte Leslau and Wolf Leslau. *African Poems and Love Songs.* Mount Vernon, NY: Peter Pauper, 1970.
Tom Lowenstein, trans. *Eskimo Poems from Canada and Greenland.* Pittsburgh, University of Pittsburgh Press, 1973.
Natachee S. Momaday. *American Indian Authors.* Boston: Houghton Mifflin, 1972.

Generalization II: Poetry can generally be grouped into two basic categories, lyrical and narrative.

Level: Primary

Objectives:

1. To introduce the students to the style of the lyric poem.
2. To develop an understanding of the short and songlike quality of the lyric poem.
3. To simulate written expression in lyrical style through visual stimulation.

Teaching Strategy:

1. Select several poems to be presented to the children from the following books: *In My Mother's House* by Ann Nolan Clark, a book of poems by Native American children;

Beyond the High Hills, A Book of Eskimo Poems by Guy Mary Rouseliere; and *Spin A Soft Black Song,* poems from children by Nikki Giovanni.

2. Tape several of the poems so the children will be able to listen to them again after the lesson. Read and discuss the poems as they are read to the class. Examine the characteristics of the poems e.g., length, rhythm, subject. Help the class to identify those characteristics that the selections have in common. Help the students to summarize, pointing out that the selections are short, that they have a songlike quality, and that they are generally personal reactions to what the poet sees, hears, thinks, and feels. Help the class to understand that these summarizing statements are the basic characteristics of lyric poems.
3. Reread several of the selections or different ones, and have the students compare the poetic expressions of the Indian children with those written by the Eskimos. Continue by contrasting the feelings expressed by Nikki Giovanni in the poems she has written for children.
4. In an effort to help stimulate students to write in lyrical style, review the characteristics of lyric poems, and present to the class a series of pictures that should stimulate their thinking and give them a subject to write about. The pictures should be diverse in subject matter and contain a variety of settings, types of people, buildings, and other objects. Encourage each student to first select a picture and then develop a poem about that picture.
5. When poems have been completed, they may be assembled with the pictures in book form, and presented to another class as a gift or added to the library collection.

Resources:

Ann Nolan Clark. *In My Mother's House.* New York: Viking, 1941.

Nikki Giovanni. *Spin a Soft Black Song: Poems for Children.* New York: Hill and Wang, 1971.

Guy Mary Rouseliere. *Beyond the High Hills: A Book of Eskimo Poems.* New York: World, 1961.

Level: Intermediate

Objectives:

1. To introduce the students to the style of the lyric poem.
2. To develop an understanding of the short and songlike quality of the lyric poem.
3. To stimulate written expression in lyrical style through personal reactions.

Teaching Strategy:

1. In an effort to help students learn about the characteristics of lyrical style, read selections to them from the book *Eats: Poems* by Arnold Adoff. Discuss the characteristics of the poems and conclude with the class that these are poems about how one person feels and thinks about food. Further stress the short and songlike quality of the verse and aid the students in understanding that these are the basic characteristics of lyric poems.
2. Have the class listen to the recording "The Reason I Like Chocolate" by Nikki Giovanni. Read to the class the "Message to the listener" found on the recording cover. Talk about how this collection of poems differs in content from those in the book *Eats.* It will be important to spend some time discussing and comparing the background of the two poets, stressing that they were reared in different parts of the country and their environments may have influenced the content and style of their writing. The fact that Adoff is a white man and Giovanni an African-American woman is an additional point for consideration.

3. Continue the discussion of the poetry by identifying the different kinds of food mentioned in the poems by Adoff. Make a list of the kinds of foods the class likes and encourage the students to tell why they choose a certain item. If there appear to be ethnic and cultural variations among the foods listed, guide the class into a recognition of these differences. It may be interesting to see how many different ethnic backgrounds are represented by the suggestions.
4. After a review of the characteristics of lyrical verse, stress the characteristic of expressing one's personal reactions to things. Invite the students to write a lyric poem based on the title of Nikki Giovanni's record "The Reason I Like Chocolate," only substituting their favorite food for chocolate, e.g., "The Reason I Like Strawberries," or "The Reason I Like Pizza."
5. Culminate this activity several days later by having a party for the class. During the party, students may share their poems and taste several of the favorite foods mentioned by them in their work.

Resources:

Arnold Adoff. *Eats: Poems*. New York: Lothrop, Lee & Shepard Books, 1979.

Nikki Giovanni. "The Reason I Like Chocolate and Other Children's Poems." New York: Folkways Records, 1976.

Level: Advanced

Objectives:

1. To describe and give types of narrative poetry.
2. To introduce students to an early writer of narrative poetry, Phillis Wheatley.

Teaching Strategy:

1. Mention that poetry may be classified as lyric or narrative but focus the discussion on narrative poetry, which tells a story. Define some examples of narrative poetry such as ballads, odes, and elegies.
2. Read an example of an eighteenth-century elegy, "On the Death of J.C., an Infant," found in Poems and Letters of Phillis Wheatley, edited by Charles Heartman. For this reading, it will be helpful for each student to have a mimeographed copy of the poem. Have the students underline unfamiliar words and allow time for them to consult a dictionary. Have a student reread the poem.
3. Identify the author of the poem as Phillis Wheatley, a slave purchased in Boston in 1761, when she was about seven or eight. Give a brief summary of her life, including the time spent in Europe, her book published in 1773, her marriage to John Peters, and her unfortunate death in 1784. Explain that she often wrote poetry on patriotic themes, including odes to heroes of the American Revolution.
4. As time permits, read "On Being Brought From Africa to America," also in Heartman. Discuss what lines of the poem might be different if it had been written today.

Resources:

William Adams. *Afro American Authors.* Boston: Houghton Mifflin, 1972.

Shirley Graham. *The Story of Phillis Wheatley.* New York: Washington Square Press, 1969.

Charles F. Heartman. Poems and Letters of Phillis Wheatley. Miami: Mnemosyne, 1969.

Langston Hughes. *The Panther and the Lash.* New York: Alfred A. Knopf, 1967.

Generalization III: Some understanding and an appreciation for the cultural heritage of an ethnic or racial group can be gained through the study of that group's poetry.

Level: Primary

Objectives:

1. To help students realize that Chinese poets often write poetry about nature because it is important to them.
2. Help students understand some ways the English language differs from Chinese.
3. To motivate students to write a short poem about nature.

Teaching Strategy:

1. Introduce this experience by discussing ways in which people communicate. Guide the discussion so that the class will focus on forms of written communication.
2. Have the students name several different languages, including Chinese. Continue the discussion with some ways in which English differs from Chinese. The fact that there are several dialects, including Mandarin, within the Chinese language should be noted. Discuss ways in which Chinese and English are similar; for example, both consist of many dialects and both are forms of communication. Introduce the term pictographs (pictures for writing) and encourage the students to use the new terms in their comparisons between the two languages. Discuss the following:

   - The Chinese began developing their writing system more than 3,500 years ago.
   - Pictographs are also referred to as characters.

- There are 50,000 characters in the Chinese writing system.
- Everyone living in China uses the same writing system, and this helps to unify or bring them closer together.
- Not all Chinese pronounce the written symbols in the same way; therefore there are many dialects in China.
- Chinese poets generally write their poetry in Chinese.

3. Write the Chinese symbols for the following words on the chalkboard one by one:

Have students volunteer to write the numbers 1–10 on the chalkboard from a prepared chart that may be displayed. Once the class appears to have grasped the obvious differences between the two writing systems (Chinese and English), begin a discussion on how a poem in Chinese might appear.

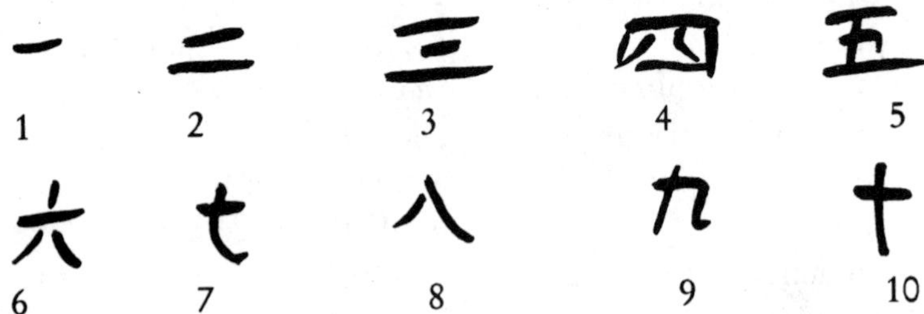

4. Read two Chinese poems to the class in English "South Wind" by Tu-Fu and "A Summer Day" by Li Po, and show the class how the poems look written in Chinese. These

poems may be found in *Do You Not See,* edited and adapted by Sally F. Nichols.

5. Reread the poems to the class and ask them what the poems are about. Summarize the discussion with the idea that many Chinese poems are about nature because nature is very important to the Chinese.
6. Select several Chinese poems from *The Moment of Wonder,* edited by Richard Lewis, to read to the class. Discuss what in nature the poet is describing and how the poet appears to be feeling about what it is he or she is writing.
7. Have the students describe some of the things they might have noticed walking to school or what they can see from the window in the classroom.
8. Have each student select a subject from nature that they would like to describe in a short poem. Encourage the students to be as brief as possible but convey the freedom they have to create their own poem.
9. Encourage the students to give a one- or two-word title for their individual poems and, with the help of a simple Chinese dictionary, aid the students in writing the title of their poem in Chinese.
10. Follow this experience by giving the students an opportunity to illustrate their poems in a manner of their choice, e.g., watercolor, chalk, or crayon.

Resources:

Richard Lewis, ed. *The Moment of Wonder: Collection of Japanese and Chinese Poetry.* New York: Dial, 1964.

Sally F. Nichols, ed. *Do You Not See: Sixteen Chinese Poems.* New York: Harper & Row, 1980.

Erwin Rosenfeld and Harriet Geller. *Afro-Asian Culture Studies.* Woodbury, NY: Barron's Educational Series, 1974.

Level: Intermediate

Objectives:

1. To introduce haiku, a form of Japanese poetry, to the students.
2. To help develop a greater appreciation for the imagery created through poetry.
3. To stimulate the students to create their own haiku.

Teaching Strategy:

1. Put several descriptive phrases, one at a time on the chalkboard, e.g., "the cold winter day," "the tall slender tree." Have the students read the phrases silently as well as in unison. As they read, have them clap for each syllable. After the class has done this several times together, ask for individual volunteers. Alternate by having the students write descriptive phrases on the board and then challenge the class to clap the rhythm of the syllables.
2. Read several haiku poems to the class. Have the students clap the syllables line by line. After trying this for several poems, help them discover the pattern for haiku. After they have discovered that haiku consists of seventeen syllables, usually five in the first line, seven in the second, and five in the third, introduce the following characteristics that may also be found in Japanese haiku:

   - Refers to a particular event.
   - Event is written about in the present, not in the past.
   - Appeals to as many senses as possible (hearing, seeing, smelling, touching, tasting).[2]

3. Discuss with the class the subjects of the haiku that were read. Lead the students to discover that haiku are generally about nature.

4. Continue the lesson with a discussion of events in nature, e.g., weather changes, seasonal changes, events of the morning, afternoon, or evening. If possible, take a brief walk around the school and have the class identify things in nature that would make interesting subjects for haiku. Upon returning to the classroom, have each student identify his or her own event to illustrate. These illustrations can be done in any medium or combination of techniques. This experience, if coordinated with an art specialist, could serve as the subject for a learning experience during an art session before moving to the next step.
5. After the event in nature has been completely illustrated, use several of the illustrations to motivate the students to think of words that would describe the subjects of their artwork. Talk about whether or not the words being suggested appeal to the senses. Make a list on the chalkboard or on chart paper of the words. Combine a few of the words and stress those that describe (adjectives) and words that name (nouns). Count syllables in a few of the words and word combinations or phrases. With the class, construct several five-syllable lines that describe one or two of the illustrations. When the class is ready, have them create haiku to describe their illustration. Stress the relationship between pictures and words. Illustrations and the poems may be shared with other classes by setting up an art gallery in an empty classroom, auditorium, or gymnasium. Invite other classes to visit the art gallery and have the students serve as tour guides.

Resources:

Ann Atwood. *Haiku: The Mood of the Earth.* New York: Charles Scribner's Sons, 1971.

Richard Lewis, ed. *In a Spring Garden.* New York: Dial, 1965.

———. *The Moment of Wonder: Collection of Chinese and Japanese Poetry.* New York: Dial, 1964.

Level: Advanced

Objectives:

1. To help students appreciate poetry of different cultural groups.
2. To introduce students to the works of contemporary Mexican poets.
3. To discuss the use of color imagery in some Mexican poetry.

Teaching Strategy:

1. Have students close their eyes and listen for references to color as you read the poem "A Monterrey Sun," in *Anthology of Mexican Poetry*, edited by Octavio Paz. Then ask students to identify approximately where the poet lives, and why.
2. Identify the title of the poem and its author, Alfonso Reyes, a Mexican poet. Show on the map where Monterrey is located.
3. The poet has painted a rainbow in this poem. Reread one verse, "Every window was a sun...," and discuss the way in which the poet has done this.
4. Note that color imagery is not limited to Mexican poets and Mexican poets are not limited to color imagery. But vibrant color images are found in Mexican written and visual arts. Use pictures, slides, or even travel brochures to show the dominance of color in the arts. A good picture source is *The Art and Architecture of Mexico* by Pedro Rojas.
5. Compare another poem, "Memories of Iza," by Carlos Pellicier, found in *New Poetry of Mexico,* edited by Octavio Paz and Mark Strand. Note that Pellicier was born in 1889 and was the winner of the *Premio Nacional de Literatura* in 1964. If at all possible, particularly if there are Spanish

speakers in the classroom, have the poem read in Spanish before the English translation is read. What does the poet mean when he says that "The women and the flowers spoke the dialect of colors"?

6. For another description of a small village, read the first fragment of "*Vuelta*" ("Return") by a contemporary poet, Octavio Paz. This poem may be found in Paz's *A Draft of Shadows.* Introduce the poem by telling something about the life of this widely known Mexican author (born 1914; has served time as a Mexican ambassador, is widely translated, is also a translator of at least four languages, and so forth). Paz has various poetic styles including poetic prose. In "*Vuelta*" he uses fragmented lines that may be compared to bits of a kaleidoscope. Just as one doesn't concentrate on each piece in the kaleidoscope, but rather on the whole image, encourage students to listen to the poem "as a whole."
7. What do we know about a village where "letters rot in the mailboxes" or where time is "stretched to dry on the rooftops." Does it sound like paradise? Why?

Resources:

Octavio Paz. *Anthology of Mexican Poetry.* Bloomington, IN: Indiana University Press, 1958.

Octavio Paz and Mark Strand, eds. *New Poetry of Mexico.* New York: E. P. Dutton, 1970.

Octavio Paz and Eliot Weinberger, ed. and trans. *A Draft of Shadows.* New York: New Directions, 1979.

Pedro Rojas. *The Art and Architecture of Mexico.* Prague: Paul Hamlyn Publishing Co., 1968.

Young Poetry of the Americas. Washington: General Secretariat of the Organization of American States.

Notes

1. Depending on the maturity of the students, these are amusing modernized folktales told in frank, authentic language.
2. Erwin Rosenfeld and Harriet Geller, *Afro-Asian Culture Studies* (Woodbury, N.Y.: Barron's Educational Series, 1974), pp. 372–73.

9
Generalizations and Teaching Strategies for Mathematics

Introduction

Far too often the question is asked, "Is it possible to include the subject of mathematics in multicultural instruction?" The answer to this question is definitely "yes." In fact, the history and development of mathematics is an interesting and exciting avenue for helping students to understand the contributions of different groups of people to the mathematics we use today—counting and numerations systems, methods of measurement, algebra, geometry, trigonometry, mathematical games, and much more. In fact, the foundations for a great deal of the mathematics studied in precollege classes were laid centuries and millennia ago, in Africa and Asia. By studying mathematics, students learn to respect the contributions of all cultures, including their own.

Mathematics is the science in which we think about numbers, space, and patterns. As students investigate the important relationships between culture and mathematics, they discover that mathematics arose out of the real needs and interests of human beings. They learn how mathematics is related to other subject areas—social studies, science, language arts, and fine arts.

The first topic in this chapter concerns the development of number systems, including number words, signs for numbers, and systems of written numerals. The discussion of the way numbers are used in trade, measurement, and data-gathering, both in historical eras and in the world today, will allow students to apply their knowledge to their own lives and to their communities.

The second major topic deals with space. Students will investigate factors that influenced the size and shape of dwellings built by people of different societies. These include the ordinary dwellings in which people lived as well as monumental structures such as the pyramids. Students will be introduced to mathematics in art through discussion of the geometry of design and repeated geometric patterns in several cultures.

Numbers, Numerals, and Their Uses

Suggested Content Outline

I. Systems of Number Words, Based on Grouping
   - A. Ten (decimal)
   - B. Twenty (vigesimal)
   - C. Five (quinary)
   - D. Two (binary)
   - E. Other

II. Numerals: Abstract Representation of Numbers
   - A. Positional notation
   - B. Multiplicative base
   - C. Repetition of symbols
   - D. Use of zero

III. Recording and Computational Devices
   - A. Incised bones, tally sticks, quipu
   - B. Counting board, abacus
   - C. Calculator, computer

IV. Applications of Numbers
   A. Money and trade
   B. Measurement
   C. Statistical data

Generalizations:

I. People have invented many ways to express and write numbers.
II. We use numbers in many aspects of our lives.

Generalization I: People have invented many ways to express and write numbers.

Level: Primary

Objectives:

To help students understand:

1. The need to have signs, words, and symbols for numbers, even in simple societies.
2. People speaking different languages have sets of number words unique to their own language.

Teaching Strategy:

1. Discuss with the students the many ways we use number words in everyday speech. Make a list on the chalkboard.
2. Ask students to pretend that they are visiting a foreign country and don't understand the language spoken there. They would like to buy three oranges. How would they indicate that they want exactly three? Encourage them to use their fingers. Ask them to think how they would use their fingers, and then raise them when you give the signal. As they look at their classmates, how many different

As students investigate the important relationships between culture and mathematics, they discover that mathematics arose out of the real needs and interests of human beings.

combinations of fingers do they see (thumb, index finger, etc.)? Do they use left hand, right hand, or both hands? Emphasize that there are many solutions to the problem. Repeat this activity with different numbers, some requiring two hands, or possibly hands and feet. Note that many people have specific ways of using their fingers and other parts of the body in counting. Read to them Zaslavsky's *Count on Your Fingers African Style*.

3. Encourage children to note that our system is based on grouping by tens, probably because we have ten fingers. *Eleven* means "one left" after counting on ten fingers, and *twelve* means "two left." Discuss the meanings of *thirteen* (three plus ten) and *thirty* (three times ten). Ask for other examples of adding to ten and multiplying with ten.

4. Ask the students whether any of them can count in languages other than English. Many children learn Spanish number words by watching "Sesame Street." Students who are familiar with other languages can teach the counting words to their classmates. Parents might be invited to contribute. Ask the students to write the words on the chalkboard, or you might write them if they cannot. Compare them with English number words. Are they based on ten or another base? Note that the French word for *eighty* means "four twenties." Twenty is the base of many counting systems in West Africa, Middle America, and among the Inuit (Eskimo).

Resources:

Irving Adler. *Numbers Old and New.* New York: John Day, 1960.

Building Bridges to Mathematics: Cultural Connections, Level Two, #12 ("Playing Gallitos"). Reading, MA: Addison-Wesley, 1992.

Jeanne Bendick and Marcia Levin. *Take a Number.* New York: McGraw-Hill, 1961.

Philip Carona. *The True Book of Numbers.* Chicago: Children's Press, 1966.

Iron Eyes Cody. *Indian Talk: Hand Signals of the American Indians.* Healdsburg, CA: Naturegraph Publishers, 1970.

Muriel Feelings. *Moja Means One: Swahili Counting Book.* New York: Dial Press, 1971.

Jim Haskins. *Count Your Way Through....* Minneapolis: Carolrhoda Books. Series of books describing the counting words and cultures of many lands.

Claudia Zaslavsky. *Africa Counts: Number and Pattern in African Culture.* Brooklyn, NY: Lawrence Hill Books, 1979.

———. *Count on Your Fingers African Style.* New York: T.Y. Crowell, 1980.

———. *Zero: Is It Something? Is It Nothing?* New York: Franklin Watts, 1989.

Level: Intermediate

Objectives:

To help students understand that:

1. As civilizations developed, people needed systems of numerals, written symbols for numbers.
2. The various systems of written numerals differed in their structure and their efficiency for computation.

Teaching Strategy:

1. Ask the class to choose several ancient civilizations, including Egypt, India, and the Roman Empire. Help them to locate these regions on a world map. Guide the discussion to identify the need for counting, written records, and computation. Topics should include trade, taxation, and calendars.
2. Have each student select one of the societies and work in a small group to research its numeration system. Each group can prepare a document in the form of a poster, using the numerals of that culture in a relevant context.
3. Compare the systems of numerals with one another and with the Indo-Arabic system we use. For example, ask students to write the number 879 in each system on the chalkboard. How many symbols are required? Are some symbols repeated? If the symbols were mixed up, would it be possible to read the numeral correctly? Does the system have place value (positional notation)? What is the base of the system, or is there more than one base? Is there a symbol for zero? How were the numerals used in computation?
4. Here are some of the characteristics of various systems. The ancient Romans wrote nine as VIIII; the subtractive form IX came later. Both Roman and Egyptian numerals involve repetition of symbols. Neither system had a symbol for zero. Egyptians multiplied by doubling, while Romans used place-

value counting boards for computation. Greeks and Hebrews used letters of the alphabet as numerals. Babylonians used the stylus to form wedge-shaped numerals; grouping was based on sixty, with ten as a second base. The Chinese formed stick numerals on the counting board. The Maya had a system based on groups of twenty, and used three symbols—bar, dot, and zero symbol—with positional notation.

Resources:

Irving and Ruth Adler. *Numbers Old and New.* New York: John Day, 1960.

Isaac Asimov. *How Did We Find Out About Numbers?* New York: Walker, 1973.

Building Bridges to Mathematics: Cultural Connections, Level Six, #1 ("Count Like an Egyptian"). Reading, MA: Addison-Wesley, 1992.

Lancelot Hogben. *The Wonderful World of Numbers.* New York: Doubleday, 1968.

Georges Ifrah. *From One to Zero: A Universal History of Numbers.* New York: Viking, 1985.

Beatrice Lumpkin. Senefer: *A Young Genius in Old Egypt.* Trenton, NJ: Africa World Press, 1992.

———. *Senefer and Hatshepsut.* Trenton, NJ: Africa World Press, 1992.

Glory St. John. *How To Count Like a Martian.* New York: Henry Walck, 1975.

Seattle Public Schools. "Ancient Systems of Numeration" (#3); "Pa-Kua: Ancient Symbols of the Orient" (#11). *Multicultural Mathematics Posters and Activities.* Reston, VA: National Council of Teachers of Mathematics, 1984.

David Eugene Smith and Jekuthiel Ginsburg. *Numbers and Numerals.* Reston, VA: National Council of Teachers of Mathematics, 1953.

Dirk J. Struik. *A Concise History of Mathematics.* New York: Dover, 1987.

Claudia Zaslavsky. Activities #1, 2, 3, 4, and 6. *Multicultural Mathematics: Interdisciplinary Cooperative-Learning Activities.* Portland, ME: J. Weston Walch, 1993.

Level: Advanced

Objectives:

1. To help students understand that as civilizations developed, so did numeration systems.
2. To help students realize that the need for calendars stimulated the creation of written records and the extension of the numeration system.

Teaching Strategy:

1. Through class discussion, identify at least four civilizations that are familiar to the class, including the ancient Maya of Mesoamerica. Locate these societies on a world map. Discuss the need for keeping track of time at various stages in the development of these societies.
2. With the class, generate a series of questions about life in these societies at several stages in their history, leading to the creation of sophisticated calendars. In what year (in our system) did each calendar begin? Discuss the Ishango bone, an incised bone dated to 18,000 B.C.E. or earlier, found at Ishango, in eastern Zaire. It is assumed that the markings represent a six-month lunar calendar. Similar calendar bones have been found in other parts of Africa and in Europe.
3. Have each student select one of the societies and work in a small group to answer the questions they have just formulated, using classroom resources and the library. Each

group should prepare a report in an interesting format, such as a skit or mock radio or television show, with a display of calendars.

4. Compare these calendars with the Gregorian calendar we use, considering year of origin and compatibility with the solar year of 365.24 days and the lunar cycle of 29.53 days.
5. Many students are familiar with some aspects of the Chinese calendar. A field trip to a Chinese-American community to learn more about the calendar should be a stimulating experience.
6. Students may be interested in photographs of Maya stone tablets, called stelae, on which are engraved Long Count numerals and calendar dates based on a period that started in 3114 B.C.E. (our calendar). The Maya recorded dates as far back as one and a quarter million years! They used a 260-day sacred calendar interlocking with a 365-day solar calendar and referred as well to the cycles of the moon and of the planet Venus.

Resources:

Irving Adler. *Mathematics.* New York: Doubleday, 1990.

Marcia Ascher. "Before the Conquest." *Mathematics Magazine 65* (October 1992): 211–218. Mathematics of the Inca and the Maya.

Joyce Marcus. "First Dates." *Natural History* (April 1991): 26–29. Mesoamerican calendars.

"The Maya." *Multiculturalism in Mathematics, Science and Technology.* Reading, MA: Addison-Wesley, 1992: 111–114.

Seattle Public Schools. "Mayan Numerals" (#10). *Multicultural Mathematics: Posters and Activities.* Reston, VA: National Council of Teachers of Mathematics, 1984.

Lawana Hooper Trout. *The Maya.* New York: Chelsea House, 1991: 29–32.

Claudia Zaslavsky. "The Amazing Maya Calendar" (Activity #5). *Multicultural Mathematics: Interdisciplinary Cooperative-Learning Activities.* Portland, ME: J. Weston Walch, 1993.

Generalization II: We use numbers in many aspects of our lives.

Level: Primary

Objectives:

1. To help students realize the need for numbers and measurement in keeping track of time, as well as for other aspects of daily life.
2. To help students appreciate the contributions of Benjamin Banneker, the eighteenth-century African-American scientist and mathematician.

Teaching Strategies

1. Discuss with the students how they know when to get up in the morning, when to come to school, and when to watch a favorite television show. Ask each student to write a schedule of a typical schoolday, e.g., the previous day, and draw a clock face showing the time for each activity. Then have students form small groups and compare their schedules. Ask one student in each group to report to the class on similarities and differences in the schedules. Discuss the importance of clocks in allowing people to keep to a schedule.
2. Discuss with the students some of the subdivisions of time. Which divisions are based on nature and which were established by people? For example, the length of the year depends on the time it takes the earth to orbit the sun. The length of the day depends on the rotation of the earth, the period of alternating light and darkness. How the day was divided into smaller units was determined arbitrarily by people.

3. In early societies, people scheduled their activities by looking at the position of the sun—sunrise, high noon, sunset. This is still true in many parts of the world. Why would this practice not be useful in our culture? In what type of society would this work?
4. Inform the class that in 1753 Benjamin Banneker, a free 22-year-old African American, constructed the first striking clock that had all parts made in America. He carried out this task by taking apart and analyzing a pocket watch he had borrowed from a merchant. Few people in the American colonies had clocks or watches. Because Banneker was a self-taught mathematician, he was later able to join the team that surveyed the site for Washington, D.C., and to write several almanacs. You may want to read to the class selections from Lillie Patterson's *Benjamin Banneker* or a similar biography of this remarkable man.

Resources:

Mitsumasa Anno. *Anno's Sundial.* New York: Philomel Books, 1987.

Joseph Bruchac and Jonathan London. *Thirteen Moons on a Turtle's Back.* New York: Philomel, 1992. The Iroquois thirteen-month calendar.

Building Bridges to Mathematics: Cultural Connections. Level One, #14 ("Benjamin Banneker's Clock"); Level Four, #3 ("Astronomer Banneker"). Reading, MA: Addison-Wesley, 1992.

Kevin Conley. *Benjamin Banneker: Scientist and Mathematician.* New York: Chelsea House, 1989.

Margaret Cooper. "The Nature of Time." *FACES* (January 1987).

Louis Haber. *Black Pioneers of Science and Invention.* New York: Harcourt Brace, 1970.

Lillie Patterson. *Benjamin Banneker: Genius of Early America.* Nashville, TN: Abingdon Press, 1978.

Claudia Zaslavsky. *Africa Counts: Number and Pattern in African Culture.* Brooklyn, NY: Lawrence Hill Books, 1979.

Level: Intermediate

Objectives:

1. To help students appreciate the importance of numbers, numerals, and computation in trade.
2. To help students understand that money became necessary as trade expanded.
3. To help students understand the use of the abacus as a calculating device.

Teaching Strategy:

1. Ask students to share with the class a recent experience in purchasing items at a store or ordering by mail or phone. How did spoken numbers, written numerals, and computation enter into the transaction? They should discuss prices, taxes (if appropriate), and the means of payment—cash, check, or credit card. Which means of payment is most convenient? Was a calculator or computer involved in the course of the transaction?
2. Have students research the history of barter and money. Did money always enter into an exchange of goods? What objects have been used as currency in the past? They should find out about cowrie shells and beads, two common forms of money, about the origin of coins and paper money, and locate the societies that used each type. Each type of currency might be assigned to a different group of students. They might create posters illustrating the types of currency and locating the regions in which they were used.
3. Have students form groups to plan a simulated transaction in a Chinese shop. They will use paper money and calculate on a Chinese abacus, which they can make with beads, string, and cardboard. Each group can then perform for the class. The Chinese were the first to use paper money, about twelve centuries ago. Two hundred years later, they established a

government-run bank to print and regulate the issuance of paper money. Soon after that, they invented the suan pan, a form of abacus that is still in use today. It is based on calculating by groups of fives and tens. Many Chinese shops use them today.

4. Discuss with students that each country has its own form of currency. Help them to refer to the "Foreign Currency" column of a daily newspaper to discover the units of currency in several foreign countries and the conversion rate to U.S. dollars.

Resources:

David Adler. *All Kinds of Money.* New York: Franklin Watts, 1984.

Building Bridges to Mathematics: Cultural Connections. Level Four, #15 ("Paper Money"); Level Six, #4 ("The Chinese Abacus"); Level Seven, #2 ("The Japanese Abacus"). Reading, MA: Addison-Wesley, 1992.

Joe Cribb. *Money* (Eyewitness Books). New York: Alfred A. Knopf, 1990.

R. V. Fodor. *Nickels, Dimes, Dollars.* New York: William Morrow, 1988.

Georges Ifrah. *From One to Zero: A Universal History of Numbers.* New York: Viking, 1985. Chapter 8 deals with the abacus.

Seattle Public Schools. "The Calculator's Ancestors" (#1). *Multicultural Mathematics Posters and Activities.* Reston, VA: National Council of Teachers of Mathematics, 1984.

Claudia Zaslavsky. "Counting on the Japanese Abacus" (Activity #8); "Mental Arithmetic: Money in West Africa" (Activity #18); "Mental Arithmetic: More Cowries" (Activity #19). *Multicultural Mathematics: Interdisciplinary Cooperative-Learning Activities.* Portland, ME: J. Weston Walch, 1993.

———. *Africa Counts: Number and Pattern in African Culture.* Brooklyn, NY: Lawrence Hill Books, 1979. Cowries, beads, and other types of currency in Africa.

Level: Advanced

Objectives:

1. To help students realize that numbers are necessary to present information of importance to people.
2. To help students appreciate that statistical data can help people to make decisions about many issues.
3. To help students appreciate that statistical data can be presented in several different forms.
4. To help students understand that careers are open to people who can formulate and present data.

Teaching Strategy:

1. Ask students to bring to class an article in a social studies book, a newspaper, or a magazine in which numerical data are presented. Have each student concentrate on one set of data. Ask several students to give the source of the data and the form in which it is presented—in a sentence, a table, a graph, etc. Show different forms on the overhead projector.
2. The United States Census Bureau collects a tremendous quantity of information and issues many reports. You may want to contact the Census Bureau to receive its materials for schools: Census Bureau Education Program; Data User Services Division; Bureau of the Census; Washington, D.C. 20233–8300; 301–763–1510 or (FAX) 301–763–4794.
3. Ask students to select a public issue that interests them, such as the environment, homelessness, poverty, racism, funding for education, the risks of tobacco or AIDS, the views of candidates in an election, or possible elimination of high school football. Have students with the same interest work in small groups to research the issue. They may want to use government publications or consult local institutions. How can statistical data help them to make decisions about this issue? How can they use such data to influence policy-

making bodies? Ask the students to pretend that they will appear before a public body to urge it to take certain actions. Have each group prepare and then give a presentation that includes statistical data presented in an interesting way.

4. The Census Bureau conducts a census of the entire population every ten years. In 1980 it conducted the first fairly accurate census of the American Indian population, due to the work of Edna Lee Paisano, who grew up on the Nez Percé reservation. As the first Native American to work for the Census Bureau, she combined her love of mathematics with service to her people. Discuss careers that involve the collection, presentation, and use of statistical data.
5. Several large cities and states have sued the Census Bureau on the grounds that their population was "undercounted"—not all the people were included in the census count. Suggest that the class investigate and discuss the effects of undercounting on these cities and states. Which segments of the population are likely to escape being counted?

Resources:

Melissa and Brent Ashabranner. *Counting America: The Story of the United States Census.* New York: G.P. Putnam's Sons, 1989.

Building Bridges to Mathematics: Cultural Connections, Level Seven, #10 ("Counting Native American People"). Reading, MA: Addison-Wesley, 1992.

"Records in Knots: Making a Quipu." *Multiculturalism in Mathematics, Science, and Technology.* Reading, MA: Addison-Wesley, 1992: 81–84.

Teri Perl. "Edna Lee Paisano." *Women, Numbers and Dreams.* San Carlos, CA: Math Products Plus, 1992 revision.

United States Bureau of the Census. *Statistical Abstract of the United States* and other publications.

Claudia Zaslavsky. "Multicultural Mathematics: One Road to the Goal of Mathematics for All" in *Reaching All Students with Mathe-*

matics, G. Cuevas and M. Driscoll, eds. Reston, VA: National Council of Teachers of Mathematics, 1993. Describes how secondary students used Census Bureau data to analyze the socioeconomic levels of their community.

Space: Shape, Size, and Pattern

Suggested Content Outline

I. Factors That Influence Shape and Size in Architecture
   - A. Temporary Shelters
   - B. Permanent Homes
   - C. Outstanding and Nonresidential Buildings

II. Patterns and Symmetry
   - A. Geometric Designs in Folk Art
   - B. Repeated Patterns in Art

Generalizations:

I. A variety of factors influence the size and shape of people's homes and other buildings.

II. Geometric motifs and their repetition are important elements in the arts of many cultures.

Generalization I: A variety of factors influence the size and shape of people's homes and other buildings.

Level: Primary

Objectives:

To help students understand that:

1. In the past, people usually constructed their own homes, with the help of family members and neighbors.

2. People had to consider many factors when planning to build their homes.

Teaching Strategy:

1. Ask students to name the types of dwellings with which they are familiar, such as single-family home, apartment house, tent, etc. Write each type on the chalkboard and discuss the characteristics, with emphasis on size and shape. Why do people choose to live in one type of dwelling rather than another? Depending upon the maturity of the students, discuss such factors as climate, cost, available land, permanence of the structure, method of construction (professional builders or people who will live in the home), and use (ownership or rental).
2. Discuss two different groups of Native Americans who had different lifestyles in the past; e.g., the Six Nations of the Iroquois Confederacy of the Northeast Woodlands and the Lakota, or Sioux, of the Great Plains. Discuss the homes of each group: the Iroquois longhouse and the Lakota tipi. Inform the students that the Iroquois call themselves the *Haudenosaunee,* "People of the Longhouse." Because the Lakota roamed the plains to hunt buffalo, they needed portable shelters. On the other hand, the Iroquois, who led a more settled life, built shelters that housed several families. Compare and contrast the size and shape of each type of Native American dwelling. Be sure to emphasize that you are referring to the past. Students may not know that Native American peoples today have lifestyles similar to those of other Americans, including dress, housing, and occupations. The tipi and the longhouse still exist but are used mainly for ceremonial purposes.
3. Encourage students to research the lives of the Iroquois and the Lakota in the past. They might extend their research to other Native American peoples, each group of students working with a different nation or ethnic group. Encourage

them to build models or draw pictures of the tipi, longhouse, and other types of dwellings. They should be prepared to discuss with the class the influence of climate on housing styles, tools used, means of obtaining food, religion, and other factors.

Resources:

Karna L. Bjorkland. *The Indians of Northeastern America.* New York: Dodd Mead, 1969.

Janet and Alex D'Amato. *Indian Crafts.* Sayre Publishing, 1968.

Barbara Graymont. *The Iroquois.* New York: Chelsea House, 1988.

W. Ben Hunt. *Indian Crafts and Lore.* New York: Golden Press, 1954.

Sigmund A. Lavine. *The Houses the Indians Built.* New York, Dodd Mead, 1975.

Peter Nabakov and Robert Easton. *Native American Architecture.* New York: Oxford University Press, 1988.

Carl Waldman. Encyclopedia of Native American Tribes. New York: Facts-on-File, 1988.

Charlotte and David Yue. *The Pueblo.* Boston: Houghton Mifflin, 1986.

———. *The Tipi: A Center of Native American Life.* New York: Alfred A. Knopf, 1984.

Level: Intermediate

Objectives:

To help students understand that:

1. Straight lines and right angles dominate architecture in our culture.
2. In some societies the circle is the dominant form in architecture.

3. Differences exist between perimeter and area and between linear units and square units.
4. For a given perimeter, a square is the largest rectangle, and a circle the shape having the greatest area.

Teaching Strategy:

1. Ask students to imagine that they are to build a small summer home. Have each student draw a floor plan for such a home. As the students compare their plans, ask them to note whether the floor plans feature straight lines and right angles or incorporate curved lines. Discuss which type of line is more common in our society by looking at examples of buildings.
2. Show students photographs of circular homes, such as the tipi of the Native Americans the Great Plains, the yurt of Central Asia, the Inuit (Eskimo) igloo, and round houses in Africa. Such houses are constructed by the people who are planning to live in them. They must gather all the materials; therefore, it would be logical to assume that they would like to have the largest floor space for a given amount of materials for the walls.
3. Ask students to carry out the following experiment. Have students work in pairs. Give each pair two sheets of grid paper and a piece of string 32 grid units in length. Students will help each other as they form the following shapes with the string and draw them on grid paper: a circle, an oval, a square, two different non-square rectangles, and several others. Each shape has a perimeter of 32 units. Have students count the number of grid squares enclosed by each shape and record the results in a table. They should conclude that the square is the largest rectangle and the circle encloses the greatest area of all the shapes.
4. Discuss the factors that influence the size and shape of a dwelling, such as ease of construction, climate, available

materials, lifestyles, wealth, and traditions. Many people who formerly built round houses are now living in rectangular homes. You might show the class the film *The Village of Round and Square Houses,* based on the book of the same title. As an alternative to showing the film, pass the book among the students.

5. Encourage students to research Great Zimbabwe in Zimbabwe, with its massive oval enclosure and solid conical tower (see Denyer 1978 or Zaslavsky 1979). They might also investigate geodesic domes.

Resources:

Building Bridges to Mathematics: Cultural Connections, Level Six, #14 ("The Round House"); Level Six, #16 ("People of the Longhouse"). Reading, MA: Addison-Wesley, 1992.

Susan Denyer. *African Traditional Architecture.* New York: Africana Publishing Company, 1978.

Ann Grifalconi. *The Village of Round and Square Houses.* Boston: Little, Brown and Company, 1986. The film of the same name was made by Weston Woods Studio, Weston, CT, 1989.

Peter Nabakov and Robert Easton. *Native American Architecture.* New York: Oxford University Press, 1988.

Seattle Public Schools. "The Round House" (#5). *Multicultural Mathematics Posters and Activities.* Reston, VA: National Council of Teachers of Mathematics, 1984.

Charlotte and David Yue. *The Igloo.* Boston: Houghton Mifflin, 1986.

———. *The Tipi*: A Center of Native American Life. New York: Alfred A. Knopf, 1984.

Claudia Zaslavsky. *Africa Counts: Number and Pattern in African Life.* Brooklyn, NY: Lawrence Hill Books, 1979.

———. "Multicultural Mathematics Education in the Middle Grades." *Arithmetic Teacher* 38 (February 1991): 8–13.

———. "People Who Live in Round Houses." *Arithmetic Teacher* 37 (September 1989): 18–21.

Level: Advanced

Objectives:

1. To help students appreciate the amazing achievement of the ancient Egyptians in constructing the pyramids.
2. To help students understand how to analyze the measurements of the Great Pyramid of Khufu.
3. To help students understand how Egyptian pyramids compare with those of Mesoamerica.

Teaching Strategy:

1. Discuss with students the shape of a pyramid as determined by the number of sides of the polygon forming the base.
2. Ask students to research Egyptian pyramids and Mesoamerican pyramids. When were they constructed? What function did they perform in each society? How large were the largest pyramids? What materials were used in their construction? Have the students report their findings to the class.
3. Analyze with students the dimensions, orientation, and mathematical relationships of the Great Pyramid of Pharaoh Khufu, one of the Seven Wonders of the World. Emphasize the mathematical and astronomical knowledge that underlay the construction, such as proportionality, similar triangles, cotangent relationship (called the sekat), volume of a truncated pyramid, and orientation to true north.
4. Have students form groups to draw plans and construct scale models of the Great Pyramid, along with illustrated reports about life in ancient Egypt.

Resources:

Richard J. Gillings. *Mathematics in the Time of the Pharaohs.* New York: Dover Publications, 1972.

Beatrice Lumpkin. "The Pyramids: Ancient Showcase of African Science and Technology" in Ivan Van Sertima, ed. *Blacks in Science: Ancient and Modern.* New Brunswick, NJ: Transaction Books, 1983: 67–83.

Kurt Mendelssohn. *The Riddle of the Pyramids.* New York: Praeger, 1974.

Public Broadcasting System (PBS). "This Old Pyramid" (1992). Depicts a contemporary effort to construct a small pyramid near the site of the Egyptian pyramids, using the technology of the ancient Egyptians.

Claudia Zaslavsky. "The Wonderful Pyramids of Egypt" (Activity #27). *Multicultural Mathematics: Interdisciplinary Cooperative-Learning Activities.* Portland, ME: J. Weston Walch Publishers, 1993.

Generalization II: Geometric motifs and their repetition are important elements in the arts of many cultures.

Level: Primary

Objectives:

1. To help students appreciate the use of geometric designs in cloth.
2. To help students recognize common use of geometric designs and repeated patterns.

Teaching Strategy:

1. Ask students to look at their clothing and at objects in the classroom. Do they see any patterns? Can they find shapes, like triangles, squares, and circles, or patterns of straight lines? Are some of these design elements repeated?

2. Show students several examples of geometric designs in cloth. Some examples may have repeated geometric patterns. Ask students to identify the motifs, or elements in the design. Excellent examples are cloth made by the Hmong, the adinkra of the Asante people, quilt patterns, and basketry. Some designs are symbolic. Explain the symbolism to the class.
3. Students can work in groups to create their own geometric designs on paper or cloth to illustrate an idea or occasion. In order to repeat the pattern, they can make stencils or cut the design into a half-potato. The resources below give specific suggestions.

Resources:

Building Bridges to Mathematics: Cultural Connections, Level K, #3 ("Red Light, Green Light"); Level One, #9 ("Jug of Flowers"); Level Two, #3 ("Hmong Flowery Cloth"); Level Three, #15 ("Native American Art"); Level Four, #11 ("Story Quilts"). Reading, MA: Addison-Wesley, 1992.

Deborah A. Carey. "The Patchwork Quilt; A Context for Probem Solving," *Arithmetic Teacher* 40 (December 1992).

Valerie Flournoy, *The Patchwork Quilt.* (New York: E. P. Dutton, 1985).

W. Ben Hunt. *Indian Crafts and Lore.* New York: Golden Press, 1954.

Geoffrey Williams. *African Designs from Traditional Sources.* New York: Dover Publications, 1971.

Blia Xiong. *Nine-in-One, GRR! GRR!* (San Francisco: Children's Book Press, 1989).

Claudia Zaslavsky. "Symmetry and Other Mathematical Concepts in African Life" in *Applications in School Mathematics* (1979 Yearbook), S. Sharron, ed. Reston, VA: National Council of Teachers of Mathematics, 1979.

Level: Intermediate

Objectives:

1. To help students understand how to analyze symmetry in geometric designs and repeated patterns.
2. To help students realize the importance of symmetry in geometric designs and repeated patterns.

Teaching Strategy:

1. Show students a photo or actual example of a rug or cloth in which the design has several types of line and/or rotational symmetry. Ask the students to analyze the symmetry. If the topic is new to them, discuss the various types of symmetry.
2. Show students a border in which a pattern is repeated, perhaps in the item used in #1. Discuss the various ways of repeating a specific motif to make a border.
3. Invite students to design their own *Dineh* (also spelled *Dine,* the name by which the Navajo call themselves) type of rug and color it. See the Resources for several references.

Resources:

LeRoy Appleton. *American Indian Design and Decoration.* New York: Dover Publications, 1971.

Building Bridges to Mathematics: Cultural Connections, Level Six, #11 ("Guatemalan Weaving"); Level Eight, #15 ("Navajo Weavings"). Reading, MA: Addison-Wesley, 1992.

"The Navajo: Creating a Burntwater Design." *Multiculturalism in Mathematics, Science, and Technology.* Reading, MA: Addison-Wesley, 1992: 127–30.

Mary Pendleton. *Navajo and Hopi Weaving Techniques.* New York: Macmillan, 1974.

Claudia Zaslavsky. "Symmetry and Other Mathematical Concepts in African Life" in S. Sharron, ed., *Applications in School Mathe-*

matics (1979 Yearbook). Reston, VA: National Council of Teachers of Mathematics, 1979.

———. "Symmetry in American Folk Art." *Arithmetic Teacher* 38 (September 1990): 6–12.

———. "Border Patterns" (Activity #31) and "Symmetry in Dine Rugs" (Activity #32) in *Multicultural Mathematics: Interdisciplinary Cooperative-Learning Activities.* Portland, ME: J. Weston Walch, 1993.

Level: Advanced

Objectives:

1. To help students understand why repeated geometric patterns are prominent in Islamic art.
2. To help students understand the mathematical principles that underlie the creation of tessellations.

Teaching Strategy:

1. Show students photographs or slides of repeated patterns in Islamic art. The Metropolitan Museum of Art publishes an excellent kit, "The Mathematics of Islamic Art," that includes slides and lesson plans (see Resources). Explain that some Islamic sects forbade the representation of humans or animals, thus giving prominence to geometric motifs.
2. Ask the students to analyze the repeated patterns for such features as types of polygons and the measure of their angles. A repeated geometric pattern that covers the plane completely is called a tessellation. Artists created such designs using only compass and straightedge.
3. Using either square or isometric grid paper, students should create and color their own Islamic-type patterns.

4. Have students form groups to research examples of Islamic art, such as the books celebrating the rulers of Persia (now Iran). They might write reports and illustrate them with art inspired by these works. Unlike many other Muslim artists, the Persians used human and animal figures in their illustrations.

Resources:

Building Bridges to Mathematics: Cultural Connections, Level Eight, #13 ("Architecture of Islam."). Reading, MA: Addison-Wesley, 1992.

Marina C. Krause. "Tessellations" in *Multicultural Mathematics Materials.* Reston, VA: National Council of Teachers of Mathematics, 1983: 36–40.

"Mathematics of Islamic Art." New York: Metropolitan Museum of Art, 1979.

Seattle Public Schools. "Arabic Geometrical Pattern and Design" (#9) in *Multicultural Mathematics Posters and Materials.* Reston, VA: National Council of Teachers of Mathematics, 1984.

Claudia Zaslavsky. "The Shape of a Symbol, the Symbolism of a Shape." *Teacher* 98 (February 1981): 36–43.

———. "Islamic Art: Tessellations" (Activity #36). *Multicultural Mathematics: Interdisciplinary Cooperative-Learning Activities.* Portland, ME: J. Weston Walch, 1993.

10
Generalizations and Teaching Strategies for Music

Introduction

Music is a valuable part of the school curriculum, and because it is an important part of all cultures, it is an excellent vehicle for teaching about the values and lifestyles of various groups. Robert L. Garretson, in his book *Music in Childhood Education,* reinforces this notion by stating:

> Music is an integral part of all cultures and the hopes, fears, aspirations, and beliefs of various ethnic groups are often expressed through their folk music. Complete understanding of these peoples cannot be achieved unless all aspects of their cultures, including music, are included in the units of study taught in the schools.[1]

Music not only reflects the lifestyles and values of people in different cultures. Music also has aesthetic and expressive benefits to offer in the education of young people. For these reasons, a chapter on incorporating music into a multicultural curriculum has been included in this book.

In most schools, music is generally taught by a music specialist during a time period set aside for this purpose. However, in some elementary schools, additional instruction is given in the regular classroom by the classroom teacher. This chapter will seek to provide suggestions that should help the elementary classroom teacher and also the music specialist to incorporate multicultural concepts into the teaching of music. The suggestions highlight music that is representative of a variety of cultures. Music that is multicultural can be effectively integrated into general music classes, vocal music periods, choruses, choirs, bands, orchestras, and ensembles.

Folk Music

Suggested Content Outline

I. Folk Music
   A. Definition
   B. History

II. Types of Folk Music
   A. Dance Songs
   B. Legendary Folk Songs

III. Music of the People
   A. Geographic Influences
   B. Ethnic Groups Contributions

Generalizations:

I. Folk music is generally very old music that was created by people as a part of their everyday existence and handed down from one generation to another.

II. African-American folk music originated in slave quarters on Southern plantations and has become a type of music that is broad in scope and includes several different types of songs.

III. The cultural heritage, beliefs, values, and lifestyles of groups are reflected in their folk music.

Generalization I: Folk music is generally very old music that was created by people as a part of their everyday existence and handed down from one generation to another.

Level: Primary

Objectives:

1. To help students understand that folk music is music that was created by people who were not necessarily trained musicians and that most folk songs that are sung today are very old; also that people from all ethnic/racial and cultural groups have created folk songs reflecting their lives.
2. To motivate students to create a class folk song and to make folk instruments.

Teaching Strategy:

1. Introduce this lesson by having the class sing one or two familiar folk songs selected by the teacher, such as "Tisket-a-Tasket" (African-American Game Song), "Aunt Rhody" (unidentified), or "Down in the Valley" (Kentucky). (Refer to the books listed under resources for other suggestions. Most songbooks for children contain a great variety of folk songs). After the class has enjoyed singing the songs, discuss how these songs might have come into existence. Include in the discussion ways that songs are composed and help students realize that ordinary people often make up songs. Introduce the concept of folk music, and explain that the songs they just sang are examples of songs made up by people who probably had no formal training in music but

Music is an important part of all cultures and thus an excellent vehicle for teaching about the values and lifestyles of various groups.

who liked to sing and made up those songs. Discuss with the students the ethnic/racial or cultural group that is given the credit for composing the song. Talk about possible ways that a song could be passed down from one generation to another.

2. Have the students identify other folk songs they may be familiar with and try to discover from the lyrics where the people lived and what their lives were like.
3. Ask the class to list several characteristics of their school environment that they would include if the class composed a song. Select one or two of the characteristics and help the class compose a class folk song. Two songs, "Together" and "Future Americans," were composed by a class studying diversity and have been included as examples. It may be

easier to put a song together if the class makes up lyrics to go with a familiar tune first and then moves into the creation of a completely original song. The song need not be as long as these, but the students should be involved in making decisions about how long their song should be.

4. Once the song is completed, this process may take several class periods. Interest the students in making folk instruments so they may accompany themselves when they are performing their song. An excellent source for teaching students about folk instruments and how to make them is *Simple Folk Instruments to Make and to Play.*
5. Once both the song and instruments have been completed, arrange to have the class perform for other classes or for the parents.

Resources:

Bergethon and Eunice Boardman. *Musical Growth in the Elementary School.* New York: Holt, Rinehart & Winston, 1963.

Peter Erdei. *150 American Folk Songs to Sing, Read, and Play.* New York: Boosey and Hawkes, 1974.

Ilene Hunter and Marilyn.Judson. *Simple Folk Instruments to Make and to Play.* New York: Simon and Schuster, 1977.

McLaughlin, Roberta. *Sing A Song of People.* New York: Bowmar, 1973.

Level: Intermediate

Objectives:

1. To help students understand how folk music is created.
2. To help students understand how folk music is transmitted.

Taken from Songs of Pride for Children
Words by Harriett L. Pearson
Music by Harriett L. Pearson

Taken from Songs of Pride for Children
Words by Harriett L. Pearson
Music by Harriett L. Pearson

Teaching Strategy:

1. Explore folk music from different countries by playing recordings from the album "Negro Folk Music of Africa and America." Indicate whether or not the examples played were composed by an individual or represent the creative efforts of a group. Explain that although most folk music is composed, the writers in many instances are unknown. After listening to the recordings, discuss with the class the kind of social activities with which the music is associated. Have the class determine whether the music functions in ritualistic manner or whether it exists for the sake of entertainment.
2. Show the film *Discovering the Music of Africa* as an example of oral tradition. Point out that musicians are not reading music, for they have memorized both the music and the rhythms. Explain that songs are passed by word of mouth, while instrument playing is learned by observation and imitation. Indicate also that folk musicians are usually nonprofessionals, although in Africa, some highly trained percussionists were called "master drummers."
3. Have the class make a list of the instruments in the film.
4. Show the film a second time, and ask students to observe closely the rhythm patterns, As a followup exercise, have students replicate the rhythmic patterns that are illustrated in the concluding performance.

Resources:

Bruno Netti. *Folk and Traditional Music of the Western Continents.* Prentice-Hall History of Music Series. Englewood Cliffs, NJ: Prentice-Hall, 1965.

Film:

Discovering the Music of Africa. BFA Educational Media.

Recording:

"Negro Folk, Music of Africa and America." New York: Folkways Records, FE 4500.

Level: Advanced

Objectives:

To help the student understand the music of Mexican/Chicano Americans by learning that:

1. Mexican music has distinct characteristics.
2. Mexican/Chicano folk music is a combination of many ethnic musics.
3. Many folk songs have evolved through the process of oral transmission.

Teaching Strategy:

1. Introduce the song "Cielito Lindo," Mexican folk song 49 in *Singing America*. Play the melody; sing the melody.
2. Discuss some characteristics of Mexican music; (a) melody—narrow range; scales—major, minor, modal; patterns—predominance of sequential patterns; (b) rhythm and meter—predominance of triple patterns: 3/4, 6/8, and 9/8; and rapid alternation of meter; (c) harmony—predominance of parallel thirds and sixths and implied dominant-tonic harmony.
3. Identify "Cielito Lindo" as a form of *huapango,* derived from Spanish forms with some African influence. *Huapango* is the generic name for tunes played and danced at the *Bailes de Huapango,* a kind of popular festivity common mainly along the shores of the Gulf of Mexico. Fast and complicated steps danced to intricate cross-rhythms are characteristic of these dances, as well as the juxtaposition of 2/4, 3/4, and 6/8 meter. *Huapango* is performed by instrumental ensembles that range from duos of harp and guitar to a full mariachi band. (A mariachi is the typical band that entertains people in cafes and at village and country dances and celebrations.) [2]
4. Relate the characteristics of Mexican music with "Cielito Lindo" in the following way: (a) melody—the range of this

song is less than an octave; the scale used suggests modal patterns and major/minor relationships; and the melodic line follows sequential patterns; (b) rhythm and meter—it is in 3/4 meter (waltz) and has triple patterns with a feel of 4 plus 2 creating syncopation; (c) harmony—create a second part to the melody using intervals of thirds and sixths and harmonize the selection using basically tonic-dominant chords, i.e., B major, F major, and C minor.

5. Related Mexican/Chicano music to North American music such as western (cowboy) songs with the chorus "Ay, ay, ay, ay." Perform using string instruments, such as the guitar. There are other examples in Chicano music of developing idioms combining the styles of *Norteno* music. *Norteno* is generally translated "northern" (native of the north, especially of Spain).[3] It is also helpful to know the following characteristics of Mexican and Chicano music:

Characteristics of Mexican Music

- *Norteno band*—guitars, accordions, double basses, and other instruments. Instrumentalists accompany themselves while singing.

Characteristics of Chicano Music

- Continued use of traditional Mexican forms, styles, and techniques.
- Developing idiom combining style of *Norteno* music and United States popular music.[4]

6. Play the melody to "Cielito Lindo," as presented in the book *Favorite Spanish Folksongs* by Elena Paz, pp. 30–31. The *Final Report to the National Endowment for the Humanities,* Center for Ethnic Music, Howard University, calls it "a good example of the eternal process of change in folk music is demonstrated in the case of this internationally famous waltz which in the Uasteca region of Mexico underwent surgery on both its rhythm and melody."[5]
7. Compare the two versions, the first from the book *Singing America,* which represents the modern version, and the second from *Favorite Spanish Folksongs.* Note the differences in rhythm, melodic line, and words.
8. Listen to recordings and point our similar characteristics in other songs; also point out the importance of the instruments used in Mexican/Chicano music: characteristic use of varied guitars strings only, trumpet, and then wind instruments.

Resources:

Books:

Gilbert Chase. *The Music of Spain.* New York: W.W. Norton, 1941.

Elena Paz, comp. and ed. *Favorite Spanish Folksongs.* New York: Oak, 1965.

John Donald Robb. *Hispanic Folk Songs of New Mexico.* Albuquerque: University of New Mexico Press, 1954.

Frances Tour. *Treasury of Mexican Folkways,* New York: Crown, 1947.

Zanzig, Augustus D., ed. *Singing America,* Boston, C.C. Birchard, 1940.

Recordings:

"Mexican Folk Dances and Folk Songs of Latin America." Bowmar Records. "Spanish and Mexican Folk Music of New Mexico." Folkways Records, FE 4426.

"Folk Songs of Puerto Rico." Folkways Records, FE 4412.

Films:

Marimba Music of Mexico. 8 minutes; 16 mm; written commentary in English. Produced by Robert Garfias and Harold Schultz. Archive of Ethnic Music and Dance, University of Washington, University of Washington Press, Seattle, WA 98105. For hire or purchase.

Mexican-American Border Songs. 29 minutes; 16 mm; commentary in English. Indiana University Audio-Visual Center, Bloomington, IN 47401. For hire or purchase.

Mexican-American Culture: Its Heritage. 16 mm. Communications Group West, 6335 Homewood Avenue, Suite 204, Hollywood, CA 90028.

Generalization II: African-American folk music originated in slave quarters on southern plantations and has become a type of music that is broad in scope and includes several different types of songs.

Level: Primary

Objectives:

1. To help students understand how and where African-American folk music originated.
2. To develop a greater appreciation for the folk songs of African Americans.
3. To introduce the spiritual as one kind of African-American folk music.

Teaching Strategy:

1. Play the recording "Simplified Folk Songs," arranged and sung by Hap Palmer for the class. Encourage the students to sing with the record. Most of the songs included are those the class should be familiar with, e.g., "He's Got the Whole

World in His Hands," "Paw Paw Patch," "Michael, Row the Boat Ashore," and others. Review and discuss with the class the conditions under which African Americans came to this country. Talk about the environment of the slave quarters, how the slaves must have felt, and the kind of songs they made up, e.g., work songs, religious songs, and game songs.

2. Have the class sing the spiritual "I Got Shoes." Write the words on the board and analyze what the song is talking about. Ask the class if they think the song was actually saying that all of the slaves had shoes. Help them to understand that all of the slaves did not have shoes and it is quite possible that this spiritual is a plea for shoes and other necessities the slaves did not have. Continue the questions by asking the following:

   - When does the song say they would get all of the things they wanted?
   - Who will not go to heaven?
   - Is it possible that the slaves were thinking that the slave masters might not get to heaven?

3. Read the words to the song "Didn't My Lord Deliver Daniel." This spiritual and the others suggested for use in this lesson were selected from a work written and illustrated by Ashley Bryan, *Walk Together Children*. Ask the class to tell what the slaves were saying in this song. Lead them to conclude that the slaves were questioning why they had not been delivered from slavery.
4. Conclude this discussion by having the students sing or listen to the teacher sing "Free at Last." The class should have no difficulty identifying the message in this song.

Resources:

Ashley Bryan. *Walk Together Children* (African-American Spirituals). Hartford, CT: Atheneum, 1974.

Recording:
"Simplified Folk Songs." Educational Activities.

Level: Intermediate

Objectives:

1. To help students understand how African-American folk music began.
2. To convey something of the social traditions that influenced the development of specific types of songs.

Teaching Strategy:

1. Explore with students the various types of folksongs such as the work-song, dance song, play song, field and street cries, and spirituals. Point out that the slaves' plantation songs are named according to their function in the life of the slave. Indicate that the slaves were permitted to observe only a few rites—religious ceremonies, funerals, and some other activities in which the African tradition of using music to celebrate the occasion was followed.
2. Show the film *Black Music in America: From Then Till Now,* as an example of how folk music in the United States was influenced by the presence of African Americans. Assist students in making a list of the musicians who appear in the movie. Discuss the contribution of each musician to folk music in the United States.
3. Divide the class into small groups and have each group identify the characteristics of the music that is played in the film. Show the film a second time and have the groups respond through the use of a silent signal when the musician being studied appears.

Resources:

Gilbert Chase. *America's Music.* 2nd ed. rev. New York: McGraw-Hill, 1966.

Bennett Reimer, et al. *Silver Burdett Music.* Atlanta: Silver Burdett, 1978.

Eileen Southern. *The Music of Black Americans: A History.* New York: W.W. Norton, 1971.

Film:

Black Music in America: From Then Till Now. New York: Learning Corporation of America.

Level: Advanced

Objectives:

To help the student understand the music of African Americans by learning that:

1. African-American music has many unique characteristics.
2. African-American folk music is a combination of many ethnic musics.
3. Many folk songs have evolved through the process of oral transmission.

Teaching Strategy:

1. Discuss the story of slavery in the United States, especially on southern plantations. Point out that most of the slaves were brought to the United States from West Africa and that it was the merging of the culture of West Africa with Western culture that produced African-American music.
2. Discuss the many characteristics of African American folk music as expressed through gospel music, spirituals, and the blues: rhythms and syncopation; improvisation; repetition;

oral transmission of the idiom; group participation (call and response); physical response, i.e., handclapping, footpatting, and religious dancing and shouting; vocal techniques, i.e., varying pitch (bending, sliding, and false pitch); stretching and variation on melody on the part of the lead singer; and use of falsetto; percussive-style playing techniques; and musical dramatization.

3. Outline the Euro-American influence on African-American music as evidenced primarily in form, harmony (scales), text, and singing technique.
4. Introduce the diatonic and pentatonic scales. The diatonic scale is common to both Euro-American and African-American music, and the pentatonic scale is primarily associated with African-American music.
5. Play scales that will emphasize C, D, E, G, A, C, as related to gospel music and C, E, G, A, B, and C as related to blues.
6. Introduce the song "Amazing Grace, How Sweet the Sound," found in *The Baptist Standard Hymnal.*
7. Play and sing it as written.
8. Listen to Aretha Franklin sing "Amazing Grace," Atlantic Records 2-906 (1972), or other gospel versions.
9. Identify the gospel techniques employed by Aretha Franklin, as indicated in the list of characteristics of African American folk music.
10. Perform "Amazing Grace" utilizing some of these techniques.
11. Introduce the spiritual "Listen to the Lambs," from *Singing America.*
12. Perform and identify the characteristic elements of American music as listed.
13. Perform other versions, such as John Work's and Nathaniel Dett's arrangements, that illustrated the Euro-American influence.

Resources:

Harold Courlander. *Negro Folk Music, U.S.A.* New York: Columbia University Press, 1963.

Nathaniel Dett. *Listen to the Lambs: A Religious Characteristic in the Form of an Anthem.* New York: G. Schirmer, 1914.

A.M. Townsend, ed. *Baptist Standard Hymnal.* Nashville, TN: Sunday School Publishing Board, National Baptist Convention, 1961.

Pearl Williams-Jones. "Afro-American Gospel Music: A Crystallization of the Black Aesthetics." *Ethnomusicology* (September 1975).

———. *Gospel Music.* Washington, D.C.: Howard University, Project in African Music, 1970.

John W. Work. *Folk Songs of the American Negro.* New York: Negro Universities Press, 1915, 1969.

———, ed. *American Negro Songs and Spirituals.* New York: Bonanza Books, 1940.

Augustus D. Zanzig, ed. *Singing America.* Boston: C.C. Birchard & Co., 1940.

Generalization III: The cultural heritage, beliefs, values, and lifestyles of a group are reflected in its folk music.

Level: Primary

Objectives:

1. To aid the students in seeing the relationship between the music of a people and the way they live.
2. To develop a greater appreciation for the folk music of the Native American.

Teaching Strategy:

1. Review with the class some general characteristics about Native Americans. Some of the following facts should be highlighted:

   - Native Americans were the first people to live in the United States.
   - There are many different tribes of Native Americans and therefore many different religions.
   - Each tribe differs from another in lifestyle; however, there are similarities.
   - The way a particular tribe lived many years ago was influenced by its geographical region.
   - Most Native Americans believed that some spirit power could be gained through ceremonies and other power through special people.
   - Music and dancing are a part of most ceremonies.

2. Have the students suggest reasons for Native Americans to have celebrations. Discuss the kinds of music that might be appropriate for certain types of ceremonies, such as fast or slow rhythms and loud or soft sounds.
3. Play the recording of "Butterfly Dance" from the album "Music of American Indians." After the first listening, explain that the music is from the Hopi, one of the Pueblo groups that live in the northeastern part of Arizona. Locate the area where the group lives on a large map. Explain that corn was important in the lives of the Native American and the process of grinding corn usually called for a ceremony. The "Butterfly Dance" was used in some corn-grinding ceremonies.
4. Play the recording a second time and discuss the kinds of movement that might go with the music and the grinding of corn.
5. Divide the class into three or four groups. Have each group make up a short dance to go to the music, keeping in mind

that the movements must have something to do with grinding corn.

6. If time permits, play one or two additional songs and have the students do the dance movements as suggested by the record.

Resources:

Recordings:
"Indian Music of the Pacific Northwest Coast." Folkways FE 4523.
"Indian Music of the Southwest." Folkways 8850.
"Music of Americans Indians." Radio Corporation of America.
"Music of the Sioux and the Navajo." Folkways FE 4401.
"Songs and Dances of the Flathead Indians." Folkways FE 4445.

Level: Intermediate

Objectives:

1. To help students understand the values reflected in folk music.
2. To convey the manner in which folk music is sung for various occasions.

Teaching Strategy:

1. Explore with students the various kinds of beliefs that are held by groups of people. Some examples are belief in a supreme being, belief in the sanctity of the family, belief in the good of the country, and belief in the soundness of the government.
2. Sing the song "Rocka My Soul," a spiritual, as an example of how one cultural value is reflected in the music. Explain that

the spiritual is sung with considerable emotion, and that this practice has been passed along from generation to generation unchanged.

3. Have the students look up folk songs of other countries to see if they can identify possible values and beliefs that are being transmitted through song.

Resources:

Sally Monsour and Margaret Perry. *A Junior High School Music Handbook.* Englewood Cliffs, N.J.: Prentice-Hall, 1970.

Barbara Reeder and James A. Standifer. *Sourcebook of African and Afro-American Materials for Music Education.* Washington, D.C.: Music Educators National Conference, 1972.

Level: Advanced

Objectives:

To help the student understand how the cultural heritage beliefs, values, and lifestyles of Mexican/Chicano and African Americans are reflected in their folk music by studying:

1. The history of the cultures.
2. The cultural and historical background that produced the music:
   a. Mexican/Chicano music.
   b. African-American music.

Teaching Strategy:

1. Discuss the history of Mexican/Chicano Americans as reflected in their folk music.
   a. The Spaniards/conquistadors upon arrival in Mexico discovered a highly developed system of Native American

music complete with sophisticated instruments, dance techniques, and so forth.

b. The Indians quickly adopted the music of the Europeans introduced by the Spaniards and learned western notation and employed European instruments which they themselves fashioned.

c. By the sixteenth century, Mexico, through the merging of the two cultures, was able to boast its own school of composition.

d. A blend of the musical languages of the Indian tradition and the Spanish idiom was the basis for the popular Mexican dances of today, e.g., *corrido,* a folk ballad that grew out of the Spanish romance; *jarabe,* a Mexican air that originated in the eighteen century; and *juapango,* a traditional Mexican musical form derived from Spanish forms with some African influence.

e. This is also the traditional music of the Chicanos, which in turn has been influenced by such Anglo genres as cowboy songs and popular music.

f. Indian influence on present Mexican music includes singing and dancing, and the use of drums, flutes, rattles, and scrapers.

g. Spanish influence on present Mexican music includes an emphasis on stringed instruments and the adoption of such Spanish genres as romances and *villancicos.*

2. Listen to recordings depicting Indian influence in Mexican music. Find some examples of this influence in the following selections: "Music of the Tarascan Indians of Mexico," "Modern Mayan Indian Music of Mexico," "Indian Music of Mexico (Yurchenco)," "Indian Music of Mexico," "*Corridos Canta al Hurricane.*" Follow the listening portion of the lesson by identifying elements of music that are characteristically Spanish or Indian. Ask the following questions:

a. Can the elements related to each group (Spanish and Indian) be clearly identified?
b. Which elements seem to be prominent in each of the examples? List the elements as Spanish or Indian.

3. Discuss the history of African Americans as reflected in their folk music.
   a. Music from the West Coast of Africa;
      (1) percussive instruments (polyrhythmic and polymetric techniques)
      (2) worksongs (rhythmic punctuation)
   b. Music from the United States:
      (1) spirituals
      (2) gospel
      (3) jazz

   Refer to Generalization II for characteristics of African-American music.
4. Listen to recordings illustrating the different types of American music. American folk music:
   a. "Palm Fruit Cutters' Songs," a work song from *The Topoke People of the Congo*
   b. "African Songs and Rhythms for Children," recorded and annotated by Dr. W. K. Amoaku
   c. "Music of the Western Congo"
5. Sing several songs of African-American heritage and examine the text for the message: spiritual inspiration—"My Lord, What a Mornin"; triumph—"Joshua Fit de Battle"; salvation—"Lord, I Want to be a Christian"; work—"Cotton Needs Pickin" (selections taken from *Singing America*).
6. Add drum accompaniment to "Joshua Fit de Battle," depicting African rhythms heard on recordings. Drum accompaniment to "Joshua Fit de Battle" provides the teacher and students with a contrasting activity to singing, provides an opportunity for creativity, and emphasizes the dominant rhythmic influence associated with music of African heritage.

Resources:

Laura Boulton. *The Music Hunter.* New York: Doubleday, 1969.

Vada E. Butcher, ed. "Materials for General Courses in the Music of Hispanic Citizens," *Final Report to the Endowment for the Humanities,* vol. 2, Washington, D.C.: Howard University, 1977.

Zanzig, Augustus D., ed. *Singing America.* Boston: C.C. Birchard, 1940.

Recordings:

"African Songs and Rhythms for Children." Folkways FC 7844 FE 4377.

"Indian Music of Mexico." Folkways FW 8851.

"Corridos Canta al Hurricane." Hurricane HF 10012.

"Modern Mayan Indian Music of Mexico." Folkways Asch AHM 4271.

"Music of Western Congo." Folkways FE 4417.

"The Topoke People of the Congo." Folkways FE 4477.

Jazz

Suggested Content Outline

I. History of Jazz
   - A. Early Beginnings
   - B. Its Development

II. Development of Jazz
   - A. Golden Age—1920
   - B. "Swing Era"—1930
   - C. Bop and Cool Jazz—1940
   - D. Popular Period—1950
   - E. New Directions—1960
   - F. America's Music—1970

III. International Contributions

Generalizations:

I. Jazz began as a simple form of folk music and is often considered one of the few art forms to originate in the United States.

II. Much of early jazz began in the South but soon spread throughout the nation and became an accepted form of music.

III. Jazz today represents the contributions of people from many different cultures in the United States and in the world.

Generalization I: Jazz began as a simple form of folk music and is often considered one of the few art forms to originate in the United States.

Level: Primary

Objectives:

1. To help students understand that early jazz was made up as it was being played and was usually played in a strict tempo of two or four beats to the bar.
2. To reinforce the concept of bar (measure).
3. To help students develop an appreciation of jazz as a form of folk music that began in the United States.

Teaching Strategy:

1. Play for the class portions of two or three jazz selections from recordings that represent dixieland-style music and contemporary jazz. (See references for suggested recordings.) As the music is being played, ask the class to tap or clap the beat. Help them discover that it is easier to identify the beat in dixieland jazz that it is in the jazz that is generally played

today. Point out to the class that early jazz was played in a tempo of two or four beats to the bar.

2. Review with the class what a bar is by putting simple examples on the board and have them either tap or clap the rhythm, one bar at a time.
3. Ask for volunteers to create patterns of rhythm using one bar at a time. Repeat this often enough until the class has an understanding of what two beats and four beats to a measure looks like in musical notation and how it feels through the tapping and/or clapping.
4. Help the class to understand that, just as they made up patterns to clap, early jazz musicians did the same thing; only they did not write it down, they just played. Stress the fact that the musicians played and created the sounds that they liked. Lead the students to understand that music created in this manner is often called folk music and that jazz began in the United States. Students should be made aware that when jazz was created, it was perhaps played more in the New Orleans area than in other places. It should also be pointed out that most jazz musicians then were African American and music reflected their culture.
5. Divide the class into groups of five or six. Tell them that each group is a jazz group and have them make up a name for the group. Encourage each member of the group to make up two or three bars of music using two or four beats to the bar. Using a variety of rhythm instruments, have each jazz group play the rhythm patterns together for the class to enjoy.

Resources:

Recordings:

"The Louis Armstrong Story." vols. 1, 2, 3, 4, Columbia LC-851, CI-853, CI-854.

"Dixieland." New Orleans Mainstream 56003.

"Pee Wee Russell: A Legend." Mainstream 56026.

"Portrait of Pee Wee." Counterpoint CPST 562 (Stereo).
"The Red Nichols Story." Brunswick BL-54008, BL-54047.

Level: Intermediate

Objectives:

To help students understand:

1. The roots of jazz.
2. The cultural significance of jazz.
3. Jazz as an art form.

Teaching Strategy:

1. Explore with students the kinds of music that preceded the emergence of jazz. For example, students will need to know that ragtime was associated with the piano. Point out that rag music is characterized by the maintenance of a steady beat with the left hand, while the right hand carries a syncopated melody. Illustrate by playing a recording by Scott Joplin.
2. Discuss with the class a second type of music that preceded jazz—the blues. Explain that the blues is music designed to be sung, and that blues represent a continuation of the slave work songs, field hollers, and sorry songs. Play a recording in which this early folk secular music is illustrated.
3. Divide the class into small groups for the purpose of having each group identify the characteristics of ragtime and the characteristics of blues.

Resources:

LeRoi Jones. *Blues People.* New York: William Morrow, 1968.
Charles Keil. *Urban Blues.* Chicago: University of Chicago Press, 1968.

Recordings:
"Golden Age of Ragtime." Riverside 12-110.
"History of Jazz." The New York Scene, Folkwas 2823.
"Piano Rags by Scott Joplin." Nonesuch H-71248.
"Roots of the Blues." Atlantic 1348.

Level: Advanced

Objectives:

1. To help students understand that jazz roots are in Africa.
2. To convey that jazz was born as a result of the merging of the African- and Euro-American cultures.

Teaching Strategy:

1. Discuss the background of jazz in the United States. Illustrate, using recordings from previous lessons on Africa and African-American music, the elements of jazz found in African music, especially the music of West Africa. This is music with very complex rhythms (syncopation, polyrhythms, polymeters) and with highly developed use of drums. The music represents a tradition of group improvisation performed by a master drummer or chorus leader leading a group of drummers, singers, and/or dancers.
2. Point out that many features of West African music are preserved in African-American folk music: work songs, field hollers, spirituals, ring shouts, singing sermons, and eventually, as societal changes were made, blues, rag, and jazz.
3. Introduce the blues as an early form of jazz, music depicting the daily living of a group of people primarily in the southern part of the United States. Early blues were normally sung, sometimes accompanied by banjo or guitar.

4. Review "Listening to Jazz," Part IV, a filmstrip and record by Billy Taylor, and learn about the development of the blues, the influence of the blues style and blues feeling on jazz, and the structure of the twelve-bar blues. The standardization of the blues was the beginning of creating an art form unique to the United States.
5. Play on the piano blues chords in the key of C structured into three phrases:

<table>
<tr><td>slow tempo</td><td></td><td>beats</td><td>1 2 3 4</td><td>1 2 3 4</td><td>1 2 3 4</td><td>1 2 3 4</td></tr>
<tr><td>1st</td><td>$\frac{4}{4}$</td><td>chords</td><td>C | | |</td><td>F | | |</td><td>C | | |</td><td>C^7 | | |</td></tr>
<tr><td>2nd</td><td></td><td></td><td>F | | |</td><td>F^7 | | |</td><td>C | | |</td><td>C | | |</td></tr>
<tr><td>3rd</td><td></td><td></td><td>G^7 | | |</td><td>F^7 | | |</td><td>C | | |</td><td>C | | | ||</td></tr>
</table>

Each chorus in the traditional blues setting is twelve bars long and fashions the pattern of chords similarly to the above.

6. Chant, in syncopated rhythms as needed, the following words to the above chord pattern fitting the word(s) to the beat(s).
7. Create a melody to fit the rhythm of the chant and chord patterns.
8. Sing variations on the newly created melody by changing the rhythm and pitches; refer back to the blues recordings.

Resources:

Leonard Feather. *The Encyclopedia of Jazz.* New York: Horizon, 1960.

———. *The Book of Jazz.* New York: Bonanza, 1957.

Richard Hadlock. *Jazz Masters of the Twenties.* New York: MacMillan, 1965.

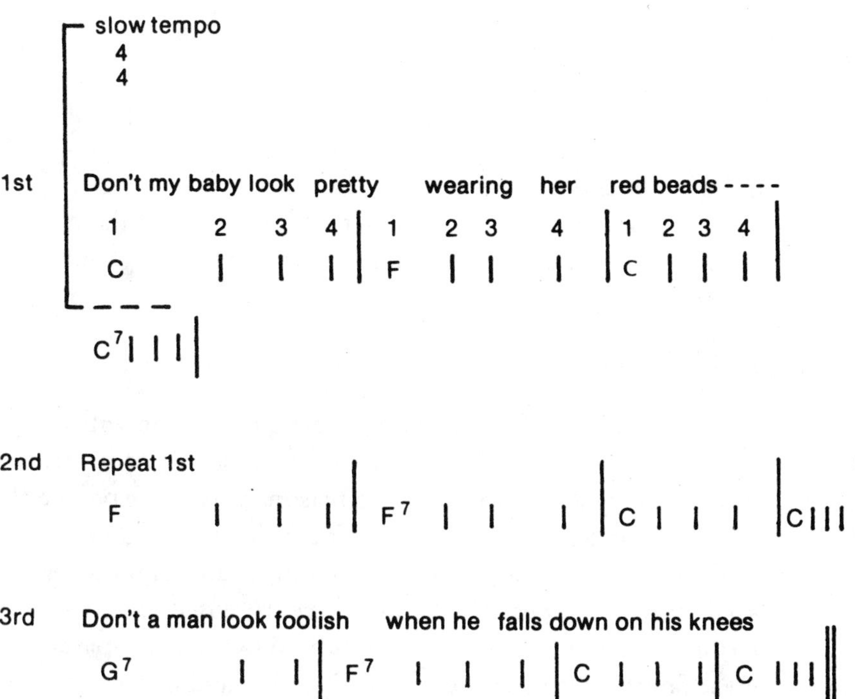

Recordings:
"The Bessie Smith Story," vol. 3. Columbia CL-857.
"The Encyclopedia of Jazz on Record," vol. 2. Decca DL 8399.
"Guide to Jazz." RCA Victor LPM-1393.
"Listening to Jazz." Sound filmstrip set, records with teacher's notes by Billy Taylor. Pleasantville, N.Y.: Educational Audio Visuals, 1971.

Generalization II: Much of early jazz began in the South but soon spread throughout the nation and became an accepted form of music.

Level: Primary

Objectives:

1. To help students understand that jazz had its beginnings in the South because the people who developed it lived there.
2. To help students develop an appreciation for the songs and music of the slaves.

Teaching Strategy:

1. Using a map of the United States, begin a discussion with the class about the kinds of people who live in the different parts of the country and have them give reasons why some people live in certain geographic regions. Focus the discussion on the South and have the class talk about how different the way of life may be for people who live there from that of people in other places. For example, people who live in some parts of the South have little need for warm coats and boots. People in the southern states have access to different kinds of foods for longer periods of time than those who live in cold climates. Discuss the kinds of things that grow in the South, including cotton. Help the students to see the relationship between the cotton industry and the fact that large numbers of African Americans live in the South. Talk about how African Americans were brought to this country from West Africa. Help the students identify those aspects of West African culture that the slaves could bring with them. Guide the discussion so the list will include language, songs, music, and rhythm.
2. Explain how the music and rhythm that the slaves brought with them to this country influenced the kinds of music the slaves developed in this country. Have the students suggest the kinds of situations the slaves might have made up songs for—e.g., songs to work by, songs for play, and religious songs.

3. Play selections from the album, "Songs of the American Negro Slaves." The album includes an excellent historical review of the music of slaves by John Hope Franklin. After the students listen to such selections as "I Stood on the River," "My Lawd's Getting Us Ready" and "Before the Sun Goes Down," have them analyze the lyrics for the meaning of the song.

Resources:

"American Negro Folk, and Work Song Rhythms." Follett FA 7654.
"Songs of the American Negro Slaves." Folkways FH 5252.

Level: Intermediate

Objectives:

1. To help students understand how early jazz functioned in the United States.
2. To show how people in the United States became aware of jazz.

Teaching Strategy:

1. Explore with students music that is associated with dance. Explain to the class, for example, that African music was very closely allied with dance and poetry. Discuss dance types such as the waltz, jitterbug, the soft shoe, the twist, meringue, and ballet. Point out that all dance forms coexist with music.
2. Play a Folkways Library recording of jazz during the 1920s. Indicate that, as far back as the 1900s, African-American syncopated dance orchestras were organizing in cities for the purpose of providing music for white and African-American social-group activities. Point out the unusual makeup of the

orchestras. For example, musicians played banjos, mandolins, saxophones, drums, violins, string basses, and a few brasses.

3. Divide the class into small groups for the purpose of having each group prepare a mock dance. Let each group decide where the dance will be held, the theme or occasion for the dance, the kinds of dancing that will take place, and the orchestra type to be engaged for the dance. After each dance presentation, allow time for members of other groups to comment on the performance.

Resources:

Edith Borroff and Marjory Irvin. *Music in Perspective.* New York: Harcourt Brace Jovanovich, 1976.

Allain Locke. *The Negro and His Music—Negro Art: Past and Present.* New York: Arno/The New York Times, 1969.

Eileen Southern. *The Music of Black Americans: A History. New York*: W.W. Norton, 1971.

James A. Standifer and Barbara Reeder. *Source Book of African and Afro-American Materials for Music Educators.* Washington, D.C.: Music Educators National Conference, 1972.

Recordings:

Folkways Library of Recordings, 1972.

"The Smithsonian Collection of Classic Jazz." Smithsonian Institution, 1973.

Level: Advanced

Objectives:

1. To help students understand how jazz was first received by the United States general population.
2. To show how one group's folk music became a part of the daily lives of the general populace.

Teaching Strategy:

1. Present to the students a chronological and geographical outline of the growth and development of jazz in the United States. The blues had developed throughout the Southland as a part of African-American folk music, along with work songs and spirituals. With the societal changes in the United States during the late 1800s and into the 1900s, African Americans' need for social mobility gave rise to the extension and development of a new kind of music, jazz. The elements of jazz as we understand them, were already present in African-American folk music, and these elements were extended and developed.
2. The hub of this development was New Orleans. The new music, jazz, was first considered "black folk music." This popular trend in music in the United States was developing in many forms. Around the 1890s, Scott Joplin was writing and performing music called ragtime. Like most folk music, the blues were being performed with an improvisational style, combining the melodic compositional emphasis of ragtime and the improvisational variational emphasis of blues. This became the basis for Jelly Roll Morton's principle of thematic variations, a style that became very popular during the 1920s. Jelly Roll Morton was considered the first great master of giving form to jazz music. Between ragtime and the rise of New Orleans jazz, the blues gained added respectability with the publication of W. C. Handy's "St. Louis Blues" and "Beale Street Blues." Southern musicians, who were accustomed to playing to African-American audiences in the South, traveled north up the Mississippi River to places like Chicago and east to New York, spreading the sound of this new music. Later, this music would be called jazz. During this period of the 1920s Euro-Americans became interested in this music and produced musicians who made outstanding contributions to the widespread growth of jazz in the late 1920s and 1930s.

3. Arrange listening sessions centered around recordings of the early periods in jazz.

   Examples:

1900s–1920s:	King Oliver, Louis Armstrong, Bunk Johnson, Bessie Smith, and Jelly Roll Morton
1920s–1930s:	Kid Ory, Duke Ellington, Benny Goodman, Glenn Miller, and Jimmy Lunceford

   Help students to identify:

   - syncopated rhythms, e.g. short/long, accented, unaccented
   - chord patterns, e.g., same/different, major, minor, dominant
   - styles, e.g., swing, dixie, blues, pop
   - form, e.g., AB, ABA, AABA, blues (12 bars)

Resources:

Benny Green. *The Reluctant Art.* New York: Horizon, 1963.
Andre Hodeir. *Jazz: Its Evolution and Essence.* New York: Grove, 1956.
Nat Shapiro and Nat Hentoff. *Hear Me Talkin' to Ya.* New York: Dover, 1955.
Recordings:
"The Bix Beiderbecke Story," vols. 1, 2, 3. Columbia CL-844, CL-845.
"Great Jazz Pianists" (one track). Camden 328.
"Guide to Jazz (one track). RCA Victor LPM-1393.
"Jazz Odyssey: The Sound of Chicago." Columbia C3L-32.
"Jazz Odyssey: The Sound of New Orleans." Columbia C3L-30.
"Young Louis Armstrong." Riverside 12-101.

Generalization III: Jazz today represents the contributions of people from many different cultures in the United States and in the world.

Level: Primary

Objectives:

1. To introduce the students to the life and music of a famous African-American musician, Duke Ellington.
2. To help the students understand the concept of an ambassador.

Teaching Strategy:

1. Select any recording by Duke Ellington and have the students listen to his music for five or ten minutes. Ask the students if they know anything about Duke Ellington. List the information on the chalkboard. If the students do not, tell them he was known as an ambassador of music. Add this to the list.
2. Discuss with the students the concept and meaning of "ambassador." Inform the students that President Kennedy sent Duke Ellington abroad as an ambassador of music in 1963.
3. Read to the class the book *Duke Ellington: Ambassador of Music* by Pamela Barclay. Follow up the reading of the story of Duke Ellington's life by asking the class to retell the story by recalling as much information as they can about his life.
4. One of the first pieces of music written by Duke Ellington in 1920 was "Soda Fountain Rag." Discuss the kind of music that is implied in the title. Tell the class to imagine that they

have been asked to design a record cover for this recording. Have the designs done on paper cut the size of a 1920s 78-rpm record album.

5. Once the designs are completed, display them on a bulletin board that has as its caption the title of the book.

Resources:

Pamela Barclay. *Duke Ellington: Ambassador of Music.* Mankato, MN: Creative Education.
Recordings:
"The Best of Duke Ellington." Capitol Records N-16172.
"Duke Ellington Rockin' in Rhythm," vol. 3. MCA Records MCA-2077 (formerly OC7-9247).
"Ellington '55." Capitol Records SM-11674.

Level: Intermediate

Objectives:

1. To help students understand how jazz styles have been shaped.
2. To convey how jazz has become music of the world.

Teaching Strategy:

1. Discuss with students the various styles of jazz; e.g., traditional, swing, bebop, cool, and modern. Explain to students that the styles were influenced by migratory social and economic conditions that prevailed in the South and in the North during each succeeding decade.
2. Play recordings in which the various jazz styles are demonstrated. Have students list characteristics of each style

that are evident in the performance. Discuss with the class the concept of collective improvisation.

3. Divide the class into groups and have each group list the cultures that have contributed to the growth of jazz. Discuss the contributions in terms of emphasis on elements of music such as melody, harmony, rhythm, instrumentation, and texture.
4. Discuss with the class reasons why jazz has become so well received in various parts of the world.

Resources:

Alan P. Merriam and R. Benford. *A Bibliography of Jazz.* Philadelphia: The American Folklore Society, 1954.
Robert Reisner. *The Literature of Jazz: A Selective Bibliography.* San Diego: San Diego State College Library, 1970.
Recording:
"The Smithsonian Collection of Classic Jazz." Smithsonian Institution, 1973.

Level: Advanced

Objectives:

1. To help students understand that jazz has become a multicultural expression in the United States.
2. To convey that jazz has become a universal language.

Teaching Strategy:

1. Discuss the extent to which jazz has developed in the United States and demonstrate through recordings and harmonic and form analysis (visual aids) how today's jazz differs from

that of the early periods. Jazz is basically an improvisational art form. Musicians representing New Orleans jazz, dixieland, swing, bebop, cool jazz, and rock have developed throughout the years a highly technical approach to the art of jazz. It is no longer possible to identify jazz musicians with any single ethnic group. Nor is it possible to single out any one group as the chief consumer or the chief producer of jazz. The techniques used in modern jazz improvisation today are as highly developed as those found in any other art form.

2. Arrange listening sessions. Identify jazz elements in the "New World Symphony" by Antonin Dvorak, "Rhapsody in Blue" by George Gershwin, and selected pieces by Leonard Bernstein and others. Listen to jazz music of Japanese pianist/composer/arranger Toshiko Akiyoshi. Compare the music of the 1920s, 1930s, 1940s, 1950s, and 1960s/1970s as represented by the following:

   1920s—Jelly Roll Morton, Louis Armstrong, and Bessie Smith
   1930s—Duke Ellington, Dorsey Brothers, Count Basie, Benny Goodman, and Glenn Miller
   1940s—Charlie Parker, Dizzy Gillespie, and Billie Holiday
   1950s—Miles Davis, Art Blakey, and Billy Taylor
   1960s/1970s—John Coltrane

3. After the listening session, engage the students in the following activities:
   - List the jazz elements found in the music of Dvorak, Gershwin, and Bernstein.
   - Discuss why this music is not considered jazz.
   - Discuss the differences found in each jazz period, 1920–1970.

   (Look for changes in harmony, rhythm, instrumentation, and style.)

Resources:

Ralph De Toledando, ed. *Frontiers of Jazz.* New York: Durrell, 1947.

Benny Goodman and Irving Kolodin. *The Kingdom of Swing.* Harrisburg, PA: Stackpole, 1939.

Nat Shapiro and Nat Hentoff, eds. *The Jazz Makers.* New York: Grove, 1958.

Martin Williams, ed. *The Macmillan Jazz Masters Series: Jazz Masters of the Twenties, Jazz Masters of the Thirties, Jazz Masters of the Forties, Jazz Masters of the Fifties, Jazz Masters in Transition 1957–69, Jazz Masters of New Orleans.* New York: Colliers.

Recordings:

"The Be-Bop Era" (two tracks). RCA Victor LPV 519.

"Charlie Parker Memorial," vols. 1, 2. Savoy 12000, 12009.

"The Indispensable Duke Ellington." RCA Victor LPM 6009.

"Jazz," vol. 7. Folkways FP 67.

"Lang and Venuti: Stringin' the Blues." Columbia C2L-24.

"Tales of a Courtesan," Toshiko Akiyoshi/Lew Tabackin Big Band. RCA JPL 1-0723.

"Thesaurus of Classic Jazz." Columbia C4L-18.

Notes

1. Robert L. Garrison. *Music in Childhood Education.* New York: Appleton-Century Crofts, 1966.
2. Wili Apel, ed., Harvard Dictionary of Music, 2nd ed., Cambridge, MA: Belknap Press of Harvard University Press, 1977.
3. Cassell's Spanish-English Dictionary. New York: Macmillan, 1978.
4. Vada E. Butcher, Final *Report to the National Endowment for the Humanities.* (Washington, D.C.: Howard University, August 1977), Grant No. ES 5962-72-76, vol. 2, p. 1.
5. Ibid., p. 20.

11
Generalizations and Teaching Strategies for Science

Introduction

It is generally assumed that language arts and social studies are the most logical areas through which the teaching of multicultural concepts can occur. The nature of these two subject areas perhaps does allow for more integration of relevant content. However, science, particularly natural science, provides an excellent opportunity for helping students to think more logically about why things are the way they are. Through science education, students can begin to think objectively about differences of all kinds and learn how to analyze and evaluate myths and stereotypes from an intelligent perspective. This does not mean that the physical sciences, such as physics and chemistry, are not to be involved. Quite to the contrary. Logic and reasoning are enhanced through the physical sciences and they can provide the scientific explanations for certain natural phenomena. Too, this may be an area through which the involvement and contributions of scientists from different ethnic and cultural backgrounds can be introduced. The possibilities are endless for helping students understand the world in which they live. Young children can begin to understand differences through simple scientific investigations as early as preschool and kindergarten. The earlier children learn to accept and understand differences of all kinds, the easier it will be for them to accept and understand differences that exist among and between groups of people later in life.

In addition to the role that science can play in helping to improve relationships between people, it can help to be sensitive to the needs and concerns of all people as decisions and changes are made to resolve problems confronting our very fast-developing, complex society. The involvement of science education in the process of establishing a multicultural curriculum is essential.

The two units presented in this chapter are a study of the human body and food. Through a unit of study on the human body, much can be learned about racial and cultural differences. Also integrated into the unit on the human body is a focus on differences caused by physical disabilities. A study of food, its value to the body, where it comes from, how it is processed, who is involved in this process, and the relationship of food to culture can contribute also to a broader appreciation for diversity.

The Human Body

Suggested Content Outline

I. Structure of the Body
   A. Racial Differences
   B. Similarities
   C. Physical Disabilities

II. Skin
   A. Differences in Color
   B. Similarities in Composition

III. Hair
   A. Differences in Texture
   B. Common Characteristics

Generalizations:

I. The structure of the body may differ, depending on the racial group to which one belongs.
II. Racial characteristics affect skin color and hair texture.
III. The structure of the body may differ because of a physical disability.

Generalization I: The structure of the body may differ, depending on the racial group to which one belongs.

Level: Primary

Objectives:

To help students understand that:

1. All people belong to the same species, called Homo sapiens.
2. Homo sapiens have many physical characteristics that are similar.
3. Some differences in the physical structures of people are due to the racial groups to which they belong.

Teaching Strategy:

1. Assemble a stack of old magazines and introduce this lesson by having students look through the magazines and cut out pictures of people.
2. Once the pictures have been cut out, have students describe the physical appearances of the individuals in the pictures. Classify the differences by listing those characteristics people are born with as physical and others as acquired.
3. Introduce the term "Homo sapiens." Have one or two students look the term up in the dictionary and/or encyclopedia and share the meaning with the class. Help the class to conclude that all people belong to the same species.

4. Once the students have grasped the concept of Homo sapiens, have the students make a listing of all the characteristics they can think of which Homo sapiens have in common.
5. Help students, through continued discussion, understand that the similarities in physical characteristics cause human beings to be grouped into the same species.
6. Guide the class into a discussion as to how people might be further subdivided into groups. Approach a discussion about race and/or racial characteristics by informing the students of the following:

   - Scientists, at one time, divided people into three major groups by color—"white," "black," and "yellow." These groups were called races and given the scientific names of Caucasoid, Negroid, and Mongoloid, respectively.
   - Through the years, scientists have changed the way they classify people. Natural selection, mutations, genetic shift, and race mixture make three groupings inadequate. (This discussion should be handled with great care and the causes discussed in terminology that will help the students understand some of the reasons for the differences in people. Background material may be readily obtained from the *World Book Encyclopedia* under the discussion of "Races of Man.")
   - Inform the students that there are several different ways to group people and that *one* of the ways that scientists do this today is to group according to regions of origin. Such a classification system would include groups like Africans, American Indians, Asians, Australians, and so on.

7. Conclude the lesson by having the students assemble a collage of the pictures they have cut from magazines, entitled "Peoples of the World."

Resources:

"Races of Man." *World Book Encyclopedia.* 1976, vol. 16.

Level: Intermediate

Objectives:

1. To introduce one method of classifying human beings.
2. To help students understand that all people belong to the same species, called Homo sapiens.

Teaching Strategy:

1. Using a large map of the world, begin the discussion by reviewing the names of the continents and locating them on the map. Proceed by asking the class about the kinds of people who live on the various continents. Guide the discussion so the class will discuss the physical characteristics of the people who live in different parts of the world.
2. Have students volunteer to work with a group to explore the kinds of people who live on a specific continent. Once students have formed groups, review with them all the possible resources available in the library that will aid them in their explorations. Encourage the students to develop a list of the kinds of people they discover are living on the continent they are studying. Have them develop a list of the physical characteristics. This lesson will require a block of time to complete the research.
3. Once the research is completed and the lists are developed, have each group report their findings to the class. Summarize by making two major lists: one a list of general differences in physical characteristics and one of similarities.

4. Introduce the term Homo sapiens and discuss the meaning. Give the Latin translation which is "man" and "wise." Help the students to understand that while people differ physically one from another, they have many similar characteristics because all people are from the same species and the term Homo sapiens is used to denote the classification. Refer to the class list of similar characteristics and identify those characteristics that could be thought of as being unique to Homo sapiens.
5. Conclude this lesson by guiding the students to discover that classifying people by the regions where they live is one way scientists group people.

Resources:

Generally the resources available in a school library will provide what is needed for this lesson.

Level: Advanced

Objectives:

To help students understand:

1. The similarities and differences in body structure that exist among various racial groups.
2. The interaction of geographic environment and heredity in bringing about racial differences in body structure.

Teaching Strategy:

1. Using a commercially prepared set of pictures showing diverse groups of people or pictures the teacher has collected from magazines and other sources, begin a discussion on the

differences that exist between people. Or do this by having the students in the class identify at least one way in which they differ from each other and from the teacher.

2. Continue the discussion by identifying those characteristics that all people have in common. Review with students the term "Homo sapiens," the genus and species classification of all humans.
3. Discuss with the class as many different reasons as possible that people differ from each other. Focus on those differences that could be explained by geographic conditions (environment) and heredity (genetics). Classify differences according to these categories, where possible, and discuss areas of overlap.
4. Following the discussion on differences, focus on two or three ways people differ as a result of heredity, i.e., hair texture, skin, or eye color. Divide the class into groups according to their interest in learning more about how the difference is explained (either by heredity or genetics). Instruct the class that the assignment for each group is to complete an appropriate amount of research that will give them the information needed to present a documentary on each one of the causes. Help the groups organize their findings so they can prepare to share them with the class by presenting a mock television documentary. If possible, have the presentations put on videotape and shown to the class and to other classes as well. If videotape equipment is not available, the same information could be presented live and in the style of a documentary.

Resources:

Isaac Asimov and William C. Boyd. *Races and People.* New York: Harper and Row, 1955.

John Fried. *The Mystery of Heredity.* New York: John Ray, 1971.

E. Mayr. *Populations, Species, and Evolution.* Cambridge: Belknap Press of Harvard University Press, 1970.
Ruth Moore and the Editors of *Life. Life Nature Library: Evolution.* New York: Time, 1962.

Generalization II: Racial characteristics affect skin color and hair texture.

Level: Primary

Objectives:

1. To help students understand that one of the differences between racial groups is skin color.
2. To convey the causes of the differences in skin color.

Teaching Strategy:

1. Review with the class some of the physical characteristics that are apparent in the collage made earlier by the class or, if this activity was not completed, use pictures the students can obtain from magazines. Guide the discussion so that there is a focus on skin color.
2. Read to the class *Red Man, White Man, African Chief* by Marguerite Rush Lerner. This story of skin color, written by a physician, gives a simple but scientific explanation of the differences in color among some living things and introduces the concept of "cells" and "melanin."
3. To aid children in the understanding of cells, draw pictures of cells on the board and set up a microscope with several prepared slides so that the students will be able to observe cells from first-hand experience.

4. Discuss thoroughly the importance of "melanin" and "melanocyte" cells. Include in the discussion the color of hair, freckles, moles, and spots found on some animals.
5. Have the class develop a list of sentences or several paragraphs that will summarize their findings.

Resources:

Marguerite Lerner. *Red Man, White Man, African Chief.* Minneapolis, MN: Lerner, 1972.

Level: Intermediate

Objectives:

1. To review, expand, or introduce the concept of geographical classification of people.
2. To reinforce the fact that skin color and hair texture are influenced by racial identification.
3. To introduce students to the kind of work anthropologists do.

Teaching Strategy:

1. If the class has had a previous introduction to the geographical approach to classifying people, this lesson can build on that. If this is an introduction, the teacher will need to provide an experience that will have students thinking about the different kinds of people who live on the various continents.
2. Discuss the reasons why earlier ways of grouping people (the three-race approach) are not valid. If the students are not familiar with the terminology used in this classification system—Caucasoid, Mongoloid, and Negroid—introduce the terms and explain their meanings. Have the class suggest reasons why this approach is not valid.

3. Read to the class *Why People Are Different Colors* by Julian Mays and focus on the section that discusses the kind of work done by anthropologists. Help students grasp the concept that scientists who study the way people live and behave (culture) are called anthropologists.
4. Draw on information presented in the book and the fact that another more recent method used by some anthropologists to group people is to do this through the classification of people by their geographic locations. One such system includes the following nine groups: African, American Indian, Asian, Australian, European, Indian, Melanesian, Micronesian, and Polynesian.
5. In order to encourage the class to learn more about the work of anthropologists, suggest that each one of them is to become a junior anthropologist. The focus of their work will be to investigate the kinds of people who live in each one of the regions and provide answers to the following questions: What do the people look like? How do they live and how does their environment affect the way they look and live?
6. Allow each student to select the group he or she is most interested in learning more about. Discuss possible ways of collecting the information needed.
7. Provide a large blank outline map of the world showing only continents and bodies of water. Label the map to differentiate clearly between the nine regions used in this form of classification. (An appropriate map can be made from large brown rolled paper usually found in most schools or by stapling together large sheets of newsprint. A map can be developed by using an opaque projector and projecting a map found in an encyclopaedia or by drawing free hand.) The map should be large enough to allow each group to place pictures, drawings, and/or written information on their respective regions that will help to provide answers to the questions they are researching.

8. Each group should have time to discuss their findings with the class. This lesson will require ample time for the research and for the reporting.

Level: Advanced

Objectives:

To help students understand that:

1. There are differences in hair texture and skin color.
2. The basic structure and function of the skin and hair are the same in all peoples, regardless of their racial group.

Teaching Strategy:

1. Using a globe, discuss and identify areas of the world with warm or hot climates, and those with colder climates. Ask if there seems to be any relationship between geographic environment (especially temperature) and the physical appearance of individuals, including skin color and hair texture.
2. Explain that skin color is a result of heavy deposits of melanin in the skin, and that melanin is a dark pigment that is found in larger amounts in the skin of people who live in warmer parts of the earth. Provide students with background information on melanin and discuss why it is necessary for people who live in areas that receive large amounts of direct sunlight to have heavier deposits of melanin.
3. Show the film "Heredity and Environment." Discuss why most physical traits, including skin color and hair texture, are a result of the interaction of heredity and environment.
4. Obtain several strands of curly, very curly, straight, and very straight hair. With a hand lens or microscope, have students observe differences in the texture of the hair strands. Next,

have students feel the various hair samples, and describe any noticeable differences.

5. Have students work in small groups of three or four for the purpose of constructing brief paragraphs that summarize the information presented during the lesson. Have the paragraphs put on the board or on transparencies, and use them to review and to compare understandings of the material presented in the lesson.

Resources:

Books:

Isaac Asmiov and William C. Boyd. *Races and People.* New York: Harper & Row, 1955.

Robert Cohen. *The Color of Man.* New York: Random House, 1968.

Marguerite Rush Lerner. *Red Man, White Man, African Chief: The Story of Skin Color.* Minneapolis: Lerner, 1973.

E. Mayr. *Population, Species, and Evolution.* Cambridge: Belknap Press of Harvard University Press, 1970.

Film:

"Heredity, and Environment." Coronet, B/W-color.

Generalization III: The structure of the body may differ because of one or more physical disabilities.

Level: Primary

Objectives:

To help students understand that:

1. Some differences in the physical structures of people may be caused by disabilities.
2. Physical disabilities may be the result of illness, injury, and/or accident at birth.
3. Such people are often referred to as the physically disabled.

Teaching Strategy:

1. On the chalkboard or on a large sheet of paper, sketch an outline of a human body. Briefly discuss the structure of the body and label the parts such as the head, neck, trunk, legs, and arms.
2. Discuss with the class and list on chart paper or on the chalkboard as many ways as the class can think of that people differ from one another physically, (e.g., height, weight, shape of head, color of eyes, skin, and head). Guide the discussion, if necessary, to lead the students into thinking about how people differ because of the loss of eyesight or a limb, loss of hearing, insufficient development of parts of the body, and so on.
3. Discuss the term "physically disabled." Encourage the class to define the term and, with the help of the dictionary and/or other resource material, develop a definition of the term that the class understands.
4. Continue the lesson by discussing the possible causes of physical disabilities such as birth defects, illness, and accidents, and explore with the class the possibilities for helping people with physical disabilities to learn how to live comfortably and to function as people do without those disabilities. Introduce the idea of correcting some physical disabilities through medical intervention. Discuss kinds of equipment designed to help individuals with physical disabilities.
5. Tell the class that you are going to introduce them to a friend whose name is Pablito. Inform them that Pablito was born in Puerto Rico, is about their age, and that Pablito is confined to a wheelchair because he cannot walk. Explain that the reason he cannot walk is because he had polio (this may require an explanation depending on the background of the students). Read to the class the story *Pablito's New Feet* by Dawn C. Thomas. The story includes several Spanish words

and phrases that the students should become familiar with, such as *por favor.*

6. After the reading of the story, review the following questions with the class:
   a. What was Pablito's disability?
   b. What was the cause of the condition?
   c. How did he feel and how did his family feel about his disability?
   d. What was done to correct the disability?
7. Conclude the lesson by reviewing how people differ physically from one another, emphasizing that people adjust to differences in a variety of ways and that Pablito's solution is one way people who have physical disabilities can be helped.

Resources:

Hanne Larsen. *Don't Forget Tom* (A John Day Book). New York: Thomas Y. Crowell, 1974. (mentally handicapped)

Nancy Mack. *Tracy.* Milwaukee, WI: Raintree Publishers, 1976. (cerebral palsy)

Diana Peter. *Claire and Emma.* New York: John Day, 1976. (deaf)

Palle Petersen. *Sally Can't See.* New York: John Day, 1974. (blind)

Jeanne Whithouse Peterson. *I Have a Sister, My Sister Is Deaf.* New York: Harper & Row, 1977. (deaf)

Margaret Sanford Pursell. *A Look at Physical Handicaps.* Minneapolis: Lerner Publications, 1976. (general)

Dawn C. Thomas. *Pablito's New Feet.* New York: J.B. Lippincott, 1973. (polio)

Bernard Wolf. *Connie's New Eyes.* New York: J.B. Lippincott, 1976. (blind)

Bernard Wolf. *Don't Feel Sorry for Paul.* New York: J.B. Lippincott, 1974. (birth defect—hands and feet)

Level: Intermediate

Objectives:

1. To help students understand that some physical disabilities may contribute to differences in the appearance and function of the human body.
2. To introduce cerebral palsy and blindness as two of the conditions that can affect the appearance and function of the human body.
3. To aid students in understanding the advantages of integrating individuals (mainstreaming) into the activities of everyday living, including classrooms.

Teaching Strategy:

1. Review with the class some of the facts they have learned about how and why people differ one from another. Have the students express each fact in a complete sentence and list these on the chalkboard.
2. If the list does not contain facts about differences that might result from physical disabilities, ask the students to think of people they might know or people they have seen who are different because of a physical disability. Encourage the class to think of names for several conditions that can affect the appearance and functioning of the body.
3. Focus on the condition of blindness. Have the students develop a list of some of the things they do, such as going to and from school, attending classes, playing in the park, and going to the grocery store, and to think about how their participation in these activities might be affected if they were blind. Discuss the kind of help they would need to be able to do each activity. It is important for the students to understand that, although the level of involvement might be different, they could still participate in most of the activities

with some assistance. For example, blind people learn to read with the help of the braille system.

4. Introduce the term "cerebral palsy" and help the students understand that generally individuals who are born with this condition lack the ability to control their muscles. This lack of control, stemming from damage to the brain, can affect the way an individual walks and talks.
5. Introduce the film *Nicky: One of My Best Friends* by telling the class about Nicky. Nicky was born blind and also has cerebral palsy. He is different but the differences in the way his body appears and functions have not prevented him from going to school and from having friends. As the children view the film, have them imagine themselves as being one of Nicky's classmates.
6. Follow the viewing of the film by discussing how Nicky's parents, friends, and teachers helped to involve him in the activities of the school. Introduce the term "mainstreaming" and have the students identify the advantages of mainstreaming for both the physically disabled and the non-physically disabled.
7. Conclude the lesson by having the students write short stories about their imaginary friend Nicky, telling about something they could enjoy doing with him.

Level: Advanced

Objectives:

1. To help students understand that some of the differences in the appearance and function of the body are caused by physical disabilities.
2. To explore ways that people who are physically disabled can be helped to participate in the everyday activities of living.

3. To introduce students to legislation that has helped to eliminate forms of discrimination against individuals with physical disabilities.

Teaching Strategy:

1. Prior to this lesson, write each of the following terms of words below on a small piece of paper. Fold each slip of paper and put the slips in an envelope. Tell the class that the envelope contains the names of some of the conditions that contribute to physical differences among people. Inform the class that they are going to develop a dictionary of terms for physical disabilities. Discuss how a dictionary presents a brief definition, and tell the class that they are to take one of the slips of paper from the envelope and prepare a two-sentence definition of the word or term found on the paper. Give the class about twenty minutes to complete this portion of the lesson. Depending on the resources of the school, the teacher may want to have a collection of books for the students to use already assembled in the classroom, or instruct the students to use the library, which may require more time.

   blind
   deaf
   braille
   multiple sclerosis
   polio
   paralysis
   cerebral palsy
   wheelchair
   quadriplegic
   stroke
   sign language
   birth defects
   nervous system
   muscle
   artificial limb
   brace
   prosthesis
   muscular dystrophy
   mental retardation
   mongoloidism
   epilepsy

2. Once the definitions have been completed, have the students present them to the class. Follow this by having the class

decide what form the dictionary should take. For example, students may choose to design a bulletin board using the words and terms. Or each student may create a printed list, with definitions, in the form of a dictionary.

3. Discuss with the class why the kinds of physical differences resulting from the conditions in the list are unlike differences resulting from race and sex. Include in the discussion the following questions:

   - In what ways have some people from each group been prevented from fully participating in society because of their physical difference?
   - What has been done through the passage of legislation to help prevent discrimination on the basis of skin color and sex?
   - Identify specific results of the passage of Section 504 of the Rehabilitation Act of 1973, which prohibits discrimination against the physically disabled in any federally funded or assisted project.
   - Discuss the advantages of this kind of legislation.

Resources:

Louise Albert. *But I'm Ready to Go.* Scarsdale, NY: Bradbury, 1976.

Robert J. Atonacci and Jene Barr. *Physical Fitness for Young Champions.* 2nd ed. McGraw-Hill, 1975.

Judy Blume. *Deenie.* Scarsdale, NY: Bradbury, 1973.

Fern G. Brown. *You're Somebody Special on a Horse.* Chicago: Albert Whitman, 1977.

Larry Callen. *Sorrow's Song.* Boston: Little, Brown and Co., 1979.

Vera and Bill Cleaver. *Me Too.* New York: J. B. Lippincott, 1973.

Bernice Grohskopf. *Shadow in the Sun.* New York: Atheneum, 1975.

Jaap Ter Haar. *The World of Ben Lighthart.* Bussum, Holland: Delacorte Press/Seymour Lawrence, 1973.

Jill Krementz. *How It Feels To Live With A Physical Disability.* New York: Simon and Schuster, 1992.

Jean Little. *Listen for the Singing.* New York: E. P. Dutton, 1977.

V. Corinne Renshaw. *Thalassine.* London and New York: Frederick Warne, 1971.

Harriet May Savitz. *Wheelchair Champions.* New York: John Day, 1978.

Gene Smith. *The Hayburners.* New York: Delacorte Press, 1974.

Food

Suggested Content Outline

I. The Importance of Food
   A. Growth
   B. Energy

II. Kinds of Food
   A. Animals
   B. Plants

III. Food Production

IV. Food Processing

V. Culture and Food
   A. Race/Ethnicity
   B. Religion
   C. Geography

Generalizations:

I. People from all cultural/ethnic groups have contributed to the development of foods.

II. Some ethnic groups are more directly involved in certain aspects of the production and processing of food.

III. The kind of food people eat is often influenced by such factors as race, ethnicity, religion, and geography.

Generalization I: People from all cultural/ethnic groups have contributed to the development of food.

Level: Primary

Objectives:

1. To introduce the students to George Washington Carver and his work with the sweet potato and the peanut.
2. To help the students learn how to plant and nurture the growth of peanut or sweet potato plants.

Teaching Strategy:

1. Prior to this lesson, read to the class the biography of George Carver by Augusta Stevenson. To introduce this lesson, review the life and work of Carver.
2. Divide the class into four teams and see which team can list the most kinds of products Dr. Carver discovered and made from the peanut.
3. Discuss the environment in which the peanut grows and talk about how that kind of environment could be reproduced in the class.
4. Share with the class the food value of the peanut. Explain that the peanut contains all three of the main classes of food the body needs— fats, proteins, and carbohydrates.
5. Plan to grow peanuts in the classroom. If it is too difficult to grow peanuts, substitute the sweet potato and have the students grow plants from sweet potatoes.
6. Chart the growth of the peanuts and/or sweet potatoes.

Resources:

Augusta Stevenson. *George Carver: Boy Scientist.* New York: Bobbs-Merrill, 1944.

Level: Intermediate

Objectives:

1. To develop appreciation for the different kinds of foods Native Americans have introduced to this country.
2. To explore the food value of corn and beans.
3. To help students learn the importance of starch and protein to the body.

Teaching Strategy:

1. With the class, list the different kinds of foods that most people eat on Thanksgiving Day. Ask the students if they know where most of these foods originated. Examine each item, such as the turkey, corn, tomatoes, and pumpkin. Encourage the class to explore the possibility that many of these foods were a part of the diet of Native Americans prior to the landing of the first groups of people from Europe.
2. Tell the class a story, which can be prepared from portions of the book *Indian Corn and Other Gifts* by Sigmund A. Lavine. This book contains information about foods and myths surrounding their origin.
3. Assign the students the responsibility for discovering the food value of corn and beans.
4. Explore the importance of starch, which is derived from both corn and beans, and the value of starch to the body. Help the students to grasp the following:

    - Starch is a carbohydrate.
    - Starchy foods are important sources of energy.
    - Carbohydrates are one of the three main classes of foods essential to the body; the others are fats and protein.

5. Explore the importance of protein, which is found in large quantities in beans. Help the students to learn the following:

- All living things require protein in order to live.
- Proteins are responsible for building new tissues in the body and repairing damaged cells.

6. Review the list of foods generally found in the Thanksgiving Day menu. Identify all of the foods that were introduced to this country by Native Americans.

Resources:

Sigmund A. Lavine. *Indian Corn and Other Gifts.* New York: Dodd, Mead, 1974.

Level: Advanced

Objectives:

To help students understand that:

1. Food plays an important role in the everyday life of all peoples.
2. The methods of cultivation, growth, and preparation of various foods are attributable to many groups of people.
3. Many foods that originate in one country become a regular part of the diet of another.

Teaching Strategy:

1. Begin the discussion by listing the basic food types that the body should receive in its daily diet. Emphasize the body's demand for food to satisfy its growth and energy needs. Show pictures of samples of foods from the basic food groups. Help students identify the group to which each belongs; for example, fats and carbohydrates.
2. With the class develop a diagram on a large bulletin board to show the value of each food. Display pictures of foods native

to other countries. Ask students to speculate about how the foods were introduced to other parts of the world.

3. Obtain tourist restaurant guides of several major cities or the city in which the school is located. Have students review the guides and, with the class, list as many different kinds of foods as are represented. Discuss the differences and identify those foods that are related to ethnic groups.
4. Have each student select a meal they would order in a restaurant of their choice and analyze the selection to see how many food groups are represented. Choices and analogies can be shared orally and by organizing a bulletin board.

Resources:

William L. Ramsey, et al. *Holt Life Science Series.* New York: Holt, Rinehart & Winston, 1978.

Sara R. Reidman. *Food for People,* 2nd ed. Scranton: Crowell/Harper & Row, 1976.

Weekly City Tour & Restaurant Guides (available at city tourist bureaus and hotels).

Generalization II: Some ethnic groups are more directly involved in certain aspects of the production and processing of foods.

Level: Primary

Objectives:

1. To help students identify the various kinds of steps involved in the production and processing of foods.
2. To explore the contribution of the migrant worker.
3. To examine why most migrant workers are Native Americans, Mexican Americans, African Americans, or Puerto Ricans.

Teaching Strategy:

1. Introduce the lesson by asking the students to share with the class what they had for one of their meals the previous day. Make a list of the many different kinds of foods that are named. Take one or two of the foods named, e.g., milk or fruit, and have the students describe the steps the food must go through to reach the table. As the steps are being identified, have the class give the names of the type of worker involved in each step, e.g., the farmer, the harvester, the truck driver. Help the class to understand that there are many people who are involved in the production and processing of food. The concepts of production and processing might need to be explained.
2. Divide the steps the students have listed that are necessary to get the food to the table; divide the list where production ends and processing begins.
3. Talk about the kinds of things the people who are involved in the production stage of one of the food items will need to know in order to be effective at the production stage. For example, the farmer must know about the best way to grow the wheat that will eventually be made into flour and then bread. Discuss how important it is to have a scientific knowledge of weather, soil, fertilizers, and sprays.
4. Discuss the processing stages and begin with harvesting. Ask the class if they have ever picked grapes, strawberries, apples, tomatoes, or other kinds of fruits and vegetables. Discuss the time it took, how they felt, and if they would like to do that kind of work for a living. Introduce the migrant worker. Ask for reasons why the migrant labor force is dominated by Native Americans, Mexican Americans, African Americans, and Puerto Ricans. Include in the discussion reasons such as the effect of job discrimination by skin color, language, or inadequate training. The students should be made to understand that inadequate job training may be the result of discrimination in schools and training situations.

5. Conclude this lesson by having the students draw a picture of one particular food worker. Arrange completed pictures around the room or in the hall in sequence so as to represent the states of production and processing.

Resources:

"Food." *World Book Encyclopedia,* vol. 13, 1975.
"Migrant Labor." *World Book Encyclopedia,* vol. 7, 1976.
Anne Neigoff. *Dinner's Ready.* Chicago: Albert Whitman and Co., 1971.

Level: Intermediate

Objectives:

1. To help the student better understand the steps involved in food processing.
2. To introduce the concept of migrant worker.
3. To explore the process of canning as one means of food preservation.

Teaching Strategy:

1. Briefly help the students to understand the difference between the production and processing stages of food. (This can be approached in several ways but at this level the students will probably be able to define the difference based on their knowledge of the terms.)
2. Focus the discussion on the food-processing stage. Select a fruit or vegetable and list the processing stages for that item. For example, if apples are selected, begin the processing stage with the picking of the fruit. Talk about who does the picking. Introduce the concept of the migrant worker. Discuss the kinds of conditions the workers live under, their

way of life, and the reason that most migrant workers are minorities. Include in the discussion the role discrimination plays in this phenomenon. Point out that people are discriminated against for reasons such as skin color and language and this not only affects the kinds of jobs they get but also the kind of education and training they receive.

3. List the various ways that foods are processed and the forms in which foods may be obtained, e.g., canned, dried, frozen, and fresh.
4. Discuss the canning process and the need for preserving food. (If a cannery is nearby, plan a trip during the study of the unit.) Be sure to include a discussion on how food spoils and highlight the fact that the canning process destroys microorganisms, e.g., yeast, molds, and bacteria that cause food to spoil.
5. Ask for volunteers who will prepare a brief report to be shared with the class on "How Food Spoils."

Resources:

"Canning." World Book Encyclopedia, vol. 3, 1976.

Level: Advanced

Objectives:

To help students understand that:

1. The food production and processing done by some ethnic groups is a vital contribution to society and deserves the respect, appreciation, and recognition that other occupations receive.
2. The lifestyle of a migrant farm family differs from that of a permanently residing family.
3. Explore the importance of freezing as a method of food preservation.

Teaching Strategy:

1. Discuss ways that foods may be processed and the reasons they are processed. Include in the discussion how people preserved food prior to the discovery of modern methods of food preservation.
2. Have the students, in small groups, make a list of the steps involved in the processing of frozen foods. When the steps are shared with the class, make a composite list that begins with the harvesting of the food. Discuss with the class the importance of the harvester and introduce the concept of the migrant worker.
3. Show the film "Yo Soy Chicano," which is an excellent film on the history of the Mexican-American and includes a description of the plight of the Mexican-American migrant worker. Following the film, discuss with the class why many migrant workers are Mexican Americans. Ask questions like these in order to lead the students to a better understanding of the value of the migrant worker to food processing and the problems of the minority migrant worker:

   - What could replace the migrant worker?
   - Is there any way the food industry could do without the workers?
   - Why are most migrant workers members of minority groups?
   - In what ways do you feel discrimination contributes to this phenomenon?
   - Are there possible solutions to the problems?

4. Review the process of freezing foods both at home and in commercial settings. Discuss the temperatures needed for quick freezing and methods of commercial freezing, such as air-blast freezing, indirect contact freezing, nitrogen freezing, and dry-ice freezing.

5. Have the original groups list the steps in the processing of frozen foods. Research the various methods of commercial freezing, and assign one group to investigate home freezing.
6. During the study of this section of the unit, an additional activity could include a trip to a freezing plant, if one is nearby, or the actual preparation and freezing of food using the home-freezing method. The food frozen could be put into a simple menu and used later in the school year for a special celebration.

Resources:

Mark Day. *Forty Acres: Caesar Chavez and the Farm Workers.* New York: Praeger, 1971.

"Frozen Food." *World Book Encyclopedia.* vol. 7, 1976.

August Meier and Elliott Rudwick. *From Plantation to Ghetto,* rev. ed. New York: Hill and Wang, 1970.

Ronald B. Taylor. *Chavez and the Farm Workers.* Boston: Beacon, 1975.

Sandra Weiner. *Small Hands, Big Hands: Seven Profiles of Chicano Migrant Workers and Their Families,* New York: Pantheon, 1970.

Film:

"Yo Soy Chicano." Berkeley, CA: Tricontinental Films.

Generalization III: The kind of food people eat is often influenced by such factors as race, ethnicity, religion, and geography.

Level: Primary

Objectives:

1. To help the student understand that food has deep spiritual significance for some Indian People.
2. To explore the kinds of food that are eaten by the Pueblo and Navajo.

Teaching Strategy:

1. On a large map, help the students identify the region of the country where the Pueblo and Navajo live.
2. Using the book *Pueblo and Navajo Cookery* by Marcia Keegan, select information to share with the class about the importance of food in these cultures. Some of the following should be appropriate for this level:

    - The Indians take a pinch of food and throw it to the winds to express gratitude to the spirit that helped grow the food.
    - Sometimes food is used for medicine, as in the placing of slices of wild potatoes on the head for a headache.
    - Each meal is preceded by a prayer.
    - Corn is important to the Indian; often the grinding of corn is accompanied by singing and dancing. The Indian's diet has consisted of food that they could grow and hunt.

    Share the pictures in this book with the class. If possible, obtain an additional copy of the book, and have the pictures individually laminated.
3. Discuss the importance of corn to the Indian. Have the students list different ways corn can be used. Introduce the fact that there are six main kinds of corn: dent corn, sweet corn, flint corn, popcorn, flour corn, and pod corn. (For uses and description of each kind of corn, consult an encyclopedia.)
4. Conclude this lesson by popping popcorn and/or making Pueblo cookies. (Recipe for the cookies can be found in the Keegan book listed under Resources.)

Resources:

"Corn." *World Book Encyclopedia,* vol. 4, 1976.
Marcia Keegan. *Pueblo and Navajo Cookery.* Dobbs Ferry, NY: Earth, 1977.

Level: Intermediate

Objectives:

1. To explore how race and the geography of China influences the way many Chinese Americans eat today.
2. To develop an appreciation for the types of food Chinese and other Asian Americans and Pacific Islanders eat.

Teaching Strategy:

1. The kinds of food Chinese Americans eat will probably not be new to most students. Encourage the class to discuss experiences they may have had eating in Chinese restaurants or eating Chinese food at home. Focus the discussion around the fact that rice is the basic food of the Chinese and many other people who are Asian or Pacific Islanders. Discuss possible reasons for this. Continue the discussion by asking the following questions:

    - How does geography influence the rice-eating habits of Chinese Americans?
    - What conditions might influence the heavy inclusion of vegetables and fruit in the diet of most Chinese Americans?

2. Draw a diagram on the board, showing the class that rice consists of 80 percent starch, 12 percent water, and 8 percent protein. Discuss the value of starch and protein to the body.
3. Initiate a discussion on how rice grows. With the class, make a list of questions they would like answered about the way rice grows. Have individuals or small groups of students investigate and provide answers for these questions.
4. Obtain several different menus from Chinese restaurants, and try to recognize the differences in the foods, depending on whether the restaurant serves Cantonese, Mandarin, Szechwan, or other styles of food. Help the students to see

the relationship between the kinds of food that are eaten in China and the eating habits of Chinese Americans.

5. Plan with the class to make a simple Chinese dish or, if possible, make arrangements for the class to visit a Chinese restaurant for a tour of the kitchen and for a meal. Arrangements sometimes can be made if the class is able to go when business is slow.

Level: Advanced

Objectives:

1. To help students understand and experience the immense diversity in food and food tastes.
2. To show that foods that are easily grown or obtained in an area tend to become diet staples.
3. To show that diet and food habits of racial and ethnic groups are affected by the socioeconomic status of the group.
4. To help students understand that religious beliefs impose diet constraints upon the people of a cultural group.

Teaching Strategy:

1. Provide a few samples of foods that are common to several different cultural groups. Have students taste the samples. Discuss students' reactions to the tasting of the various foods. Explain that the "taste" of food is acquired over a period of time, and that identical foods prepared differently will taste different. Have the class name seasonings from herbs and spices that are commonly used by some cultural groups to give familiar foods a different taste.
2. Explore reasons why some cultural/ethnic groups have a diet that consists mainly of fish and game, while other groups' diets consist of plant foods, and still others eat a variety of

foods. Ask students if there is any relationship between the geography of a region and the type of foods eaten. With the students, list the different kinds of foods eaten in distinctly different regions in the United States.

3. Initiate a discussion of the influence that religion has on dietary habits. Relate the fact that some religious groups exclude certain foods from their diet.
4. Make a chart listing the daily food requirements of the body. Using the groups named in Step 2, chart the kinds of food that are generally eaten by each group to show the vitamin substitutions that are often made, e.g., collard greens eaten by southerners are a good vitamin C substitute. This step will require students to research the vitamin content of certain foods.
5. Have students discuss the relationship between socioeconomic status and the foods people eat. Explain that the financial condition of an ethnic/cultural group often determines its dietary habits.

Resources:

Yeffe Kimball and Jean Anderson. *The Art of American Indian Cooking.* Garden City, NY: Doubleday, 1965.

Seymour Fersh, ed. *Learning About Peoples and Cultures.* Evanston, IL: McDougal Littell, 1974.

August Meier and Elliott Rudwich. *From Plantation to Ghetto,* rev. ed. NY: Hill and Wang, 1970.

12 Generalizations and Teaching Strategies for Social Studies

Introduction

In addition to reading and mathematics, most elementary schools generally have substantial programs in social studies. Usually the course offerings in secondary schools contribute generously to solid programs in social studies. The nature of social sciences provides a logical place for multicultural instruction to begin. In fact, historically much of the early curriculum work in multiethnic and multicultural education began through social studies instruction. The reason for this is primarily that social studies deal with people: how they live; where they live; how they think, behave, and interact with each other. Because social studies are interdisciplinary, they are an excellent resource for helping students develop skills that will enable them to understand themselves better and to learn how to interact effectively with other people. James A. Banks states that:

> The social studies should assume the major responsibility for helping children become adept at making important decisions that affect their relationships with other human beings

and the governing of their local communities and the nation.[1]

Effective decision making in the eighties and beyond will require a broad base of knowledge, a base that can be provided for by the interdisciplinary approach used in the teaching of social studies. Social studies draw their content from more than one discipline. John Jarolimek describes it best when he writes that "the social studies as a part of the elementary school curriculum draw subject matter from the social sciences; history, geography, sociology, political science, social psychology, philosophy, anthropology, and economics."[2]

It is most appropriate that this chapter on social studies be included and present material that may serve to further promote the integrative aspects of making education multicultural. In this chapter, two subunit topics, on communities and on families, will be presented. Both topics are rather broad in scope but were chosen for just that reason. Each topic will allow for an inclusive exploration of where, how, and why people live as they do, as well as with whom and for what purpose.

Communities

Suggested Content Outline

I. Characteristics of a Community
   - A. People
   - B. Location
   - C. Organization
   - D. Purpose

II. Types of Communities
   - A. Neighborhood
   - B. Local
   - C. County
   - D. State
   - E. Nation
   - F. World

III. Responsibilities of Communities
   A. Economics
   B. Protection
   C. Education
   D. Recreation
   E. Communication
   F. Transportation
   G. Religion

Generalizations

I. A community consists of people who live in a common area and who share common concerns.

II. Large communities are made up of smaller communities of people with common ethnic and cultural lifestyles.

III. Communities generally supply what citizens need but often what is provided is determined by the ethnic and racial identification of the person and/or group.

Generalization I: A community consists of people who live in a common area and who share common concerns.

Level: Primary

Objectives:

1. To help students grasp the concept of community.
2. To expose them to a community that may differ from theirs.
3. To introduce them to a few Spanish words.

Teaching Strategy:

1. Introduce the lesson to the class by making several statements about the school and the neighborhood they live in. Use the word *community* in each statement: for example,

"most of us in this room live in the same community"; "the school community includes all students who attend this school, their family, and neighbors"; "people who live in the same community often have several things in common." Follow this by asking the children for the word that was used in each one of the statements. Repeat statements if necessary.

2. Write the word *community* on the chalkboard. Discuss each statement with the class to ascertain its accuracy.
3. Make a list of things on the chalkboard that all the people who live in the school community have in common.
4. Introduce the book *Song of the Swallows* by Leo Politi by telling the class that the main character in the story is a boy whose name is Juan. Explain that Juan lives in a Southern California community and that his community may differ from theirs. Have a student identify Southern California on a map of the United States. Encourage the class to suggest some things that Juan and his friends and neighbors might have in common since they live in the same community.
5. Tell the class that many of the people in Juan's community speak Spanish and the story contains four Spanish terms that some of them may not know. If there are students in the class who speak Spanish, involve them in teaching the Spanish phrases to the class. If not, proceed to introduce the following terms to the class with meaning and pronunciations so they will be familiar with them when they are introduced in the story. The terms introduced in the story are: *buenos dias* (good morning), *las golondrinas* (the swallows), *pobricito* (poor little one) and *vienen las golondrinas* (the swallows are coming). When the phrases appear in the reading of the story, point to the appropriate phrase and have the class repeat it.
6. Upon completion of the story, discuss with the class the differences between their community and Juan's. Conclude the lesson by summarizing those aspects of both communities that are the same.

Resources:

Leo Politi. *Song of the Swallows.* New York: Charles Scribner's Sons, 1949.

Level: Intermediate

Objectives:

1. To reinforce the concept of community.
2. To broaden students' concept of community to include the neighborhood and/or school community.

Teaching Strategy:

1. Have the students bring a current newspaper to class for use with this lesson. Or the teacher may wish to obtain sufficient outdated copies from a local newspaper company. Discuss the concept of community and make a list of those characteristics all communities have, e.g., schools, churches, stores, and parks.
2. Take a newspaper, an issue that the students will not be using later, and with the class, select and circle with a felt pen those articles that make reference to something that has happened in a particular type of community. The class will learn that different sections of the paper will contain articles and information about different sections of the city, state, nation, and world.
3. Have the students work in small groups to examine their copies of one or two newspapers for articles with headlines and captions that make reference to a type of community. Once the captions and/or articles are identified, have groups cut out several to use in the next stage of the lesson.
4. Encourage the students to label the type of community each article makes reference to and have them justify the type of community they are referencing by using the list of

characteristics for communities the class established earlier in the lesson. Once the justification is considered valid by the class, e.g., state, region, or national community, then the article or caption can be placed on the bulletin board. Articles should be grouped according to type of community. To make the bulletin board even more exciting, add an interesting heading such as "Communities come in all sizes" or "It takes all kinds of communities to make a universe" or "People make things happen in all communities."

Level: Advanced

Objectives:

1. To introduce the students to the concept of community through the exploration of the Japanese internment camp.
2. To develop an understanding of the historical events that have affected the way Japanese live in the United States.
3. To help the students understand that people sometimes are forced to live in certain areas and under certain conditions because of racial discrimination.

Teaching Strategy:

1. In preparation for the viewing of the film *Guilty by Reason of Race,* give the class a brief historical perspective of the Japanese in the United States. This can be done very effectively by listing important dates, beginning with the arrival of the Japanese in Hawaii in 1868. The book *Teaching Strategies for Ethnic Studies,* by James A. Banks, contains an excellent chapter on Asian Americans, which includes a summary of important dates in the history of Japanese Americans. Explore with the students this history up to 1941. Discuss the impact of Executive Order 9066 on

Japanese Americans and on the nation. Students should be helped to understand that the internment camp was a kind of community but was formed under undesirable conditions.

2. Show the film *Redress: JACL Campaign for Justice* and have the students look for those aspects of the internment camp that would classify it as a community. Have the students identify the reasons for the Executive Order.
3. The film is long and the discussion that should follow will need to be scheduled when there is time to discuss the two aspects stated above as well as the effects of this type of treatment on the Japanese and on the nation as a whole.
4. After students are familiar with the history of the Japanese in the United States up to 1946, when the last camp was closed, have them write individual papers on how they might have felt if this situation had happened to them. Have them include feelings that might still exist in the Japanese communities today. Also explore the reasons why some Japanese live in communities that are predominantly Japanese. Is this by choice? If yes, what contributes to the desire to live with other Japanese? If not, what conditions cause some communities to be dominated by Japanese Americans? This discussion could be expanded to include communities inhabited by other ethnic groups.
5. The role of the federal government in internment should provide an opportunity for the students to understand the institutional nature of unfair treatment toward groups or individuals. This provides an opportunity to explore the impact of racist treatment toward certain groups of people.
6. Depending on the class, the above discussion might provide the basis on which to discuss immigration legislation.

Resources:

James A. Banks. *Teaching Strategies for Ethnic Studies,* Boston: Allyn and Bacon, 1979.

Noel L. Leathers. *The Japanese in America.* Minneapolis, MN: Lerner Publications, 1967.

Film:

Redress: *JACL Campaign for Justice,* National Japanese American Citizens League, San Francisco. 1991.

Generalization II: Large communities are made up of smaller communities of people with common ethnic and cultural lifestyles.

Level: Primary

Objectives:

1. To extend the concept of community to other countries by using Mexico as an example.
2. To help the students compare a Spanish-speaking community in the United States with one in Mexico.
3. To continue to develop an appreciation for the Spanish language.
4. To help the students understand why some people prefer living in communities where there are people who are similar to them.
5. To introduce the concept of the barrio.
6. To help students understand that racial discrimination and economics also influence where people live.

Teaching Strategy:

1. This lesson is a natural followup to the one suggested under Generalization I. Review with the class the characteristics of a community. Focus on the Spanish-speaking characteristics of Juan's neighborhood and briefly compare it to other communities where other languages are spoken.

2. Discuss the locations from which people who speak Spanish generally come to the United States. Identify Mexico as one place and locate it on the map. Introduce *Carlos and the Brave Owl* by Josephine Camille by telling the students that they will meet a boy whose name is Carlos and that Carlos also speaks Spanish but lives in a village in Mexico. Tell the class that in this story they will meet some new Spanish words. Write the following words on the chalkboard or on chart paper, and introduce them to the class as previously described: *tienda* (store), *Senor Dio* (Dear God), *tortillas* (a type of Mexican food), *por favor* (please), *un buho* (an owl).
3. Follow the reading of the story by discussing the things that people who come from Mexico to the United States to live would look for in a neighborhood or community. Once a list has been established and the ability to communicate with one's neighbors has been established as one of the characteristics, introduce the concept of the barrio. Explain that the word *barrio* is used to describe the communities in which many Mexican Americans live in the United States. Point out that there are small and large barrios located in many sections of the country, such as El Paso, Texas; Denver, Colorado; Chicago, Illinois; and Los Angeles, California. It should also be pointed out that due to discrimination in housing and economic factors, some people who may not want to live with people who share similar lifestyles are forced to do so.
4. If time permits, or in an additional art period, review the story and discuss the "Blessing of the Animals Festival" as described in the story. Encourage students to create their own animals from large pieces of brown wrapping paper and conduct a mock festival in the room. The replicas of the animals can make an attractive decoration for the classroom or in the hall. Once displayed, label each animal with its appropriate Spanish name.

Resources:

Ruth M. Baylor. *Moving Day for Manuel,* New York: Reader's Digest, 1969.
Josephine Camille. *Carlos and the Brave Owl.* New York: Random House, 1968.
Patricia Miles Martin. *Chicanos: Mexicans in the United States.* New York: Parents Magazine Press, 1971.

Level: Intermediate

Objectives:

1. To help students understand that some neighborhoods/ communities are made up of people who have similar values and lifestyles.
2. To help students explore ways that discrimination contributes to the development of communities in which people share similar lifestyles.
3. To help students understand the concepts of "integrated neighborhoods," "assimilation," "stereotypes," and "blockbusting."

Teaching Strategy:

1. Prior to this lesson, read at least one-half of the book *Iggie's House,* by Judy Blume, to the class. Before reading the book to the class, discuss the types of neighborhoods that exist in the city in which the school is located. Point out that there are sections in all cities where certain groups of people live and have the class discuss reasons for this. The discussion should include the notion that some people choose to live with others who share similar lifestyles and/or cultural values but there are those who do not have a choice and are

not allowed to live where they want to even if they can afford to do so. The story *Iggie's House* introduces several ideas that will help the students to analyze housing discrimination. First it introduces the idea of "restricted integrated neighborhoods." Those neighborhoods are generally integrated by those who are able to assimilate. Next, it introduces a situation where a black family moves into an all-white neighborhood. The story continues with the concept of "blockbusting." The story sets the scene for an open class discussion not only of "blockbusting" but of the causes for racial discrimination and how such discrimination affects housing patterns and therefore the development of communities across the nation.

2. Once the entire story has been read to the class (it is suggested that the book be read in two periods), then the stage is set for a discussion of the following questions: Why was Iggie's family, who was Japanese, accepted in the neighborhood and the Garbers, who were African American, not accepted? What ethnic and cultural factors may have contributed to the acceptance of the Japanese family? What ethnic and cultural factors may have influenced the manner in which the Garbers were treated? Can you identify the stereotypes that Wine, Mrs. Landon, and Winnie's parents were operating on? Why do you think Mrs. Landon did not want to have the Garbers for neighbors? How do you think the Garbers felt about living in an all-white neighborhood? Why do you think they chose that particular community? What is "blockbusting" and who profits from it? What are the consequences of "blockbusting" for the people who remain in the neighborhood and for the neighborhood as a whole? Have students imagine they are one of the Garber children and they are going to write to Iggie in Tokyo to tell her what has happened since they moved into the house she used to live in. The letter is to include a description of how they feel about what has happened.

Resources:

Judy Blume. *Iggie's House.* New York: Dell, 1970.

Level: Advanced

Objectives:

1. To assist students in identifying the distinctive qualities of Native American community life in a number of socioeconomic and geographic settings.
2. To assist students in developing an appreciation for the value system of Native American people which is supported through community life.
3. To explore with students the universal characteristics of Native American values and traditions and the effectiveness of Native American community life in supporting these values and traditions.

Teaching Strategy:

1. Before showing the film *The Divided Trail,* discuss with students their perception of the features of Native American community life. Identify the sources the students used in developing their perceptions. Determine if students have a fundamentally accurate and positive or a negative perception at this point.
   a. The film was produced by Jerry Aronson, a Native American. It is a documentary film depicting the struggle of a Midwest tribe of Native Americans in establishing a land base in their relocation neighborhood in Chicago, and also in their traditional homeland. The film explores the emotional and economic distress of one of the women leaders of her group, how the disruption

of a community support system aggravates this distress, and how the reestablishment of that support system assists in the resolution of her difficulties.

b. Alert students to focus attention on the film in line with the concepts previously discussed in Generalization I and the objectives for this lesson.

2. The film contradicts stereotypic representation of Native American life and often has an immediate and overwhelming impact on viewers. After viewing the film, allow students to express their emotional reactions to the film.
3. Discussion of the film should lead students through the objectives for the lesson.
   a. How is its depiction of Native American life different from students' previous perceptions? Help students focus on the contemporary, dynamic depiction of Native American people, rather than the depiction of "vanishing race" from a static past.
   b. Consider a discussion of the following:
      - What are the distinctive qualities of community life? How are these expressed in urban and rural settings?
      - What values and traditions of Native American people are supported by community life? Focus attention on attitudes toward land.
      - What are the values of Native American people that are universal? How do their communities support these values? Focus student attention on protection of family life and assistance to individual members of a community who are in distress.

Resources:

Film:

Jerry Aronson, producer. *The Divided Trail.* Distributed by Phoenix Films.

Generalization III: Communities generally supply what its citizens need but often what is provided is determined by the ethnic and racial identification of the person and/or group.

Level: Primary

Objectives:

1. To introduce the class to a Japanese-American family who lives in a city.
2. To compare the needs of people who live in different types of communities.
3. To identify how a community satisfies the ethnic/cultural needs of a given group of people.
4. To introduce several Japanese characters to the students.

Teaching Strategy:

1. Review with the class the types of communities they have studied thus far and talk about their differences. Lead the discussion to focus on large communities, namely cities. Discuss their physical differences and how these differences influence the way people live.
2. Draw the Japanese character for Mo Mo (see Figure 12.1) and have the class try to guess what language the character is from and what it means. Once the figure has been identified as a Japanese character, lead the class to discover that it is a name for a young girl whom they will meet through the story *Umbrella* by Taro Yashima.
3. Ask for volunteers to read individual pages of the story and as a new Japanese character appears on the pages, add it to the other characters on the board, or have the characters already drawn on large pieces of tagboard and display them when needed for the class (see Figure 12.1).

Figure 12.1

4. Once the story has been read, review it with the class and identify again how the city community differs from other types. Lead the class into a discussion as to what kinds of services a community needs to supply, e.g., transportation, recreation, protection, and restaurants.
5. Discuss with the students where Mo Mo's mother and father were born and what they probably looked for in deciding where to live in New York City. Be sure the discussion includes people they could communicate with and therefore their need to be near people who spoke Japanese. Also point out their need to have grocery stores that could provide the kind of food they ate and restaurants that served what they were used to eating and liked to eat. The discussion should also include the desire for churches, entertainment, and so forth, with which they were familiar.
6. Conclude the lesson by having the children cut and design city buildings from newspaper. Draw window and doors with black felt pens. If possible, have some of the buildings labeled with a few Japanese signs to indicate some obvious and distinguishing characteristics that a Japanese community might have.
7. Use these buildings and signs to construct a community on a bulletin board and label it "Mo Mo's Community."

Resource:

Taro Yashima. *Umbrella.* New York: Viking, 1970.

Level: Intermediate

Objectives:

1. To introduce students to the concept of the "migrant worker."

2. To expand students' awareness of communities to include that of migrant workers' camps.
3. To reinforce the idea that communities often respond to the ethnic and cultural needs of groups.

Teaching Strategy:

1. Explain to the class that they are going to play a game called "Find Out." Have the class divide into groups of three or four. The instructions for playing the game are as follows: First, the objective of the game is to see how much each group can "find out" about something in a short period of time through any type of resource available to them. In this instance, each group is to find out as much as they can about "migrant workers" in twenty minutes. The only rules are that they must use the resources available to them in the classroom and in the school building. At the end of the twenty minutes the groups are to report the information to the class. Some of the groups will use the resources in the classroom, others will go to the library, and some may even use the telephone.
2. Once the twenty minutes are up and the students have returned to the room, then each group reports to the class on the kind of information they have discovered.
3. Once the information has been shared, then have the class write a set of statements about migrant workers that will include who they are, where they live, and how their needs are supplied. As these statements are being developed, the following generalizations should be pointed out. Many migrant workers are members of minority groups, migrant workers live in communities called migrant workers' camps, the migrant worker is important to the food industry, and many migrant workers suffer from poor housing conditions, inadequate schooling, lack of day care for children, and low pay.

4. Continue the discussion with an introduction to Cesar Chavez. Tell the students that they are going to play "Find Out," again, only this time they are to find out as much as they can about Cesar Chavez and his work overnight. Encourage students to use a variety of resources, e.g., libraries, radio stations, informal interviews.
5. Continue the lesson on the following day by having the students report on the information they have found about Cesar Chavez. Once the information is shared, then have the students write a brief biography of Chavez. Assign sections to small groups. Have the unified, completed biography typed and duplicated for the students' use in the classroom and in the library.

Resources:

Ruth Franchere. *Cesar Chavez.* New York: Thomas Y. Crowell, 1970.

Patricia Miles Martin. *Chicanos: Mexicans in the United States.* New York: Parents' Magazine, 1971.

Clark Newlon. *Famous Mexican Americans.* New York: Dodd-Mead, 1972.

Louise Shotwell. *Roosevelt Grady.* New York: Grosset and Dunlap. 1963.

Florence White. *Cesar Chavez: Man of Courage,* Westport, CT: Garrard, 1973.

Level: Advanced

Objectives:

1. To help the students explore the reasons why some communities are homogeneous.
2. To analyze the effects of segregation on the development of racially impacted communities.

3. To become aware of ways in which communities supply the needs of their inhabitants.

Teaching Strategy:

1. With a city map, have each student identify and mark on the map, using a felt pen or another means of identification, the place he or she lives. Try to make some generalized statements about the pattern. For example, students may all live in the same area and then additional generalizations can be made about things they have in common, such as socioeconomic status, religion, race, or other factors.
2. Read the following statement to the class and/or reproduce it for easy reference:

> On the whole, people live in the best part of the city they can afford. What any family considers best depends partly on how many people there are in the family, what their ages are, where they work, and what they like to do in their spare time. It also depends on what other kinds of people live there and whether those other people will give the family a chance to buy or rent living quarters. Thus, the way people are distributed throughout the city is not an accident, nor something decided by law, but a pattern which each person who rents or buys living quarters helps to make. If we know the patterns we can predict with fair success where a family would like to live and where it actually will live.[3]

3. Examine each sentence in the paragraph and discuss the validity of the statement with regard to all ethnic and racial groups. Does the first sentence hold true for African Americans? For Hispanics and other groups? Continue until each sentence has been examined.
4. With the class, develop a list of factors that contribute to homogeneous neighborhoods. Label those factors that are the result of discrimination.

5. Conclude this lesson by identifying ways in which communities provide for the needs of the people living there.

Families

Suggested Content Outline

I. Society's Basic Unit
   A. Production
   B. Survival
   C. Training
   D. Protection

II. Types of Families
   A. Patriarchal
   B. Matriarchal
   C Egalitarian
   D. Extended
   E. Single-person-headed
   F. Other

III. Function
   A. Legal
   B. Customs
   C. Relationships

Generalizations

I. The family is society's basic unit for perpetuating and continuing the human race.
II. The ethnic, racial, and cultural characteristics of groups often influence the structure of the family unit.
III. The traditions and customs of ethnic and cultural groups are supported, celebrated, and preserved by the family unit.

Generalization I: The family is society's basic unit for perpetuating and continuing the human race.

Level: Primary

Objectives:

1. To increase students' awareness of the differences in family size and structure.
2. To emphasize the major functions of the family unit.
3. To help students understand that the individual roles and responsibilities of the members of the family are determined by the needs of the family.

Teaching Strategy:

1. Several days before the lesson is scheduled to be taught, ask students to bring in a snapshot of their families or several snapshots that represent the family unit.
2. Allow time for each student on several days prior to the full initiation of the unit to spend one or two minutes describing their families to the class. This will serve several purposes, but most important it will allow the teacher and class to be more familiar with the variety of family units in the class, create an awareness of the differences in family structure and size, and help to develop an interest in the unit to be explored.
3. Initiate the unit of study by having each student draw a family tree with a branch for each member and assemble the pictures on a tree using a variety of methods. Assemble all drawings on a large bulletin board or wall that will help to set the scene for the study on families.
4. Continue this lesson by discussing with the students the major functions and responsibilities of the family. Include in the discussion a listing of responsibilities and discuss with the students which family members assume various responsibilities for the family. The important concept to stress, in addition to function and responsibilities, is that

these responsibilities are satisfied in many different ways and by various members of the family. Encourage children, if the ideas do not appear to be in opposition to cultural values, to see that roles and responsibilities are not assigned according to sex except where biological needs are to be fulfilled, e.g., giving birth.

5. Conclude the lesson by having children write a brief paragraph on what their family does for them and what they do for their family.

Level: Intermediate

Objectives:

1. To aid children in understanding the basic function and responsibilities of families.
2. To help students realize that the size and structure of families vary.
3. To develop an understanding and an appreciation for the one-parent family.

Teaching Strategy;

1. In preparation for having the students view the film *The Blue Dashiki: Jeffrey and His City Neighbors,* have the students share the size of their families with the class. Ask the students to close their eyes and to think about one thing that they enjoy doing with their families. Ask for volunteers to report to the class about their favorite family activity. Encourage the students to tell why the activity is their favorite. Ask the class if their favorite activity could be done with people who were not a part of their family; if "yes," continue with a question as to whether or not the activity

would be as enjoyable. If the answer is "no," have the student explain why not. This activity can lead to a discussion as to why families are important and what the family unit provides for its members.

2. Prior to viewing the film, ask the students to keep in mind as they watch it, the kinds of things that Jeffrey must be responsible for in his family. Point out that Jeffrey's responsibilities are affected by the size of his family. (Jeffrey is an only child and lives with his mother.)
3. After viewing the film, discuss with the class the various ways in which Jeffrey earned money to make his purchase. Compare these tasks with those the class feels Jeffrey might be responsible for at home.
4. Once Jeffrey's responsibilities appear to be clear, have the class identify the responsibilities of Jeffrey's mother.
5. Conclude the lesson by reviewing with the class the major function of the family, the variation in sizes of families, and the way size affects the roles of the family members.

Resources:

Books:

Raynor Dorka. *This Is My Father and Me.* Chicago: Albert Whitman, 1973.

Christine Engla Ebner. *Just Momma and Me.* Chapel Hill, NC: Lollipop Power, 1975.

Beth Goff. *Where Is Daddy?* Boston: Berron Press, 1969.

Katherine Leiner. *Ask Me What My Mother Does.* New York: Franklin Watts, 1978.

Hanns Reich. *Children and Their Mothers.* New York: Hill and Wang, 1964.

Films:

The Blue Dashiki: Jeffrey and His City Neighbors. Chicago: Encyclopedia Britannica Educational Corp.

Level: Advanced

Objectives:

1. To develop a greater appreciation for the role and responsibilities of the family.
2. To increase students' awareness of the differences in family size and structure.
3. To introduce the concept of genealogy through a brief study of the ancestry of each student.

Teaching Strategy:

1. Begin the discussion by having the students discuss what role each one plays in his or her family. Then include descriptions of the roles other family members play. Continue by identifying the relationship between the roles of individual members and the responsibilities of the family.
2. Through the discussion, the students should become aware of differences in family size. Take a brief poll of the sizes of families represented in the class. Discuss the structure of the families. Help the students understand that families are diverse in size and structure but roles and responsibilities are basically the same.
3. Most of the students will be familiar with the work of Alex Haley through his book *Roots.* Discuss the way he went about conducting his study on the history of his ancestors. Have the class list procedures they would go through to conduct a genealogical study of their own.
4. Allow the class to decide how much time they would like to spend on the study, how many generations they would like to cover, and how they would like to report their findings.
5. Conclude this lesson by reviewing the importance of families by listing the roles and responsibilities of the family unit.

Generalization II: The ethnic, racial, and cultural characteristics of groups often influence family structure and lifestyle.

Level: Primary

Objectives:

1. To introduce the concept of sharing space when a family lives in a small apartment in a city.
2. To help students understand factors that help determine where and how families live.

Teaching Strategy:

1. Begin this lesson by having the students discuss where they go in their homes to be alone. Discuss the concept of space and allow the students to discuss how their family unit uses its space. Depending on the lifestyle of the students, compare and/or contrast a few of the different ways people live that may be different from the way most of them live, e.g., apartments, small houses, large buses, trailers, condominiums, tents, or hogans.
2. Prepare the class for viewing the film *Evan's Corner* by asking them to count the members in Evan's family and to try to think of more than one reason why Evan had a corner.
3. Following the viewing of the film, discuss the size of Evan's family, the reason he wanted a corner, and the things he did to fix up his space. Compare this with the way the members of the class decorate their space in their homes.
4. Have the class imagine that they are going to be asked to design a cover or a brochure that will be used to advertise the film. Have them create a design that would in itself give the viewer an idea of what the film is about.

Resources:

Film:
"Evan's Corner." New York: Stephen Bosustow Production, BFA, 1970. Color, 24 minutes.

Level: Intermediate

Objectives:

1. To assist students in understanding the structures of Native American families.
2. To explore with students the value of these family structures in meeting the needs of Native American cultures.
3. To encourage students to appreciate the universal and contemporary value of the family structures in meeting the needs of many peoples.

Teaching Strategy:

1. Begin the lesson by asking the following questions:
   - How do you think a Native American family might spend a day?
   - What are your perceptions of Native American family life? Roles of mother and father? Roles of children?
2. Have the students give their own definitions of an extended family. Discuss the roles of grandparents and the roles of uncles, aunts, and cousins.
3. Explore the meaning of kinship patterns and how these might interact with clans. If kinship and clans and tribes are new concepts, have volunteers research the meaning and report to the class. Or define these yourself.

4. Read selected passages from some of the Resources to enrich students' perceptions of Native American family life.
5. Students might view the paintings of George Catlin on American Indian life and photographs by Edward Curtis for fairly accurate depictions of tribal life.
6. Students should be encouraged to work analogously through the lesson, identifying similar structure patterns (or each of them) in their family community life. Discuss the following:
   a. awareness of ancestry and homeland
   b. oral traditions in the family
   c. roles of uncles, aunts, grandparents
   d. What in Western European culture is similar to a clan?
      - Do families tend to stay in similar occupations?
      - Are unions, associations, and professions like clans?

Resources:

Thomas Berger. *Little Big Man.* New York: Dial, 1964.

John Lame Deer. *Lame Deer: Seeker of Visions.* New York: Simon and Schuster, 1972.

N. Scott Momaday. *The Way to Rainy Mountain.* New York: Ballantine, 1970.

John G. Neidhardt. (Fleming Rainbow). *Black Elk Speaks: Being the Life Story of a Holy Man of the Oglala Sioux.* Lincoln, NE: Bison, University of Nebraska Press, 1971.

Maria Sandoz. *Crazy Horse.* Lincoln, NE: Bison, University of Nebraska Press, 1961.

Level: Advanced

Objectives:

1. To develop a better understanding of the life of Puerto Rican families in the United States.
2. To introduce the concept of "extended family."

Teaching Strategy:

1. Present to the class some historical facts about Puerto Ricans in the United States. Relevant material can be obtained for this from the Resources and, in particular, from James A. Banks's book *Teaching Strategies for Ethnic Studies.*
2. Explore with the class the differences between Puerto Ricans, African, Japanese, and Mexican Americans. The following are areas for comparison:
   a. Under what conditions did each group come to the United States?
   b. Which groups are immigrants or migrants?
   c. What characteristics of each group make it difficult for them to participate fully in the mainstream of society? Why? Are there differences in family structure? How might the responsibilities of the family differ in these groups?
3. Read the following passage to the class:

> The family came: mother, father, sisters, brothers, cousins, and just friends who, because of living with us so many years, had become part of the family. An old Puerto Rican custom. Many times we asked mother about someone who had been living with us for years. "In what way is Jose related to us?" And my mother after a lot of genealogical hemming and hawing in which the more she explained the more she got involved and confused, would end with a desperate whimsical gesture: "He is just part of the family." And there it ended.[4]

   Tell the class this was taken from a short story about a Puerto Rican family in New York entitled "How to Rent an Apartment Without Money," taken from *A Puerto Rican in New York* by Jesus Colon. Ask the class the following questions:

- What kinds of conditions would cause grandparents, cousins, and friends to move in and live with a family?
- Would the responsibilities of the family change when the unit becomes extended?
- Does the size of a family have any effect upon the role of its individual members?
- What kinds of accommodations would most families need to have adequate living facilities?
- How do you think the practice of extending the family became a custom?
- Is it possible to generalize and say that all Puerto Rican families follow the practice of living in extended family units?

4. Conclude the lesson by reading to the class the entire short story this passage was taken from. If time permits, the story "Grandma, Please Don't Come," also found in the Colon book, is an interesting story to read aloud. This story describes conditions in the city and the cold climate of New York that are not particularly pleasant for older people to experience when they have spent most of their lives in warm climates and in rural areas.

Resources:

James A. Banks. *Teaching Strategies for Ethnic Studies.* Boston: Allyn and Bacon, 1979.

Jesus Colon. *A Puerto Rican in New York.* New York: Mainstream Publishers, 1961.

Helen MacGill Hughes, ed. *Cities and City Life.* Boston: Allyn and Bacon, 1970.

Kal Wagenheim and Olga Jimenez de Wagenheim, eds. *A Documentary History: The Puerto Ricans.* New York: Praeger, 1973.

Generalization III: The traditions and customs of ethnic and cultural groups are often supported, celebrated, and preserved by the family unit.

Level: Primary

Objectives:

1. To introduce students to a Navajo family in the southwest.
2. To help students understand the importance of the family in helping to maintain family traditions and customs.

Teaching Strategy:

1. Introduce the book *Annie and the Old One,* by Miska Miles, to the class by exploring the title. Have the students try to guess what the story is about. Once it has been established that the story involves an elderly person, perhaps a grandparent, ask the class to listen closely for things that the family in the story does that appear to be things they have done for many years.
2. After reading the story, list those things the students identify as having occurred over and over again in the family and call these "customs and/or traditions," e.g., weaving, grinding corn, relating to nature, handling death, storytelling by the grandparent. Have the class develop another list of customs and traditions that their families maintain. Stress this as one of the major functions of families.
3. Review the list the class has established and try to identify those customs that are different from family to family and examine to see if the background of a family contributes to the differences.

4. Have the class select several customs and traditions they would like to learn more about. Schedule times when family members can join students in giving a presentation to the class. These presentations can be scheduled throughout the year and those that are based on holidays can be presented at or around the appropriate days. This manner of proceeding might even extend throughout the year and enrich the curriculum in a variety of ways. Aspects of some customs can be shared with the entire school.

Resources:

Miska Miles. *Annie and the Old One.* Boston: Little, Brown, 1971.

Level: Intermediate

Objectives:

To help students understand that:

1. Jews are a religious and cultural group.
2. Jews observe many customs and holidays.
3. The family is the center for most of the Jewish traditions, customs, and celebrations.

Teaching Strategy:

1. The first twenty to thirty minutes of this lesson should take place in the library. Or make provisions for having a large number of books about Jews, Judaism, and related subjects in the classroom. Prior to the lesson, prepare a number of questions about the Jews and Judaism to equal the number of students in the class. Number each question and place each one in a separate envelope. Have the students select one question to research the answer for the twenty- to thirty-

minute periods. The following list represents some of the questions the students could find answers to:

- What is the basic belief of the Jewish religion?
- Name three types of activity that take place in synagogues.
- What are the three major religious groups that Jews belong to?
- What is an Orthodox Jew?
- How does Conservative Judaism differ from Reformed Judaism?
- What does "Kosher" mean to Jewish people?
- How does a Bas Mitzvah differ from a Bar Mitzvah?
- What is the significance of the Sabbath?

Suggestions for additional questions may be found in the Resources listed.

2. Following the research period, randomly select, by number, the questions to be answered. Continue the process until all questions have been answered. The teacher may want to limit the answers to one minute to cover as much information as possible in once class period. Or the activity could last for several periods.
3. Summarize this lesson by listing the traditions and customs that the family takes primary responsibility for.

Resources:

David A. Adler. *The House on the Roof: A Sukkot Story.* New York: Bonim (A Division of Hebrew Publishing Company), 1976.

Sophia Cederbaum. *The Sabbath, A Day of Delight.* New York: Union of American Hebrew Congregations, 1960.

Margery Cuyler. *Jewish Holidays.* New York: Holt, Rinehart & Winston, 1978.

Theodore Gaster. *Festivals of the Jewish Year.* New York: William Morrow, 1953.

Harry Gersh. *When a Jew Celebrates.* New York: Behrman House, 1971.
Sulamith Ish-Kishor. *Pathways Through the Jewish Holidays.* New York: KTAV Publishing House.
Eliyahu Kitov. *The Book of Our Heritage: The Jewish Year and Its Days of Significance,* 3 vols. New York: Feldheim, 1970.
Seymour Rossel. *Judaism.* New York: Franklin Watts, 1976.
Yuri Suhl. *An Album of the Jews in America.*
Vaacov Vainstein. *The Cycle of the Jewish Year.* Jerusalem: World Zionist Organization, Department for Torah Education and Culture in the Diaspora, 1953.

Level: Advanced

Objectives:

1. To assist students in gaining an understanding of the structures of Native American families.
2. To explore with students how family units provide the support base for the values and traditions of Native American people.
3. To assist students in gaining an appreciation for the special strengths and beauty present in Native American extended family life.

Teaching Strategy:

1. The resource for this lesson is N. Scott Momaday's *The Way to Rainy Mountain.* Assign the reading of this book prior to this lesson or read portions of the book to the class. This is a poetic and impressionistic autobiography of a contemporary Native American who journeys back to the land and time of his Kiowa ancestors to discover his own reality and his place within his group. Students may need some preparation for

beginning this work. The book shifts from simple narrative description to the poetic presentation of sacred belief, myths, and legends. The ease with which Native American peoples move between a very practical grasp of "what is actually going on"—rain, snow, birth, death—and sacred realities and the meaning of practical reality is central to an understanding of Native American culture; it is the family that provides the "laboratory" for these two realities, allowing members to integrate them through traditional symbol systems, practices, and oral traditions.

2. Discussion of the book should encourage students to explore the concepts introduced in Generalizations I and II and in the object for this lesson. Questions for discussion are:

   - What are the structural characteristics of the Native American family?
   - What is the function of the extended family?
   - How is the family—the kinship line—linked to the larger social structures of the group?
   - What is the clan system?
   - Why is Momaday's need to journey to the land of his ancestors so critical to his sense of well-being? (Explore the role of ancestors in terms of personal and social identity and the necessity for a sense of "homeland.")
   - How do families sustain and transmit the values and traditions of Native American culture? (Focus student attention on the role of oral tradition and the importance of role modeling within Native American families.)

3. The impressionistic qualities of this work may take students some time to become familiar with, but it is valuable because it does closely parallel the thought processes supported by the culture. However, it may be helpful to supplement the book with some other readings, such as Dee Brown's *Bury My Heart at Wounded Knee,* which is written in a straight narrative form and has some excellent depictions of Native

American family life. Also, *Passages from Black Elk Speaks,* as interpreted by John G. Neidhardt, is superb for this purpose. The students might also be introduced to the paintings of George Catlin and photographs of Edward Curtis to enrich their sense of the Plains Indians as Momaday describes them.

4. This lesson should conclude by emphasizing the present reality of Native American families and their maintenance of tribal traditions in a contemporary world. It is recommended that students become aware of the Native American communities within their state and the organizations and activities currently implemented to sustain family and community life. Often a person or organizational group affiliated with the office of the governor in each state is responsible for representing the interests of the Native American peoples in that state, and many state Departments of Education designate a person for this purpose. The class may be interested in inviting a resource person from one of the appropriate offices to discuss some of the issues in greater detail.

Resources:

John Lame Deer. *Lame Deer, Seeker of Visions.* New York: Touchstone Books, Simon and Schuster, 1972.

N. Scott Momaday. *The Way to Rainy Mountain.* New York: Ballantine Books, 1970.

Notes

1. James A. Banks with Ambrose A. Clegg, Jr., *Teaching Strategies for the Social Studies: Inquiry, Valuing and Decision-Making* (Reading, MA: Addison-Wesley, 1973), p. 12.
2. John Jarolimek. *Social Studies in Elementary Education* (New York: Macmillan, 1971), p. 4.

3. Helen MacGill Hughes, ed., *Cities and City Life* (Boston: Allyn and Bacon, 1970).
4. Jesus Colon, *The Puerto Rican in New York* (New York: Mainstream, 1961), p. 44.

Index